How to MAKE $100,000 A YEAR in DESKTOP PUBLISHING

Thomas A. Williams

D1413833

Also by the same author

Mallarme and the Language of Mysticism
Eliphas Levi, Master of Occultism
We Choose America
The Bicentennial Book
Tales of the Tobacco Country
How to Make Money Publishing Real Estate Guiaes
How to Write a Living Family History
How to Publish Poetry
The Freelance Writer's Indispensable Start-up Kit and Success Guide
How to Form a Non-Profit Corporation, on Your Own and without a Lawyer

How to MAKE $100,000 A YEAR in DESKTOP PUBLISHING

Thomas A. Williams

BETTERWAY PUBLICATIONS, INC.
WHITE HALL, VIRGINIA

Author's Note: *How to Make $100,000 a Year in Desktop Publishing* is my work alone. No endorsement by Williams & Simpson, Inc. of the ideas or information this book contains, implicit or explicit, is implied.

Tom Williams

Published by Betterway Publications, Inc.
P.O. Box 219
Crozet, VA 22932
(804) 823-5661

Cover design by Rick Britten
Typography by Park Lane Associates

Library of Congress Cataloging-in-Publication Data

Williams, Thomas A. (Thomas Andrew), 1931-
  How to make $100,000 a year in desktop publishing / by Thomas A.
Williams.
    p. cm.
  Includes bibliographical references and index.
  ISBN 1-55870-160-5 (pbk) : $18.95
  1. Desktop publishing. 2. New business enterprises. I. Title.
II. Title: How to make one hundred thousand dollars a year in
desktop publishing.
Z286.D47W5384 1990
686.2'2544--dc20   90-38810
                                                                          CIP

                  Printed in the United States of America
                          0 9 8 7 6 5 4 3 2 1

For my wife Christina,
whose loving encouragement infuses the pages of this book.

Contents

Introduction

I went into business four years ago with a Mac Plus, a LaserWriter, and two used desks. This year my company will gross $800,000. Next year we will top $1,000,000.

What I did, you can do too. I had no special qualities beyond a burning desire to succeed in the field of local and regional publishing. And I learned to appreciate and harness for my own purposes the enormous potential of the microcomputer hardware and software required for what has come to be known as "desktop publishing."

I learned by trial and error. At that time there was no other way. The books all told you how to operate your equipment and even how to draw pretty pictures with it. But none really told you how to make money with it.

I asked a lot of questions and came up with a lot of ideas. If an idea worked — as most did — I added it to my repertoire and repeated it as often as possible. If it didn't, I scrapped it and tried something else. Gradually, on evenings and weekends while I worked my day job as a teacher, I acquired the necessary information.

The effort paid off. Today I publish *NCEast*, a regional magazine with statewide circulation; the *North Carolina Travel and Tourism Guide*; *Welcome to Wilmington*, a full color, slick paper newcomer's guide to this major metropolitan area; *Homebuyer's Handbook*, a real estate buyer's guide; *Washington and Beaufort County Magazine*, a city magazine; and *Renter's Helper Apartment Directories* in nine cities. I have also published both hardcover and softcover books, and I plan a major expansion of the book publishing part of my business with a nationally distributed line of how-to books in the niche market of small-business entrepreneurship.

I am able to do all of this on my original Mac and a additional one I bought along the way so that two people could work at the keyboard simultaneously. As the business has grown I have added a bevy of commissioned salespeople, two full-time art people, and I have begun to use the services of free-lance writers.

But in the beginning I did almost all of it myself and, to tell the truth, I could have remained at that one-man shop level and done very well for myself financially. The great thing about desktop publishing is that you can grow as big or remain as comfortably small as you wish. Whatever level you choose, you can make a handsome profit.

I know how to publish magazines, directories, guides, books, and pamphlets and how to make money doing it. This knowledge I have put into the pages of this book. You can use this information to make money — sometimes considerable amounts of money — as a desktop publisher.

1.

Getting into Desktop Publishing

This book contains detailed, step-by-step instructions. The person who studies and follows them will make money — sometimes considerable amounts of money — in the field of independent publishing. All that is required is the ambition, the know-how, and the latest desktop publishing equipment.

You have the ambition, or you would not be reading this book. You can purchase or lease the desktop publishing equipment you need for less money than it would take to buy a good used car. I have the know-how, and that's precisely what I intend to reveal to you in this book.

I can personally vouch for the workability and profitability of these publishing projects because I have carried each of them out myself. Each was easily manageable, even those undertaken while I was working full-time as a college professor. Each made real money. And each was begun with little or no up-front cash investment.

Clearly, when you put down this book there will still be a great deal more that you can learn — there always is. But these pages constitute a map to the unknown territories of independent desktop publishing, a map you can rely on and chart your course by. When you have read the book you will know far more than I did when I proudly printed "Thomas A. Williams, Publisher" on the title page of the first book my brand new little company brought out.

Each chapter represents a doorway through which any ambitious writer, salesperson, or businessperson can enter the world of publishing at the head of his or her own company — with all the satisfaction and financial security that comes with owning your own business.

A REVOLUTION IN PUBLISHING

There is a revolution taking place in the publishing business today. One aspect of this revolution is a matter of scale. The large publishing companies are getting bigger and bigger, leaving the very lucrative local, regional, and specialized markets open to all comers. The big New York publishers have become "blockbuster" oriented, abandoning the sure but (for them) relatively modest profitability of the

"The importance of desktop publishing technology? I firmly believe that I could go into any town, anywhere, set up my Mac and — starting from scratch — establish a niche publication that would bring me a very livable income within eight weeks time."

Tom Williams
How to Make Money Publishing Real Estate Guides
Venture Press

short-run book or magazine to what used to be known as the "small presses," which are now referred to more and more frequently as the "independent publishers."

Coupled with this restructuring of the publishing business itself is the truly revolutionary appearance of the astonishing new desktop publishing technology. Thanks to the new equipment that this revolution has spawned — in all its forms and permutations — independent publishing companies can now be run from *any location in the country* — from the spare bedroom in your own home if necessary. One of the most successful independent publishing companies I know of is run from a small apartment built in a former dry-cleaning shop in a town of 200. My own shop is in a small guest apartment I built in the upstairs of my home a few years ago. There I routinely receive and transmit manuscripts by modem. I fax contracts and requests for quotes on publications in progress. I write, lay out, and design more than twenty publications each year with a $2000 computer and laser printer. I do business with printers in Ann Arbor, color separation houses in Colorado, and book wholesalers in Atlanta. In publishing, the much-heralded "electronic cottage" is very much a reality. And it works!

Immensely powerful and ever more affordable microcomputers, driven by very sophisticated page layout and typesetting software, now put into the hands of an entrepreneurial publisher the means to control planning and production of the product at every step of the way — sometimes even including printing. In the "publishing on demand" techniques developed and pioneered by my friend Carole Marsh of Gallopade Books, books are not even printed until the orders come in. At that point the laser printer grinds out the pages, which are then spiral-bound in house and sent out. This procedure may not work on all — or even most — books or magazines, but it does very well indeed where it is appropriate. (See Chapter 10 on selling information by mail.) This new technology gives the entrepreneurial publisher advantages that would have been simply unbelievable just ten years ago:

- Its use produces great savings in pre-press production costs and, as a result, a substantial increase in profitability. Projects which once might have been marginal are now quite profitable.

- Since it does so much, so well, desktop technology creates the possibility of operating with a very small staff. A one-person shop is quite feasible, since with this equipment one person can do almost everything.

- It permits more efficient schedule management. You are doing everything in-house, so there are almost no outside people whose work schedules, holidays, and down-time you have to accommodate.
- It creates more efficient general operations, since the same computers that produce your books and maintain mailing lists can send bills and do all other necessary accounting operations from accounts receivable to general ledger.

Another great benefit of the new technology is what I call the SOB factor. When you develop your business there are three ways that you can finance yourself during the start-up phase. You can use OPM (Other People's Money), by going to the bank and getting a loan which you immediately have to start paying back. You can use YOM (Your Own Money) by raiding the reserves of your hard-earned savings. Or you can use SOB (Sweat of Your Brow), by doing all of the work yourself until the business is up and running. It used to be that before you could get a publication on the street you had to pay designers, typesetters, pasteup people, and printers. Now you do it all yourself. It takes longer, but it's much easier on the pocketbook.

GETTING INTO PUBLISHING

There are many reasons for going into any business, including the publishing business. The most direct and easily understood of these is the desire for financial gain. Most of us who give in to the entrepreneurial urge and crank up our own enterprises share that basic goal. Whatever other motivations there may be, we all want to turn a profit.

But our other, more personal, motivations are important, too. Because of them we turn our attention to this or that opportunity rather than to any one of the hundreds of others that a person with different interests would, perhaps, find more appealing. Strong personal motivations give us the staying power we need to make a go of it.

Dan Poynter of Para Publishing was a sports parachute and hang-gliding buff. He wrote down some tips for others interested in these activities, but found that the subject matter was too specialized to interest the larger publishing houses. Consequently, he published the books himself, marketed them aggressively, and in the end made them the cornerstones of his own publishing company. He then wrote a new book, *The Self-Publishing Manual* (Para Publishing, 5th edition, 1985), which has become a classic in its field. Almost by accident, Poynter parlayed his interest in parachuting into a successful business venture. He is now one of the leading independent publishers in the country.

Peggy Glenn had a home-based typing business. To share what she had learned about establishing and running such an enterprise, she wrote a twenty-nine page pamphlet called "How to Start and Run a Home Typing Business." People loved it. The booklet went through several editions, eventually becoming a 104-page book. Buoyed by this experience, Peggy went on to publish *Don't Get Burned: A Family Fire Safety Guide* based on her husband Gary's experience as a fire investigator.

Peggy Glenn is now the proud owner of Aames-Allen Publishing Company. Her latest book, *Publicity for Books and Authors*, is valuable reading for independent publishers.

Rod Hoyle lived at Atlantic Beach, NC, a prime summer tourist destination. Rod noted that there was no tourism guide serving the area. He began selling advertising and contacting local writers to provide needed editorial copy. The result was *Lookout Magazine*, one of the best advertising sales-driven tourism publications in North Carolina. That was ten years ago. *Lookout Magazine* is still going strong and formed the base from which Hoyle was able to undertake even more ambitious projects in periodical publishing.

Real estate developer Steve Davenport wanted to advertise his high dollar residential properties to upscale people moving into the Wilmington, North Carolina area. He looked around for a full color, slick paper magazine in which to run the ads that he had paid agencies thousands of dollars to develop for him. Unfortunately, there was no such publication. Steve teamed up with a salesman and originated *Welcome to Wilmington* magazine. It was a success. After two years of solid ad sales revenues Steve sold his magazine to another publishing company (mine) which will pay him a percentage of profits for years to come.

Jim Reid was a disabled Vietnam veteran, who, after years of struggle to overcome a physical disability resulting from his wartime service, came to work for me as a typographer and editor. Jim was quick to understand the nature of the publishing business, particularly the interplay between sales and marketing, editorial and production.

"I learned to harness the power of desktop publishing technology while working for another company, and I also know how a magazine is edited, marketed, and put together. I knew I had a magazine in me, so as soon as I was able, I looked around for a niche market. I zeroed in on the growing community of older people in our town, and started Pitt County Crossroads. *It was a modest publication, but it worked. We were able to sell the ads. Now I'm looking forward to something more substantial."*

Jim Reid

After two years Jim set out on his own and established *Crossroads* magazine, a modest nostalgia-flavored city magazine for Greenville, NC, which had no such publication. As I write this, *Crossroads* is in its fifth issue and is building an advertising base. As is true of all the other publications listed here, *Crossroads* is entirely desktop-generated.

Such stories could be multiplied many times over. There are as many doorways into the publishing business as there are publishers. The key to all of them is knowing how publishing is structured and understanding the relationship between concept, production, and sales.

Where do you find the opportunities? How do you recognize them? What steps do you take to turn ambition or idea into reality?

This book answers all of these questions. Once you know the inside story, the rest is easy. Like a magician's sleight of hand, success in publishing seems difficult and mysterious *only when you don't know how it's done.* (Pay particular attention to the "three keys to success" later in this chapter.)

HOW I GOT INTO PUBLISHING

In my own case an inborn fascination with book, words, and ink on paper were the powerful motivators that eventually led me into publishing. I don't know where, when, or how it began but somehow I always knew that I wanted to make my living by working with "words and books," as I remember saying to one close friend on the eve of undertaking my first publishing venture.

Still, in the beginning I held back. I became, instead, a college professor — a tried and true way of generating monthly paychecks to finance the hours one spends in the library or at the typewriter. At that time I was totally inexperienced in business and had neither the know-how nor the all-important self confidence to go directly into publishing. Perhaps if I had had a book like this, I might have been able to consider doing so at a much earlier stage of my life.

But things do take their natural course. Our secret inclinations, if strong enough, ultimately find ways to express themselves. One evening I noticed an article in the local newspaper. A steering committee, the article said, had been set up to coordinate the celebration of the town's bicentennial.

We are only beginning to scratch the surface of the possibilities of desktop publishing. The problem is that most of the books and magazines that talk about this technology are very long on the desktop part and very short on the publishing. Desktop publishing is an absolutely revolutionary way to carry on the business of publishing magazines, books, and anything else that can be sold and read. It is now perfectly possible to sit at your own kitchen table and run your own highly profitable publishing empire.

Such events, I knew, traditionally generated some kind of book. Be it good, bad, or indifferent, a retrospective book celebrating the town's history, people, and places would appear. Most of the ones that I had seen had been very badly and amateurishly done — on cheap paper, with poor printing and worse writing and design. I knew that I could do better.

I determined on the spot to type out a proposal and go to the committee. For a modest fee, I told them, I would compile, edit, and print a local history. It would be filled with a fabulous collection of old photographs (which I would later have to collect) and the best available writing. It would be handsomely printed and bound. Proceeds from sales, I said, would be far greater than the combined cost of my fee and production charges. It would be a money-maker, generating cash to support other bicentennial activities. It would, I promised, be a better book than the committee could obtain in any other way. (The project did make money, both for me and for the bicentennial committee.)

My proposal was accepted and I was off on my first big project. I set myself a working schedule that I know now was virtually impossible. I would research for thirty days, write and edit for thirty days, and get the book printed and bound in thirty days. It worked, and at the beginning of the third month I was holding page proofs in my hands.

As I reviewed them my eye fell to the bottom of the title page, where the imprint (name) of the publishing company usually appears. It suddenly dawned on me that I could invent a name for myself, have it printed on the title page and, presto! I would have a publishing company. I would be off and running.

And it was, in fact, just that easy. The following year I issued my second book — a reprint of a county history that had been out of print for years and had become a collector's item. This, too, bore the imprint of my new company and was sold successfully. It was published as a numbered, limited edition and found a ready market of people willing to pay the relatively high price tag I put on it.

Shortly afterward, I put my newfound publishing expertise — such as it was at that early date — to a much more substantial test when I began to publish a regional magazine. This, too, grew nicely and eventually became the statewide, full color consumer publication, *Tar Heel: The Magazine of North Carolina.*

At this point I gave up teaching altogether to become owner, editor, and publisher of a weekly newspaper, *The Mecklenburg Gazette,* in the college town of Davidson, North Carolina.

BRAINS, TIME, AND ENERGY, NOT MONEY

None of this, mind you, cost me one single cent in out-of-pocket cash. Getting into publishing, I found, took its toll in brainpower, time, and energy, but required little investment other than that.

As you gain more experience you may be willing to take on more complicated and extensive projects that require you to risk a modest amount of cash. But in the beginning you need not put up any money at all. When I have made this claim to others, they have found it hard to believe. But it is true. I have never undertaken a publishing project that did not make money from the very first. I have always been able to finance my books, magazines, and newspapers with sweat equity and ongoing cash flow.

MOONLIGHTING? IT'S HIGHLY RECOMMENDED

What about the time required? Is it manageable for someone working at another job?

It is, indeed. In fact your first plunge into publishing will work out *better* when you start slowly, build wisely, and learn as you go. The fact is that you are unlikely to generate an income to live on from publishing alone until you learn — from firsthand experience — *all* the rules of the game. You will need an established income for a while yet. You just put in the extra hours until the payoff comes.

Many individuals will be quite content to continue in this way indefinitely, deriving their major income from a "regular job" and maintaining publishing activities as a lucrative sideline. This is a very workable arrangement, especially for those whose primary employment is so remunerative or so intrinsically interesting to them that they prefer not to give it up.

Others, for whom this is not the case, will eventually discover ways, as I did, to move into publishing as a full-time occupation.

THREE SECRET INGREDIENTS FOR SUCCESS

The term "publishing business" covers a lot of territory, a good deal of it out of reach for the beginner. It would be nonsense to say that you could start, from scratch, a company on the scale of, say, Harper & Row or Scribner's. You would need to raise millions in capital to

For an analysis of trends — and problems — with the big publishing houses, read Leonard Shatzkin's book, In Cold Type *(Houghton-Mifflin, 1982). Small entrepreneurial publishers — like you and me — are actively avoiding many of the problems Shatzkin so brilliantly describes: short shelf life books, high returns, awkward and clumsy distribution systems, high costs of inventory.*

fund the publication of fifty to a hundred titles before you could begin to generate the cash flow necessary to cover day-to-day expenses, much less make a profit.

The gigantic undertaking of establishing a truly national circulation newspaper like *USA Today* required the infusion of tens of millions of dollars before the first edition ever hit the stands. Even now, after years of publication, this newspaper is just beginning to return a precarious profit to its investors.

But setting aside this high-dollar neck of the woods, there is still a lot of publishing going on out there that is viable for the start-up entrepreneur. How do you recognize the kind of opportunity that is likely to yield success and result in financial reward for the independent desktop publisher?

My experience tells me that there are *three secret ingredients* that you must look for. When one or another of these ingredients is missing, consider it a red flag of warning. You may feel that your publication idea contains other elements that more than compensate for the missing ingredient. And you may be right. There are always exceptions. My advice, however, is to stick with the tried and true, at least until you learn to navigate on your own. To do otherwise can cost you money in lost time and profits.

The secret ingredients of what I call my publishing success formula are as follows:

Choose only those projects that allow for . . .

> (1) *intensive sales*
> (2) *in a limited geographical area*
> (3) *to a well-defined (targeted) clientele*

The last two of these are closely related and, indeed, the third can sometimes take the place of the second.

Intensive Sales

When a high proportion of the businesses in a given area constitutes prospects for advertising sales, or when a book will appeal to the majority of those who buy books in a given area (a book on Atlanta for Atlantans, for instance), then that magazine or book has the possibility of intensive sales. A high percentage of potential customers will be interested in buying an ad or in buying a book.

When there is a large enough pool of potential customers that are also easy to reach (see the next section), sales to a reasonable number of them will bring success. A newcomer guide focusing on a major metropolitan area meets this test. By way of contrast, let me give an illustration of an idea, from another field, that does *not* meet it.

A year or two ago a friend suggested the idea of building personalized doll houses for sale during the Christmas season. The doll houses would be built to resemble the houses in which the family of the child for whom it was designed actually lived. My friend was excited by the idea. The doll houses would be handsomely made and unique, though expensive, gifts. The children who received them would certainly be thrilled by them.

But this business idea did not have the possibility of intensive sales. The prospects for the doll houses, I pointed out, would be limited to those few affluent individuals who could afford such a customized toy. Prospects would, moreover, be further limited to families with female children between the ages of three and ten or twelve. Additionally, they would be limited to those affluent parents of little girls who liked the doll house idea, and whose daughters did not already have a doll house. Looked at this way, our small town had a pool of only ten or fifteen prospects for customized doll houses. It was not an idea worth exploring further.

On the other hand, when you publish a tourism guide to a major resort area, virtually every business there is a prime candidate to purchase advertising, and your ad rep can call on every one of them, with confidence, year after year.

Limited Geographical Area

A single entrepreneur can easily handle a project that covers a limited geographical area, whereas expanding the coverage area beyond the reach of one or two people can create real difficulties.

A city magazine is relatively easy to publish; a regional magazine (the mountains of your state, for instance, or the coast) more difficult; a statewide magazine requires an entire staff of sales and production people. A national magazine requires all of the above, plus a high-risk investor with several million dollars of idle money in very deep pockets.

When you focus tightly several good things happen. You or your ad salesperson can make calls and sell the product without traveling anywhere overnight. Circulation and distribution are easily and inexpensively managed. You can do this job yourself if necessary. In the case of book publishing, all the major booksellers can be called on personally. Your own advertising becomes more affordable and your name recognition more readily achieved.

A Well-defined (or Targeted) Clientele

It is difficult for a small publisher to market a general interest novel because those who may want to buy it represent a diverse group of people, spread across such a wide area that it becomes prohibitively expensive to reach them all. A typical book of this kind will sell relatively few copies in a large number of bookstores nationwide. A company that does not have a national sales force simply cannot make the calls necessary to get the title on the bookstore shelves. When a few people in a great many communities constitute the potential pool of buyers, the small publisher has a problem.

The successful desktop publisher will bring out books and magazines that have a large number of readers in a very limited area. When I brought out my bicentennial history, 99% of all sales took place within a fifty mile radius of the town. No one in Detroit or Denver or San Diego was interested in a picture history of Greenville, NC. But a great many people in Greenville were. Enough, indeed, to sell out an entire first edition.

Analogous to the concept of the limited geographical area (and an acceptable substitute for it) is that of the targeted, specialized, and easily identifiable readership. This is the domain of the so-called "niche" publications, each of which has a highly specialized readership. If you bring out a magazine called *Gum Disease Today*, you know that it will appeal to every periodontist everywhere. Mailing lists of targeted readerships are readily available, so that even though this group of individuals may be spread across many geographical miles, they are still easily reached by direct mail or by telephone. They are *targeted* in such a way that even the small publisher has a chance of hitting the mark.

This book, for instance, is to a limited degree targeted. I can rent mailing lists of subscribers to writers' magazines, to *Entrepreneur*, *Inc.*, and other such "make your name in business" publications and reach the very heart of the readership for which it is intended.

A later chapter details the publication of an association directory, in this case the membership directory of the North Carolina World Trade Association. Companies dealing in export-import are easily identifiable, as are the banks, shippers, and others who want to do business with them.

Such a magazine is *doubly targeted*. Both association members and companies wishing to reach them through advertising which they place in the directory are limited in number, easily definable, and very reachable. Most of the ads in the directory mentioned above were sold by telephone.

USING THIS BOOK

The body of this book deals with specific publishing projects. Other chapters deal with general information that you will need to know no matter which of these projects you decide to undertake first. They include hard, how-to information that I have gleaned from years of experience.

Throughout this book you will read about such things as rate cards, media kits, sales reports, ad approval forms, and many other like items. What do these things look like and where do you get them?

In the appendices I have reproduced samples of the forms that I have found to be serviceable. They work, and they are included for you to adapt and use. The forms are simple. Just duplicate as many as you need. Or take the page to a printer and have some pads of them printed.

The rate card and the media kit serve as guidelines. You will want to say the same kinds of things about your publication, changing the details appropriately.

Although this book is protected by copyright, you have full permission to make whatever use you wish of the forms in this book.

A Gradual Process

Home or Office?

Equipment You Will Need

That Flood of Paper

Organization: Sole Proprietorship or Corporation

Your Management Team

Management Know-How

The Importance of Schedules

Billing and Accounting

Your Credit Line

The Value of the Customer

Your Capabilities Brochure

The Wall

Periodicals of the Trade

2.

Setting Up Shop

A friend of mine who is a very successful family-business entrepreneur says that all you really need to get into business is an idea and a pack of business cards with your name and address on them.

There is a great deal of truth in that observation. Many potentially great businesses never get off the ground because the idea person put off the start-up until he was totally prepared. That moment, of course, never arrived.

Somewhere between these two extremes of winging it on a pack of business cards on the one hand and mind-choking over-preparation on the other, the middle road of wisdom lies. There is no doubt that you can sabotage yourself if you delay too long in getting started. But there is one element, beyond the business card and the idea, that you can't do without: a customer. And when you land that customer you had better be prepared to serve him well. Every customer who leaves you singing your praises creates dozens more to take his place and fill your bank account. A satisfied customer is like the seed from which the field of wheat is grown. He multiplies himself endlessly. So you must plan carefully. Just don't get so bogged down in the planning stage that you never move beyond it.

A GRADUAL PROCESS

In my experience, setting up to do business is a gradual process. There are the bare minimum space and equipment requirements, of course, but a great many decisions can, and should, be put off until your needs become clearer and more well-defined as you go along. And, of course, as work comes in you'll create a flow of cash that will help you acquire some of the niftier and more expensive things that you need.

In my own start-up phase I found many substitutes that I pressed into service until I could afford the real thing. I did layouts on the dining room table, used wooden fruit crates for files, and made a $3 can of spray adhesive do the work of a $600 waxer. As the work flow began to build I went beyond these homespun arrangements for two reasons. The first was that I knew that I would work better and faster with the proper equipment. The second was that I simply enjoyed myself more and felt better in more professional surroundings. I believe that you will feel that way, too.

And I must confess to a third reason. I am in publishing as much for the love of the business as for the money I earn by engaging in it — as important as that is. The truth is that I simply *enjoy* the paraphernalia of writing, typesetting, pasteup, and production. I assemble it, use it, and care for it out of pure pleasure.

HOME OR OFFICE?

I firmly believe that any business that can be started in the home ought to be started in the home. You will need to nurture your start-up capital and your initial income from publishing projects, using it to build your business. There is no sense at all in leasing expensive office suites that you do not need. And once up and running there is really no reason to move out into rented space unless you grow to the point that you can't do without it.

Some conditions — rarer than you might think, though — can make a home-based business unworkable. If, for various reasons, it is difficult to create an atmosphere conducive to work you may have to set up elsewhere. Maybe you are blessed with ten active children, all under the age of twelve. Maybe you just have two of them, but they are as noisy and rambunctious as twelve would be. It would be a miracle if you could keep them out of your hair for the uninterrupted hours of work and concentration that you will need.

Or there may be a space problem that, even with the best of wills, you just can't solve. Maybe you share a studio apartment with a spouse and a child, and can't even muster up a closetful of real privacy.

But under normal circumstances space should be no problem. Carole Marsh of Gallopade Publishing Group works out of a single car garage attached to her home, augmented by one Macintosh on a small table in her kitchen.

Remember that in the beginning you will be making use of the space of your suppliers. For the first project or two you may use outside graphic designers for all the ad layout and pasteup that you do not generate with your own computers. Their studios become an extension of your own work space and supplement it. You can even start out using the services of outside desktop people for your typesetting, putting in your own computers as the work flow becomes more predictable. Buying outside services may cut into your profit

"Whenever I see a company setting up a plush layout that looks sleek and prosperous before they've earned a dime, I blanch. That prime clue is all you need to know in order to forecast their outcome."

James R. Cook
The Start-up Entrepreneur

margin a bit, but if yours is a gradual, moonlighting start-up it may be the way to go.

If you decide to establish your business in rented space, some of the best deals, I have found, come in office space with shared receptionist and answering service. This arrangement gives you many of the benefits of having an office staff without having to pay for it. In my part of the country you can get this kind of space, in new construction, for $200 to $300 a month, including utilities, though your office will be quite small. It will be a great advantage if you have the option of expanding into adjacent rooms as your space needs increase.

Another thing to keep in mind as you look for rental space is that you have to pay premium prices for prestige locations. Remember that what you need is work space, not expensive image building. Your publications will do that pleasant job for you.

EQUIPMENT YOU WILL NEED

What are you going to fill all this space up with? Precisely what equipment will you need? Let me go down the list of essentials for you. Keep in mind that after many of the items on this list you can mentally insert the phrase, "or its equivalent." There is much room for ingenuity and bargain-basement problem solving here.

The Computer Component

Computer update
I note that the latest version of my page layout program uses two megabytes of random access memory (RAM) to work well. So do updates of two other leading page programs. Add a requirement of at least two megabytes of memory to your list of desirables in purchasing or leasing your computer hardware. You will surely need the two megs for your work, especially if you are using a IBM or clone 286 processor. You may want to consider up to four megabytes of extended memory if you have a 286 machine. Heretofore one megabyte was perfectly adequate.

Your microcomputer system will be your largest single expense, but this equipment is becoming more and more affordable, even for the smallest business. It will certainly earn profits far in excess of its cost. It is truly the goose that lays the golden eggs.

The constant upgrading of computer capabilities creates some difficulties in discussions such as this one. By the time this book has been on the market for a year or two there may be some new, desirable product out there that is totally unknown today. Such a development is much less likely than in former years, however. More and more, personal computers are being built to support future expansion of capabilities. If you buy a unit that is expandable, you will go a long way toward solving the old problem of computer obsolescence.

As I write this there are two systems on the market that compete for the desktop publisher's business: IBM systems and their clones, and the Apple Macintosh series. Both systems have their advantages and disadvantages, though they are currently coming closer and closer together in terms of their capabilities.

The Apples, however, are in my opinion far superior to the IBM's in the area of graphic design — something you will be doing a lot of as you sell advertising. They are also somewhat easier to use. An inexperienced person can begin to be productive on an Apple after just a few hours of training. The Apple computers are more flexible in the use of type, and there is a vast library of type styles available.

The IBM clones tend to be less expensive (up to 30% when I last checked) and, with recent enhancements, are suitable for the work you will be doing. For setting straight type — books, for instance, or magazine articles — they are every bit as capable as Apples. They also tend to be more effective in the other uses to which you will put your computer system, uses such as mailing list maintenance and especially bookkeeping and financial management.

Whichever system you choose, make sure that it has adequate memory. As the graphic arts and page layout programs develop new features, they require more memory. You will need at least one megabyte of RAM and a forty megabyte hard drive for storage. If you plan to do a lot of image scanning (see below) you might even opt for a sixty or eighty meg hard drive. I currently operate my business with Mac Pluses and two twenty meg hard drives, but I have reached their limit. When we go beyond this level and begin to use a scanner we will increase memory needs enormously.

Since it is usually less expensive to buy the memory when you purchase the initial package than later as an add-on, my advice is to go ahead and get it while the price is right. The increase in your monthly lease or purchase payment will be minimal and the long-range usefulness of your equipment greatly enhanced.

An important note: Make sure that, wherever and from whom-ever you purchase your equipment, training and support services are readily available.

Cost? Really quite affordable. At today's prices you can put to-gether an entire desktop publishing outfit (computer, printer, and programs) for $6,000 to $10,000 — cheaper than the least expensive cars. Your monthly payments will range from $175 to $250. Many secondhand units can be found for even less.

Your Laser Printer

The words and images you create on your computer screen are printed out on your laser printer. There are several good laser printers on the market. Apple has its own LaserWriter. Hewlett-Packard produces a very good product for the IBM market. By the time you read this there will undoubtedly be others.

The essential quality you are looking for in a laser printer is the *resolution* of its type. The word "resolution" refers to the clarity of the output. At present the standard in the industry is 300 dots per inch (dpi). Some laser printers, through enhancements from third party suppliers, now provide 600 dpi. This undoubtedly will become the new standard, with 1000 dpi and better not far behind.

Purists — and professional typographers — will tell you that 300 dpi type is not suitable for publication work. They advise that once you have designed and typeset your pages you take your diskette to a typeshop or communicate your material to them by modem. There it can be run out in high resolution type on a compatible typesetting machine.

Once word gets around that you are setting up in business you may get calls from salespeople for the old-line typesetting equipment companies: Varityper, Allied Linotype (Merganthaler), and Compugraphic. You will not normally need their high-priced, high resolution products.

My experience tells me that only the purists really mind the 300 dpi resolution. I regularly produce full color, slick paper magazines using nothing more sophisticated than my Apple LaserWriter. As long as the publication is set entirely in 300 dpi, the eye of the reader does not perceive the print as of lower quality. I use 300 dpi constantly and have never gotten a complaint about the quality of the type.

When the laser printers are generally able to do 600 dpi or 1000 dpi (in the not too distant future, as I write this), the quarrel between the purists and the pragmatists such as I am will disappear altogether. For all but the very finest printing the laser printers will be perfectly and universally acceptable.

Your Scanner

A scanner is a device that reads a complete page of typewritten or printed text, line art, or photographs and stores them in the memory of your computer. It thus eliminates the necessity of retyping every manuscript that you wish to include in a publication. It even simplifies the placing of art on page layouts. This, too, is scanned and read into your layout, where it is enlarged, reduced, or otherwise altered to fit your needs.

Should you own a scanner? Probably not yet, in my opinion. A scanner is a device that, once perfected, will be very useful to you, though certainly not essential. I say "once perfected" because I recently considered an expensive memory upgrade of my computers to accommodate a scanner. I applied for the lease, had it approved, and was ready to close the deal. When I witnessed a demonstration, though, I was not satisfied. The scanner, represented to me as being top of the line, made several typographical errors on each page. Such errors, even when you find them all, are difficult to correct. And it took as much as ten minutes to scan a black and white photograph, filling up enormous chunks of the machine's memory.

Keep your eye on scanners. Once the price comes down and the quality goes up you may want to consider adding one to your system.

A Modem

A modem (short for modulator/demodulator) is a device that allows your computer to communicate with other computers, transferring data via ordinary telephone lines. A modem is useful if you are going to have other people do typesetting for you by way of an electronic computer link. However, you can achieve the same result by simply sending a floppy disk through the mail or hand-delivering it. I must say that in the five years I have been doing desktop publishing I have never once really needed a modem.

Computer Programs

Tips on Buying Software
The software for your computer can be expensive. A page layout program may cost as much as $700 or $800. But you can often get much better deals on software, often saving hundreds of dollars, by buying it at the same time as the computer itself. Just ask what software can be "bundled" with the computer you order. Since many of the layout programs are good — Ventura, Pagemaker, Quark-Express, and others — you can buy the one that you get the best price on. The same goes for word processing, data base, and accounting programs.

You will need several basic programs to bring your computer system on line. The ones I suggest here are programs that are affordable, that I have used, and that I can recommend. I have not, of course, tried them all. And there are new ones constantly coming onto the market. If you are knowledgeable in the field of microcomputer programs, your choice may differ from mine. But the ones I suggest have proven their worthiness in the hard test of day-in and day-out use. They work.

You will need a *word processing program*. I suggest Microsoft Word for the Apple and Word Perfect for the IBM.

You will need a *page layout program*. The two leaders in this field are Pagemaker and Ventura Publisher. People who design a lot of ads on the Macintosh generally prefer Pagemaker. Those who do mainly straight text and fewer ad layouts often prefer Ventura Publisher. Pagemaker was originally designed for the Mac and Ventura for the IBM. Currently, however, versions of each program are available for both computer systems.

You will find a *drawing or design program* — such as Aldus Freehand or Super Paint — quite valuable though not absolutely necessary. There are many such programs on the market, and they are not expensive. Get your dealer to show you the ones he has or has access to and choose the one that seems best suited to your purpose.

You will need a *basic accounting program.* Two of these that are quite inexpensive and that I have used in my business are Peachtree (IBM) and Rags to Riches (Apple). There are much more elaborate programs on the market, but most of us will not need them.

If you have chosen an accountant or if you are shopping around for one, ask which accounting software he uses. It will be to your benefit to use the same or a compatible program.

The more expensive accounting programs can be bought by "modules," that is, a little at a time. In the beginning you may need only to keep track of accounts receivable (the money people owe you). If this is the case, you can purchase only the receivables module, adding payables, general ledger, and others as you grow.

An accounting program is a very sound investment. Computerized billing and record keeping are two of the chief fringe benefits of owning a desktop publishing system.

Waxer

In the pasteup process, elements are held in place on a layout sheet (or board) with a thin coat of wax, applied by a waxer. Wax is a very forgiving adhesive. It holds elements firmly in place. At the same time, the wax seal is easily broken, allowing the pasteup artist to pick up an element and reposition it with ease. The rubber cement favored by some pasteup artists is bulky and difficult to use, and spray adhesive soon adheres so firmly that repositioning is impossible.

Which waxer should you buy? There are hand-held models on the market, but I have found them to be unsatisfactory for any significant work flow. An economical waxer that I have used and can recommend is the Art Waxer, available from most graphic arts supply houses. A heavier duty model, popular in newspaper layout departments, is the Daige waxer.

You will find that the old cut and paste method, although often replaced by the graphic output of your computer and laser writer, does not disappear altogether. There will be much work to be done by hand. You might want to combine elements of various computer-designed page or ad layouts. Although a very experienced operator can reopen the computer files and do the job electronically, it is often speedier and more efficient to do the job by hand.

Graphic Arts Work Station

Each person who does art and pasteup will need a "work station." A graphic arts work station consists of an inclined board (as on a drafting table); a T-square, preferably attached to the table for greater accuracy; and the assorted tapes, razor knives, technical pens, and other materials that designers need.

Drafting tables are expensive. A home-built table, constructed of 3/4 inch plywood with a hinged top, will substitute very nicely. I have built many of these. If I can do it, anybody can.

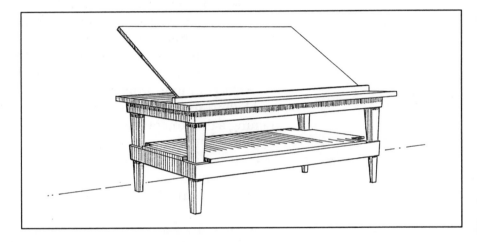

In addition to the solid-top work stations you will find a light table very useful, especially if you use pre-ruled layout sheets. A light table can be bought for less than $150, including an attached T-square. The brand that I use is the "Lucentview," built by Buckingham Graphics. I bought mine by mail from the *Printer's Shopper* catalog. Many of the other small items you need can be bought from the same source. See the suppliers listing in the back of the book for the address. Write them a note and ask for their catalog.

To these items, add files and shelving for materials and your all-important "morgue" (your file of previously used advertisements, logos, etc., from which you will draw again and again).

THAT FLOOD OF PAPER

There is no doubt about it, business is done on paper. You may complain about it and try to control it, but the fact remains that without the proper paperwork you just can't do business.

The following is a list of the basic paper items that your publishing business will need. Check your computer first. Invoices and statements appear on the list below, but they can also be generated by the Peachtree accounting package I recommend. Other forms can be designed using your data base program.

You can also buy ready-made forms of various kinds at your office supply store. You will just insert the name and address of your business in the proper place with a rubber stamp. While these preprinted forms may be good enough to get started with, they are too expensive to serve over the long run and, of course, they are not very professional either. They don't do a thing for your image.

Most of the items listed here can be bought from suppliers like Carlson Craft (this company will give you wholesale prices when you ask to be set up as a distributor) and NEBS (the Wal-Mart of business form companies). You will have a wider choice of business cards and letterhead styles and quality with Carlson Craft than with NEBS. The addresses of both these companies are given in the appendix. Other forms (such as the advertising approval forms and sales management forms) can simply be photocopied from the blank forms provided in the back of this book.

Here is my list of necessary paper:

☐ **Business cards**.

☐ **Letterhead and envelopes**. I usually buy these in two grades — a smaller quantity of good bond for special uses and "executive communications" and regular white offset for run-of-the-mill use. Buy these from Carlson Craft. You'll save a bundle.

☐ **Invoices**. An invoice is issued and sent at the time of sale. Have a separate, numbered invoice for each transaction.

☐ **Statements**. A statement is issued to a regular customer monthly. It carries a line for balance forward, a summary of the month's transactions (with invoice number), and the total balance due. Any finance or service charges are added to the statement.

☐ **Insertion orders**. These are the contractual agreements between advertisers and your company. Samples are given in the appendix.

☐ **Request for quote forms**. You fill out these forms and send them to printers from whom you want to get prices on your publications.

☐ **Ad approval forms**. You use these forms to get an advertiser's approval of the ad to be run, after you have typeset and designed it. It is his final okay to run the ad just as you have presented it to him. Signed ad approvals are a great help when the time comes to get paid. Some advertisers have a very short memory about what they asked you to do for them and what they okayed. The signed approval sheet jogs such memories very effectively.

ORGANIZATION: SOLE PROPRIETORSHIP OR CORPORATION

You will hear a good deal of discussion about company organization. Is a sole proprietorship best? Should you incorporate?

I prefer the corporate structure for several reasons, all of which I believe to be sound. It is true that under today's tax laws incorporation will not save you money; indeed it may cost a little more because of the increased accounting costs. But it can be very useful in other ways. Above all, the corporate structure will protect your personal assets in the unlikely chance that things go awry, either financially or legally.

Publishers are more open to lawsuits than many other businesses. You publish materials about other people, their lives, and their businesses. You could find yourself looking down the muzzle of a very unwelcome lawsuit.

This is not common. I have never, in all my years in this business, been sued for any reason, and I don't know many who have. In all likelihood *your* own common sense will keep you miles away from any lawsuit, too. But in the remote event that you were brought into court, and you lost, only corporate assets would be at risk.

In the financial realm, it is true than no bank is likely to lend money to your corporation without your personal guarantee. But your suppliers — printers, color separation houses, and others — will do work for your corporation and bill the corporation. In the event of bankruptcy, such creditors can obtain liens on your corporate assets. Your personal property, however, would not be in danger.

The corporate structure is more easily marketed, should the time come when you wish to sell your business. And set up as a "subchapter S" corporation, you can avoid most of the double taxation snares of regular corporations. Your accountant will guide you through all these details. But while I consider the corporate structure best, any will work, so long as it is well organized.

Your Management Team

You will want to locate an accountant and an attorney with whom you can work and feel comfortable. Consult them, and especially the accountant, early in the organizational process. A friend of mine, a CPA who specializes in business start-ups and funding, has a favorite saying. "If you want me in at the landing," he tells entrepreneurs, "then get me in at the take-off."

There is some good sense in this. Many of the first decisions you make will affect the way you do business over the long haul, and you want to make the right ones. You do not need to seek out the most expensive people in town, just good, competent professionals who take an interest in your needs. Shop around. An initial interview costs nothing. Ask what the rates are and what services are provided. Get a feel for the personalities involved. Can you work with this person? Keep looking until the answer you give yourself is "Yes, certainly."

I do not advise you to keep your books yourself, nor should you prepare your own quarterly and year-end tax returns. Accountants have bookkeepers on staff who can handle these matters for you at very reasonable hourly rates.

First of all, utilizing an accountant's staff for such routine matters can save you the cost of a staff person during your start-up phase. And when income tax time comes around your accountant will have everything in order and spend much less time doing your return than would otherwise be required. In addition, if you are like many of us, failure to use an accountant or his bookkeeper will probably result in the levy of at least some fines against you because of late filing of required tax reports. It takes a special mind to keep up with these things. I confess that my own is not one of them.

The attorney will be less necessary in the beginning, unless you decide to incorporate. In that case, although you can do the necessary paperwork yourself, an attorney can be called in to help. And thereafter he will take on the responsibility of keeping your all-important corporate minute book up to date and in compliance with the law. In my state it costs anywhere from $400 to $500 to incorporate. I paid a lawyer the first time I formed a corporation and thereafter did it myself, paying only the $50 fee required by the North Carolina Department of State.

If this is your first time around, and if you do not have a clear understanding of the legal requirements of incorporation, you should certainly use an attorney.

MANAGEMENT KNOW-HOW

As you progress in your publishing business you will learn more and more about business management. Success or failure in business is as much a result of effective management as it is the result of a good product. Even the best product can bite the dust if management (in this case, you) doesn't do its job.

You will read constantly. There are a number of good books out on small business management. Titles, authors, and publishing companies of some that I can recommend are given in the back of this book. You will attend seminars that look useful to you. My first full-time business venture was the publication of a weekly newspaper. For several months I went to every seminar on newspaper management, advertising sales, and page design that I could find and fit into my schedule. I might sit all day long in one of these sessions and glean just a single new idea. But often this idea made a major difference in the way I ran my newspaper and greatly enhanced its profitability.

But let me be more specific and tell you a few of the most important things I have learned about management over the years.

Develop a Business Plan. The first item you should generate on your new computer, if you haven't already done so, is a business plan for your desktop publishing company. This plan will be your point of reference, your road map to success.

Spend some time on your plan. Write it carefully. Don't be afraid to set challenging goals for yourself, but bear in mind that you've got to get there from here. The plan will detail both desired accomplishments and plans for achieving them. Review the plan with your accountant and other trusted advisors. Pay attention to any concrete and specific difficulties they may spot, but don't let them throw cold water on your plans either. Your accountant is not the entrepreneur. You are.

When you're satisfied with your plan take it down to the nearest quick copy shop and have it duplicated and spiral bound. Your banker may need a copy — and definitely will if you seek a loan of any kind for your business — and so may others with whom you will work.

Remember, too, that no business plan is written in stone, including yours. It exists to guide you, not to hamper you. As early as six months into your business you may well glimpse new opportunities, rule out ideas that now seem less profitable, set new financial projections, and make other basic changes. If these changes grow out of experience in your business and not out of mere vacillation, simply call up your business plan file on your computer, amend it, and print out new copies.

What items does a good business plan contain? Obviously if you were trying to raise millions of dollars in venture capital you'd have to have an extremely detailed plan. For your purposes a mini-business plan will serve very well and include everything that you will need.

You should read up on these plans. Marcuse's book (see Suggested Reading) is the most thorough that I have read, although all the examples he gives are for maxi-plans and not mini's. The Small Business Administration also has a publication explaining the ins and outs of business plans. There may also be some free consultation at your local Chamber of Commerce or community college. Many of these organizations have "small business centers" to provide information to those starting new businesses.

Here are the basic items that I include in my own mini business plans.

- **Define the concept.** Tell precisely what your business is and what you will do.

- **Outline the qualifications of the principals.** In this section you tell about yourself. Put down on paper those elements of your background, education, and experience that support you in starting your business.

- **Define your market position.** Analyze the market for your goods or services. Name and analyze the competition, if any. Specify how you will position yourself in the market so as to capture your share of the business.

- **Outline marketing strategies — the ways in which you will seek and obtain business.** For most of the projects I've developed in this book there is no substitute for personal contact. Direct mail and telephone sales can be also be used, as well as some limited space advertising.

- **Prepare a pro-forma.** The pro-forma is your detailed projection of income and expenses. Most business plans do a pro-forma for at least three successive years. Obviously the pro-forma is not expected to be absolutely accurate. It represents your best guess concerning the financial progress of your firm.

In all of these areas be simple and direct. Do not worry if you don't feel comfortable with what you turn out. Just do the best you can. Six months from now you will know a great deal more, and your plan can always be revised. If you are moonlighting during the start-up phase, just do a mini-plan for whatever limited publishing activity you undertake.

THE IMPORTANCE OF SCHEDULES

Work out reasonable schedules for yourself and then *stick to them.* For publishers — as for any business person — time is money. If you publish a magazine twice yearly you will make twice as much money as you would if you published it only once.

It is very easy, especially if you are working at another job, to let your schedule slip. You go a week over in closing advertising sales. You give yourself an extra weekend to get that lead article in. The photos come in a week or two late. Consequently, you lose your place in line at the printer's and publication is six weeks or more behind schedule.

Not only do you lose credibility with your clients and customers when you are late, you sabotage your own bank account. It does not take a mathematical genius to understand that if you make $15,000 in three months you are earning at the rate of $5000 a month. If your schedule slips and it takes you four months instead of three to get your magazine out, your personal earnings fall to $3750 a month. You have given yourself a nifty cut in take-home pay. Was that weekend off worth it?

In setting my own schedules I always work backward. I decide when I want to have the completed project in hand, or when circumstances or my customer *require* that I have it in hand. I then work out a plan that will enable me to finish on time.

In the case of a quality of life magazine or a newcomer's guide, for instance, here are the pertinent stages along the way. Each type of publication will have its own timetable for completion.

ITEMS	SCHEDULED	COMPLETED
Sales materials completed		
Sales plan established		
Sales close		

All editorial in		
All materials typeset		
Ads sent out for approval		
Ad approvals in		
Photography in		
Complete publication dummy made		
Page layout complete		
Materials sent to printer (or elsewhere) for stripping		
Press run date		
Delivery date (from printer to you)		
Distribution date or publication date (from you to the public)		

Assign a reasonable date to each of these steps and don't deviate from it. Work extra hours to make up the slack if you get behind. The beauty of desktop publishing is that there is very little you can't handle yourself if the need arises. You may not be quite as fast or quite as good as the hired help, but when deadlines press you will be able to get the job done.

There will be a bit of trial and error here as you learn the ropes, but you will be able to establish deadline schedules with some assurance fairly quickly.

BILLING AND ACCOUNTING

What blood is to the human body, the flow of cash is to your business. You need to ensure that it comes in regularly to be deposited into your bank account where it will be available for use. How do you ensure a regular cash flow? Here are some methods that I have found useful.

Because you are a publisher you will be asked to undertake a variety of projects for businesses and organizations. I have done product catalogs for manufacturers, annual reports for governmental agencies, and privately printed books for individuals. This kind of work can be very profitable and, if handled correctly, is a real shot in the arm for your business' cash flow.

I always draw up a simple agreement between my company and the client specifying precisely the work I will perform for them and the fee that I will charge for it. I then specify how the money is to be paid to me. Typically, I ask for one-third on the signing of the contract, one-third on approval of galley proofs, and one-third on final approval of page proofs and the signing of the authorization to print. This method of payment gives me money to work with during the production process. It also assures that I will have my money in hand before anything is printed.

Why do I insist on payment in full before printing? There are several reasons, all very good ones. I am obligated to the printer and the color separator; the client is not. The printed materials are of value to the client only, not to me. And many are the bankruptcies, personnel changes, and plain old opportunities for financial skull-duggery that can make it difficult to collect *after* you deliver your goods. You may want to relax this policy for the most credit-worthy and reliable clients, but my advice is to do so only when it is truly necessary. Even then, make sure that your first two payments are adequate to cover all out-of-pocket expenses and a small profit.

You cannot require clients who buy advertising in your publications to pay up front. Traditionally, advertising bills become due and payable only on publication. However, you can offer incentives for early payment — a discount, say of 2 or 3% or more, if it is to your advantage. The smaller fry will probably not take advantage of this offer, but some larger corporations have a standing policy of always taking the discount.

In addition, you will send an invoice as soon as a contract for advertising comes in. The invoice will bear the notation, if you wish, that "this is a record of our transaction. It is not a bill." Statements and tear sheets will be sent later after the publication appears. Still, many businesses will pay from the invoice, although you do not require them to do so.

It is also possible to ask for a one-third payment in advance. This technique will not work with larger corporations, but with small businesses, where the person who signs the contract also writes the checks, it is very possible to get such an advance payment.

This technique is especially appropriate for advertising sold to resort businesses, restaurants, and some other smaller businesses, in newcomer guides, as well as for advertising sold to new business start-ups. Typically you will be selling these ads well in advance of the publication date. The no-pay rate among many of these businesses — whether caused by cash flow problems or by actual bankruptcy — is rather high. It makes good sense to get something in advance if you can. In publishing the North Carolina *Travel and Tourism* guide I was able to defray the entire cost of sales, including commissions and travel expenses, through such advance payments. If your client will not go along with this policy, and you want his business anyway, simply ask for a couple of credit references and bill on publication in the normal way.

Always add service charges to bills that are over thirty days old. State laws govern the amount you can charge. In North Carolina the rate is 18% per year. Such service charges encourage clients not to hold your money too long. And they give you a negotiating edge. You can arrange to forgive the service charges in return for a check by return mail for the outstanding balance.

In almost every case, an advertising account that is more than ninety days delinquent should be turned over for collection. You will begin calling your advertiser at forty-five days. At ninety days ask your attorney or collection agency to take action. The insertion order or other agreement that your client has signed will include a clause making the client liable for all expenses of collection.

Your collection process and policy should be in writing, and you must implement it unfailingly. Failure to do so will result in the loss to you of many dollars which will have to be written off as bad debts.

YOUR CREDIT LINE

In the beginning you can operate almost totally out of current revenues. This is the way I have gotten all of my businesses under way. But as you take on more and more projects you may find that you need temporary infusions of cash that you can't generate out of the normal flow.

An example? You have, say, completed a quality of life magazine. You have sold $50,000 worth of advertising, for which you hold signed contracts. You can't collect your money until the magazine is published, but the printer — with whom you have not done business before — wants a third of his money up front.

What do you do? You go to the banker with whom you have so carefully established a positive relationship. Show him the contracts, and on that basis ask for a short term loan (ninety days, perhaps) to carry you through. Repay this loan promptly.

After you do a couple of transactions like this one, ask for an open line of credit. With a credit line you avoid having to negotiate every deal individually. Your credit line limit should be adequate to cover the largest likely short-term cash need.

Once you have a credit line, you simply call the bank, have the necessary funds transferred to your account, and write your check. Since these are very short term funds you repay them the minute the money comes in the door. The bank will expect you to pay your credit line down to a zero balance at least once during every twelve month period.

Another way to solve the problem of credit needs is by negotiating an equity credit line secured by a second mortgage on any real property that you own — your home, for instance. If you are disciplined and repay the funds just as you would with a commercial credit line, the equity line works very well. I have used this credit source with considerable success.

THE VALUE OF THE CUSTOMER

A satisfied customer will generate many more of the same kind. Many businesses fail or do far less well than they should through simple failure to recognize this basic fact. Your customer — whether an advertiser in your magazine, a sponsor of your county history, or a Chamber of Commerce executive — is your most precious asset. This is true not only for the income you currently derive from meeting his needs, but from all the future business you will derive from him and from everyone he recommends you to. A good customer recommends you to two friends, who also recommend you to two friends and so on into the future. It's a geometric progression. It takes a while to land the first client or two but after that, if you do your work well and deliver as promised, it becomes much smoother sailing.

An ill-served, dissatisfied customer, on the other hand, represents a dead end and, at worse, a dead weight that you'll drag along behind you for years to come.

Remember that you are always working not only on the assignment at hand but on all the future business you will earn from a job well done. Always go the extra mile to make your clients happy, even the smallest among them. Put the same effort into thoughtful advertising design for the guy who takes the one-twelfth page ad in the back of the book as for the bank that takes the back cover. Write your clients. Thank them for their business. Deliver complimentary copies. Refer leads to them when they come your way. Do business with them yourself. Send Christmas cards. Maintain positive contact in every possible way. When you have a complaint, go overboard in trying to resolve it in a way that will meet your customer's needs. Big businesses indeed can be built on the solid, sound base of satisfied customers.

YOUR CAPABILITIES BROCHURE

When my company was a brand new business, we designed and printed a full color, eight page brochure that described our company, ourselves, and all of the things we thought we could do for our clients. The thousand-plus dollars it cost us — a princely sum for us at that time — was some of the best money we ever spent. (We did not have to pull the money out of our pockets from one day to the next. The printer gave us very good terms and quite a while to pay on the promise from us that as work came in to us, we would channel as much to him possible.)

This high quality, glossy, and colorful piece made all the difference. Chamber of commerce executives and heads of corporations whose advertising we sought might never have heard of our company, but they could not deny that the capabilities brochure they held in their hands was top drawer and so, by inference and association, were we.

We used to call it our "credibility brochure." It generated instant believability and respect. Could we create a first-rate publication? Well, we had already done so, and the client held the proof in his hands.

THE WALL

You hear long distance running buffs talk about the wall. They will be running well, they say, over quite long distances. Then, suddenly, before they have reached their goal they hit the wall. It seems momentarily that they have reached the limits of their endurance, that they can't continue a step farther.

At this point some give up and drop out. But the real winners, those who have and reach their goals, understand about the wall. They know that if they continue on, pace by pace, and do not give in to the strain, they will pass through the wall, tap into unknown reserves of energy and strength, and carry the race through to its conclusion.

In business, too, we often hit the wall. Things are going well, according to plan. Suddenly, difficulties arise. You can't meet a deadline, ad sales just don't develop, the hoped-for contract doesn't come through. You feel so overworked and worried that you are tempted to say the heck with it and throw in the towel. This often happens just when your business seems on the verge of real and substantial success. It is a critical moment.

If you will persevere in following your plan, writing the next page, selling the next ad, making the next presentation to that bank or historical society, you can break through. The wall is gone and there's smooth sailing ahead. Often your base of satisfied customers will carry you through. At other times a new idea or opportunity will suddenly surface and come to your aid.

But nearly always, if you keep on keeping on, you will break through the wall. You never know just when or where your next great success is going to come from. After all, you can only see as far as the horizon. But when you reach that point there is always a new horizon, one that becomes visible only as you tough it out and continue — at whatever the cost in effort and dogged determination — to make forward progress toward it.

PERIODICALS OF THE TRADE

One way to keep a fresh mind for your business is to scan the trade publications for ideas. Here is a list of some good publications that are about desktop publishing. Read them, keep them and re-read them. Also refer to the suggested reading in the back of the book.

The Editorial Eye
Editorial Experts, Inc.
66 Canal Center Plaza, Suite 200
Alexandria, VA 22314-1538
(703) 683-0683
Newsletter for publications professionals. Practices and standards for writers, editors or for anybody working in publications.

PC Publishing
PC Publishing
950 Lee Street
Des Plaines, IL 60016
(312) 296-0770
A great magazine for IBM users who do any type of publishing.

Personal Publishing
Hitchcock Publishing Company
365 East Nort Avenue
Carol Stream, IL 60188
Covers the latest in equipment for both Mac and IBM computers. Excellent for product reviews and publishing tips.

Publish
PCW Communications Inc.
501 Second Street, #600
San Francisco, CA 94107
Excellent for design ideas and other related matters of desktop publishing. This publication wants to make itself an example of great desktop publishing. If your looking for the newest trend in DTP, check out this magazine.

Communication Concepts
2100 National Press Building
Washington, D.C. 20045
(703) 425-7751
Newsletter for professional communicators. Key issues: writing, editing, DTP, publication design and production . . . creative ideas that work.

Editor's Workshop Newsletter
407 S. Dearborn
Chicago, IL 60605
(312) 922-8245
This is put out by Lawrence Ragan, Inc. who also puts out the *Ragan Report*, *Speechwriter's Newsletter*, and the *Corporate Annual Report Newsletter*. This is a valuable aid for staying up with current design concepts and ideas. Covers editing, design, production, and DTP.

PROFILE OF A QUALITY OF LIFE MAGAZINE
HOW QUALITY OF LIFE MAGAZINES ARE USED
BACKGROUND RESEARCH
HOW TO USE THE CHAMBER OF COMMERCE
A DETAILED AGREEMENT
THE SALES CAMPAIGN
EDITORIAL CONTENT

3.

Publishing a Quality of Life Magazine

The so-called "quality of life" magazines, published from time to time by virtually every Chamber of Commerce in the country, represent prime pickings for the publisher-entrepreneur. Someone's will sell, edit, print, and profit from these magazines, and it should be you.

Most of the hundreds of quality of life magazines I have examined have been colorful, slick, and expensive as far as advertising was concerned, but dry as dust editorially and often poorly designed. The articles in them, ostensibly written to project a dynamic, desirable image of the Chamber's trade area, usually read like the back of a cereal box. With close attention to writing and design you can make a name for yourself in this area of the publishing business.

There is no regular publication date, since each issue is good for as many as two or three years, and does not constitute an onerous commitment to an ongoing publication — unless you want it to. If you do a fantastic job you'll be asked back. You can decide at that time whether you want to do the magazine again or not. Usually the money is very good, the time commitment reasonably small, and the public recognition for you and your new company both gratifying and valuable — a combination of benefits that is usually hard for most of us to resist.

Again you have the three pluses going for you: *intensive sales, in a limited geographical area, with targeted circulation.*

I won't say that ad sales are ever easy, but with the quality of life magazine they are as easy as they are going to get. The businesses and industries that are Chamber members have been conditioned to "participate," issue after issue, year after year. There may be a grumble or two, but most of those who bought last year will buy again this year. Ad rates are traditionally higher than those for any other regional or local magazine: up to $3100 for a full page, full color ad in a magazine I recently did in a city with a population of 35,000.

PROFILE OF A QUALITY OF LIFE MAGAZINE

What is a quality of life magazine? The best way to answer that question may be to describe to you the one I received a few weeks ago from my own Chamber of Commerce here in Greenville, North

Carolina. It is a 112 page perfect bound book (squared at the spine, with the pages glued in) and the size of a standard magazine (8½" x 11"). The cover, in full color, has been made extra glossy by the recently developed process of liquid lamination.

Inside, inserted between the cover and page one, is a three-fold brochure on the city of Greenville and its fine qualities. More about this brochure later. The first forty pages, as well as the front and back covers — inside and out — are filled with mostly full page, full color ads for major industries, financial institutions, a university, an ad agency, some commercial building contractors, etc.

These ads, which cost from $3000 to $4500 each in this book, are interspersed with editorial material in the form of short (about 700 words, tops) articles on such breathtaking topics as (and I quote the table of contents) "Recreation; Growth and Development; Education and Health Care; Real Estate; and Shopping." There are also a few pages of "useful names and addresses."

Seventy additional pages are filled with a membership directory, giving the name and address of each member of the Chamber, alphabetically. With some entries there is a mug shot, for which there is an extra charge. Judging by the number of these postage stamp-sized photos there are enough hungry egos around to make this little profit center of more than passing interest to the publisher.

Following the alphabetical listing is a listing by profession or business specialty. A large number of fairly simple black and white ads in one-third, two-thirds, and full page sizes appear in this section.

I note on the table of contents page the name of the publisher. How did he get the assignment? Very simple. He walked into the office of the Chamber executive and offered to do his next quality of life magazine.

"What's in it for the Chamber?" the executive asked.

The publisher told him, outlining a generous profit-sharing plan. Then he sold the ads, wrote the copy, laid out the book, had it printed, and collected the money for the ad sales.

I calculate that total sales reached the $45,000 level. It cost $15,000 to sell the ads and print the book. Probably $5000 went back to the Chamber. Profit: $20,000 plus. Not bad for two months' work.

HOW QUALITY OF LIFE MAGAZINES ARE USED

How does a Chamber of Commerce use its magazines once it has them? One copy will be given to each member, with additional copies going to the larger businesses and industries that buy the expensive full page ads. This local circulation is the main basis for the claim of the publication to be an effective vehicle for advertising the products and services for the membership. (This may not be a very strong claim, but it is apparently enough to raise advertising sales to profitable levels.)

The remaining copies will be held in the Chamber offices and perhaps the offices of the county development commission (as it is usually called). These they may be sold to casual inquirers. But the more important use is as the lead item in the packet of community information that the Chamber sends out to professionals, businesses, and industrial enterprises expressing an interest in locating in the area. The quality of life magazine, in fact, becomes a mainstay of the town's or the county's media kit and is used for civic advertising and promotion purposes. It must, therefore, be as handsome, slick, and professional in appearance as the publisher can make it.

BACKGROUND RESEARCH

"What is your target market? You can't sell to everyone, so don't try. Determine the most profitable market and concentrate on reaching it first. Then branch to other markets as time and money allow."

Barbara Brabec
Homemade Money

Do you need some secret knowledge to do one of these books? Is there some hidden lore secretly passed on from generation to generation about how to make money and succeed in publishing quality of life magazines? Not at all. You just need to follow a simple, basic rule that has worked time and time again: To succeed in business you find out what has worked for others and do it again for yourself. You do it better, if possible, but you do it.

To find out what has worked, assemble the largest possible collection of recent (there are fashions in these things and you want to be up to date) quality of life magazines from Chambers of Commerce in your area, large towns and small, industrial and resort. Study them. Make inquiries about the cost of advertising space. See what works − in terms of design and format − and what doesn't. Start a notebook of ideas that you find particularly interesting and that you think you can improve on. Keep a file of tearsheets of design ideas that you think you can use. Analyze organization. Read and study every word.

Chambers don't usually give these away. You may have to pay a few dollars for each copy or perhaps you can strike a deal for outdated copies of older magazines. But it is worth the investment. When you have finished your cram course in this specialized niche of publishing you will *know* what a quality of life magazine is all about, how it is put together, and what writing you are expected to supply.

You will have the all-important product knowledge necessary to sell yourself to a Chamber executive as someone thoroughly familiar with the quality of life field. You stand as good a chance as the next guy of getting the assignment.

HOW TO USE THE CHAMBER OF COMMERCE

What is a Chamber of Commerce? There are so many misconceptions, even among those of us who should know better, that I will answer the question in some detail. After all, you're going to be dealing with a Chamber of Commerce on a project involving major sums of money. You need to know who your partner in business is. The most popular misconception, I suppose, is that a Chamber of Commerce is a public organization, a department of the municipal government.

Nothing could be further from the truth. A Chamber of Commerce is a private organization, with its own director, its own aims and goals, its own agenda. While these aims and goals usually coincide with those of a progressive mayor and city council, it has no official relationship with them and, more important, usually receives no financial support from them.

A Chamber of Commerce is made up of members drawn from the business and professional community of a town or city. In non-metropolitan areas many Chambers of Commerce, while centralized in the largest town, also include county-wide membership.

The Chamber membership then hires a full-time executive director (sometimes he or she has other titles) and an office staff. It houses them in commercial space which is as upscale as its budget will permit. The function of this paid director and his assistants is to promote the growth of the business community through community development, industrial development, population growth, etc. It mounts campaigns to achieve these goals and supports those that others may mount.

For the community at large, the Chamber of Commerce becomes identified with its offices and its salaried, full-time director. It seems to have a life of its own and is often mistakenly perceived as an organ of government. When well run it has high visibility and is a major asset to the community at large.

The Chamber's budget is met by dues paid in by the membership, but these are never adequate for all the activities it wants and is expected to carry on. In order to make ends meet the Chamber itself begins to operate as a small business enterprise, doing what it can to generate additional funds for its operating budget on the one hand, and seeking out cost-cutting measures on the other.

The quality of life magazine is interesting to the Chamber for these very reasons. Without investing a cent, the Chamber is able to have a publisher deliver to its offices several thousand expensive, full color magazines for use in its work. It could never find the funds to pay for such publications directly. Furthermore, in return for its endorsement of the project, the Chamber receives from the publisher a percentage of gross advertising sales paid back into its own treasury.

A DETAILED AGREEMENT

Once you get an initial expression of interest from the Chamber with which you are doing business, write up a draft proposal and present it for review. There will be some negotiating and some give-and-take, and the draft proposal serves as a base-point for your discussion. When the details are ironed out, write up the final version. If the executive secretary of the Chamber likes it, he will then present it to his board of directors. Once he has their approval, he will sign, you will sign, and the business of making the magazine can get under way.

What is in such a proposal? In general a proposal includes two major parts. Part one specifies what you will do for the Chamber of Commerce and part two specifies what the Chamber will do for you. Although every proposal will be tailored to fit the circumstances at hand, you will be in good shape if you cover the following points.

Part 1: What You Do for the Chamber

❑ Specify that you will sell, typeset, write, and publish a quality of life magazine in accord with the desires of the Chamber.

❑ Specify the type of paper, cover, etc. that you will use. Any printer can look at your sample copies and tell you what kind of "stock" (paper) it is printed on.

❑ Specify that you will prepare editorial copy in the amount of, say, 1000 or fewer words on such topics as history, community characteristics, education, real estate, industry, retail climate, growth & development, transportation, etc.

☐ If a membership directory is to be part of the project, specify that you will include this directory in your book in both alphabetical order and in listings by trade or specialty.

☐ Specify a schedule for completing the project. This depends on your publishing and managerial experience — if any. Don't make it too hard on yourself. Ninety days is a tight schedule. On your second time around you could pare that down to six weeks. Never guarantee a publication date. There are too many things that go wrong and cause delays, and some of them undoubtedly will do so. You can include mention of an "estimated publication date," but nothing more firm than that.

☐ Specify that your company will do all selling, billing, and collecting.

☐ Specify that you will pay to the Chamber 10% (or whatever percentage you negotiate) of gross revenues actually received by you.

I say that 10% is "standard." That has been the agreed on figure for the deals I have made or know about. However, if your overhead is low, or if it is worth taking fewer dollars in profit to get a start in the quality of life business, you may offer 12% or even 15%. This will certainly give you a leg up on your competitors. The Chambers are interested in whatever course of action will maximize income to them. When you offer them more money, you become more interesting. But put pencil to paper and calculate costs carefully. Offer to share as much of the profit as you can but not one cent more than that.

☐ State that no percentage will be paid on bad debt accounts (yes, you will have some) or on filler pages. Filler, as you probably know, is used to provide copy, public service advertising, or other material for pages where no advertising has been sold and which would otherwise remain blank.

I once ran into a problem when a Chamber wanted me to pay them a percentage on a page which I had filled, for lack of anything better, with a house ad for my company.

☐ Specify the number of copies that you will print. Specify the number of these that you will distribute, free of charge, to the Chamber and to the advertisers.

❑ Specify how you will sweeten the pot — the extras that you can throw into the deal.

Earlier in this chapter I mentioned a brochure that was included in the quality of life magazine distributed by my own Chamber of Commerce. This brochure was a freebie thrown in as an incentive by the company that did the magazine. Other popular pot-sweeteners include a promotional slide show and script on the town that can be used in oral presentation to industries looking for a spot to locate or, if you have the know-how required and can do it easily, a video on the town. Easier to prepare is a slide show of, say, 100, 150, or 200 color slides that the Chamber executive can use for oral presentations.

❑ Include an escape clause. How much advertising do you have to sell to make a go of it? Calculate this figure and specify that if this amount of advertising is not under contract at the end of the selling period, then you reserve the right not to publish the magazine. This is almost never a problem when a quality of life magazine has been done several times previously. Still, it is better to be prepared.

Part 2: What the Chamber Does for You

❑ Specify that the Chamber of Commerce will endorse your publication to its membership.

This is an essential part of the agreement, and it is built on a solid community of interests. You, as publisher, and the Chamber are after the same thing: increased business — you for yourself and your advertisers, the Chamber for its community and its members. As publisher you are interested in building a profitable business, generating cash flow into your own bank account. The Chamber, dependent on income from any source it can scare up, is interested in generating cash for its own coffers.

What does an endorsement consist of? In general you will find the following parts:

• A prominent write-up in the monthly Chamber newsletter announcing the project and introducing you as the person undertaking it. (The Chamber executive will want to tell his membership that you, too, are a member of the Chamber, so you will have joined up. The dues you chalk up to the cost of doing business.) You would do well to write this note up yourself and give it to the person who edits the newsletter.

- A personal letter from the Chamber executive to every member which, again, introduces the project. But it also goes further. It suggests that members give you a close and sympathetic hearing when you call on them and consider favorably the prospect of advertising in a magazine that will do so much to generate business and economic development. The envelope also contains a postage-paid business reply card. By filling it in and returning it, the recipient can get detailed information on advertising, rates, circulation, etc. The cards that are returned constitute your first prospect list.

- Prospects on whom you or your salespeople call often call the Chamber to check on your bona fides. When this happens, the Chamber agrees to give you a warm recommendation.

☐ The Chamber will agree to share with you information about ad sales in previous editions, who the top prospects are, who the contact people are, etc.

It may even agree to make some calls on behalf of the magazine to heads of industry whom you may have difficulty seeing. The Chamber should help you with problem solving at every stage of the game. But remember that the Chamber executive, who has to go to his membership frequently for money to support this or that activity, probably does not want to get directly involved in ad sales. That is what he has you for.

☐ If you are working in a distant town, you may ask the Chamber to furnish a desk and telephone during the sales campaign.

☐ The Chamber should agree to furnish complete information about advertising rates in previous editions. It will be difficult for you to go up by more than 5 or 10%. Rates for quality of life magazines are already far higher — on a per page and per reader basis — than any other print media advertising.

☐ The Chamber will agree to furnish complete, up-to-date membership lists and to be responsible for proofreading and approving these after they have been typeset.

☐ The Chamber will review page proofs and give final authorization to print.

When you have these items written up in duplicate originals, signed both by you and by the Chamber executive, you are ready to begin.

THE SALES CAMPAIGN

The sales campaign will be tightly organized. You have fewer ads to sell in this book than in other publications, but each will cost considerably more. Since you don't want to "burn a prospect" (a salesperson's term for losing a sale or account through poor planning or bad salesmanship) you will plan carefully, day by day and week by week. You will review the history of each company. What ads have they bought in Chamber publications in the past? Ask yourself if a prospect has added a new product to his line or a new division to his company. These would be excellent motivators for advertising and getting the message out before the leaders of the community.

Show some familiarity with past advertisements placed by the prospect. Knowledgeable talk about such things will build a rapport between salesperson and prospect.

Begin with the biggest, most solid prospects: banks, major industries, big businesses. Present and past boards of directors and officers of the Chamber make excellent prospects. Contact these premium prospects first. This is a good idea for two reasons. When they buy, it builds your morale and whets the appetite of the sales force, which now smells blood. If they *don't* buy — and with a quality of life magazine that has had good sales in the past, this is, fortunately, very unlikely — you can decide very early in the game whether it is worthwhile continuing or whether you should invoke your escape clause and back out gracefully.

Of course, you need a salesperson with the right appearance, manner, dress, and personal carriage to sell an ad to the president or marketing officer of a bank. The same guy who can sell ads all day long to mom and pop retail outlets for the local free circulation shopper may very possibly not be right for this job.

But the bottom line is that you need a *good* salesperson. You're going to be insistent, to invoke the community good, the necessity for members to support the Chamber, the patriotic duty to advertise in the quality of life magazine that you are selling. If this sounds a little aggressive, it is. But a good salesperson can pull it off without seeming pushy and losing ground.

There are three reasons individuals will buy expensive advertisements in your quality of life magazine (and in you other magazines, too). The first is ego satisfaction. The second is desire for profit. The third is the desire to support the Chamber or community in promoting itself. Your salespeople must be aware of these motivations and find the hot button that will get a signature on the dotted line in each particular case.

To get your sales campaign off the ground, make careful lists of those who have bought before, those who have come into the area since the last publication and are good prospects, and those who have not bought but whom you think you can or ought to sell. Schedule these so that, when the time for closing sales comes, you will have made all the calls you intended to make.

Once the sale is made, always try to nail down the content of the ad. It can be very, very time consuming to make several trips back to help the client decide just what he wants to see in print. "We can just pick up this ad from last year. Are the address and telephone number still current?" is a good way to go. Always have some suggestions ready, culled, if possible, from previous advertising the client has done. Anytime you can repeat an ad that has been run before, it saves you important chunks of time and cash that would otherwise be spent designing new ads for approval. Even when you pass these costs back to the customer — as I suggest that you do — it is far more desirable to settle the matter up front and run what has been run before.

The larger clients will often have camera ready ads (slicks for black and white, composite film and a proof for color) which have been designed for them by their ad agencies. In these cases all you have to do is pick up the materials and go about your business.

EDITORIAL CONTENT

It is in the editorial content of your quality of life magazine that you can make a real difference. When you read through the articles in the magazines you gathered, you may well conclude that whoever wrote the copy and whoever approved it knew nothing whatsoever about effective writing.

You would be absolutely right. Remember that these magazines are usually undertaken by specialists in marketing and sales who have no experience in magazine journalism. They do not know what makes for high reader interest or effective writing. They are, more often than not, quite blind to the quality of writing in the same way that a tone-deaf person is unable to appreciate the quality of a musical performance. The New York Philharmonic or the local fireman's marching band — it's all the same to them. Just a bunch of people blowing on horns.

But some *will* know the difference, and they'll be the ones who contact you to do other magazines. Furthermore, many readers —

although they don't know why — do perceive, for instance, that the *Reader's Digest*, with its personal style, ease of reading, richness of anecdote and example, is more fun to read than the instruction manual that came with their Japanese computer.

Here are some guidelines that I have found useful for creating reader interest. If you are doing the writing, keep them in mind as you proceed. If you are paying someone else to do the work, be sure that he or she is experienced in magazine writing and understands the importance of following these rules.

Provide High Visibility to Facts and Figures

The CEOs of corporations seeking new locations or markets which offer expansion opportunities will want to know the facts about population growth, family size, business activity, and a whole range of other kinds of quantified information. The Chamber executive can provide you with a list and up-to-date numbers. (He can also let you know which items he may *not* want to include.) Don't hide this material in the body of articles. Combine it, organize it, lay it out clearly. Centralize it on one or two easily accessible pages.

Use Anecdotes and Examples

Business writing should not be any less readable or interesting than any other nonfiction writing. Just remember: Every generalization, theory, or idea deserves illustration in case history form, within the context of the space available. Success stories are always good. A word of caution, however: In using businesses or businesspeople in your anecdotes be sure that those you choose to highlight are members of the Chamber of Commerce.

Develop Strong Leads

Your lead is as important in this quality of life magazine as elsewhere. Work on it. Make sure the reader is motivated to move on to paragraphs two and three.

Use Sidebars for Emphasis

Short and sweet seems to be the name of the game these days. Check the pages of *USA Today*. They spent a million dollars-plus to research the optimum article length, and came up with the conclusion that most casual readers prefer their information in concise, albeit colorful, form.

Sidebars are those small, boxed "featurettes" that accompany and amplify major articles. A sidebar can contain detailed, related factual

"Editorial presentation is a means to an end, the end of journalistic communication . . . The successful layout is the one that helps the story come alive; it is easy to understand, interest, and therefore memorable. If it happens to be an example of [so called] Good Design, so much the better. But that is just the gravy; the meat-and-potatoes is effective communication."

Jan White
Editing by Design
R.R. Bowker

information or perhaps, along with a mugshot of the principal, a success story that illustrates the dynamic economy (or educational system, etc.) of the area your magazine covers. The possibilities are endless. Read *USA Today*, *Newsweek*, or *Time* for ideas. All three publications make great use of sidebars.

Use Testimonials when Appropriate

There's no doubt about it: testimonials are powerful selling tools. Ask the Chamber executive to go through his correspondence to find letters that might be useful. I am thinking particularly of the "We looked at your town, you gave us all the help we needed, and business has been terrific since we arrived" kind of comment. Other testimonials might focus on the excellence of a particular sector of the town: education, labor force, health care, etc.

Postage stamp-sized mug shots should accompany testimonials whenever possible. Testimonials should be in quotation marks and followed by the name and company affiliation of the person who is being quoted.

In the event that no suitable testimonials are on hand, the Chamber executive can usually pick up the phone and generate some especially for the magazine.

Use "For More Information" Items

Include a personalized "for more information call or write so-and-so" note, usually boxed in with a mugshot of the Chamber executive and copy written in the tone of a personal invitation. A signature over a typeset name at the bottom is an effective touch.

All-in-all a quality of life magazine is an attractive project. Potential profits are high, and the start-to-finish time is limited enough not to interfere with other projects you may be involved in. If you are already doing business as the publisher of a tourism guide, for instance, you can fill in the fallow, off-season months with a quality of life magazine.

And remember, every Chamber of Commerce does a quality of life magazine at regular intervals — sometimes yearly. So within a day's drive from your home there are some of these money-making projects just getting under way, some just completed, but also some now, today, up for grabs. With the proper preparation and effort on your part, one of them could be yours.

4.

Publishing a Tourism Guide

You've seen tourism guides on visits to the beach or to the mountains — those digest-sized (5½" x 8½") magazines chock full of ads proclaiming the merits of this place to go, that thing to see, do, or buy, and this absolutely unsurpassed restaurant.

Such little magazines are chock full, too, of profit for the individual who successfully undertakes the challenge of publishing one of his or her own. It is a relatively simple venture, one that will contribute mightily to your treasury and still leave you time for the other activities you may be engaged in.

These regional tourism guides can bring in the bucks, season after season and year after year. Editorially, they are a breeze, and if your magazine is attractive in appearance and circulated effectively, advertisers will get the results that keep them coming back to renew their advertising issue after issue. Such magazines all possess the magic three ingredients that bring success: 1) intensive sales; 2) in a limited geographical area; 3) to a well-defined clientele.

The first step in deciding which book or a magazine to publish is to determine what there is a market for. Then you publish whatever will attract that market. It is amazing how many of us get off to a disastrous start by writing or publishing what we like, regardless of any market that may exist for it. The market always comes first.

I came across an excellent example of a successful tourism guide recently when my wife and I spent a couple of weeks at Atlantic Beach, North Carolina. A young man named Rod Hoell had organized a small publishing company to bring out a full-color, digest-sized publication called *The Lookout Magazine*, named after nearby Cape Lookout.

I found a copy of *The Lookout* in the condo I had leased. Like all other good vacationers, I immediately set about browsing through it to check out the local restaurants to determine where we could have dinner that first evening. I found an ad for one I liked, telephoned in a reservation, and had a delightful evening.

The publication was mostly ads — which is really what I and others like me were interested in — with just enough editorial content to provide background color and heighten interest. The ratio seemed to be about 80% ads to 20% editorial, which is a successful mix for such a magazine.

It was a very manageable publication, covering a stretch of just thirty miles of resort/beach area. A single salesperson could handle the territory without difficulty. The geographical trade area was clearly definable and limited, so that editorial features could be targeted. This limited area also made saturation circulation (a copy for virtually everyone who could want or use it) possible on a bi-monthly publication schedule.

Why is it better to zero in on the main market rather than expand your area of coverage to the maximum? The answer is simple: it is just too expensive to do otherwise. When you attempt to cover a very extensive area — as my company does with its own magazine *The Vacationer: North Carolina Travel and Tourism Guide* — the cost of maintaining two or more salespeople on the road and the great expense of printing enough copies to have an impact statewide can bring down bottom line profits, perhaps eliminating them entirely. The amount of advertising sold may be somewhat greater, but without planning and sufficient up-front capital, the percentage of advertising revenues that sticks in the publisher's own back pocket may be small indeed.

The Lookout, like most successful magazines of its type, can be published by one writer-publisher or salesman-publisher with just a couple of part-time helpers. The statewide *Vacationer* requires much more in the way of staff, payroll, and risk.

So in your tourism guide think small: it's the royal road to success.

How Often Do You Publish Your Magazine?

Some tourism guides come out once a year. Most others, however, come out monthly, every other month, or quarterly, often omitting publication in the off-season.

For most small publishers the quarterly schedule is undoubtedly best. You want to do most of the work yourself, farming out to salespeople and writers as little work as possible, and this takes time. And, as you will see in Chapter 13 on dealing with printers, getting a book out takes time too — as much as six weeks more from start to finish when you don't have an art department of your own to back you up.

This would still give you the possibility of coming out twice during a seashore summer season, with one April-May-June issue and one July-August-September issue. But even *one* magazine during the season, printed in great enough numbers and filled with 80 to 85% advertising, would be quite successful and give you a base from which you could spin off other publishing enterprises.

HOW MUCH DO YOU CHARGE?

Your rate card is your most important sales piece. It lets your prospective advertiser know who is publishing the magazine, how often it comes out, where and to whom it is distributed and for how long, the sizes of the various ads, and related material.

The card also tells the advertiser how much his ad is going to cost — and there's the rub. You can easily put together the other information, but how do you fill in the price list? How do you know how much to charge? The more experience you have, the more easily this question is answered. For starters, though, here is a rate-setting method that works.

Your rate will fall somewhere between the smallest charge you can get by with and still make a profit and the maximum possible charge — which is everything the traffic will bear. Let's start by calculating the break-even charge, the minimum profitable charge, and the maximum practicable charge. Add up what you will have to pay out for the following items:

Itemization of Cost for One Issue	Amount
Printing costs (one issue)	
Distribution cost (one issue)	
Writers' fees (one issue)	
Layout and design costs per issue	
Rent and utilities for the period covered by a <u>single issue</u>	
Miscellaneous expenses	
Ad sales commission rate or salesperson's salary	
Total Cost for One Issue	$

Some of these services may come from you, but treat them as though you had to pay someone else to perform them. You want your magazine to be profitable even when success forces you to hire others to help you out. One of the ways you can make a bundle of money from your publication is to sell it later as an established entity to someone interested in acquiring an up-and-running publication. Any buyer you attract will *always* look for profit above and beyond all costs, including those that you were, as owner-publisher, happy to furnish "for free."

When you have this total, estimate the number of advertising pages you think you can sell. Now divide your total costs by the anticipated number of ad pages. This will give you your break-even point:

$$\frac{\text{Total Cost per Issue Break-even}}{\text{Number of ad pages}} = \textbf{COST PER PAGE}$$

This cost per page is what you pay out to publish the magazine. At this level nobody makes anything. Your profit will have to be added in on top of the break-even cost. To simplify matters, let's say that your magazine will come out once every two months. It's going to cost you, say, $10,000 to bring out an issue. You think you can sell thirty pages of ads. Your break-even cost per page, therefore, is $333.

In order to make the venture profitable for you, and to cover all the small expenses (they can mount up) that you forgot to include in your calculation of costs, you want to clear $5000 an issue above costs. This is the least you can get by with.

Your cost plus your profit ($10,000 plus $5000) equals $15,000. Now divide this price by the anticipated number of ad pages and you get your retail, per-page rate:

$$\frac{\text{Cost plus desired profit}}{\text{Number of ad pages}} = \textbf{RETAIL RATE PER PAGE}$$

In this case, the retail rate per page would be $15,000 divided by 30, or $500. This is your minimum profitable retail charge per page.

Next, study your market area. Is it affluent? Can businesses afford more? Study your competition. What are *they* charging per page? In comparing yourself to the local newspaper, remember that it is here today and gone tomorrow. It is in black and white. Your magazine is full-color and *targeted to your customer's chief market, the tourist or newcomer.* Your rate, therefore should be considerably higher.

If there is another well-designed tourist guide already up and running, you'll have to take their rate structure into account as well. But in general, my experience shows me that desirable and obtainable retail ad rates — as distinct from the minimum possible charge — will be approximately three times the break-even cost, and possibly more. Using this figure, the retail ad rate you should shoot for in your tourism guide is, in even numbers, $1000 — and still a bargain for the advertiser at that.

SMALLER ADS COST MORE

Let's say that your per-page retail rate is $1000. That's what you charge a customer who takes a full-page ad. Smaller ads will be proportionately more expensive.

Study samples of tourism guides that others have done. (This should be your source for many of the design details you will face. Simply find someone who has done things well and do likewise.) You will note that the usual format is to divide the page into two columns. Breaking this format down into ad sizes you come up with a half page, quarter page, and eighth page as your standard sizes for smaller ads.

If a full page is $1000, then a half page will be three-fifths of that figure, or $600. (This is a minimum. It could be higher.) Your quarter-page ad will be three-fifths of the cost of the half-page, or $360. And your eighth-page ad will be three-fifths of $360, or $216. So, although your full page rate is $1000, eight ads one-eighth page in size will gross $1728.

The rationale for this is simple. It takes as much time to sell, service, and collect a one-eighth page account — and design the ad to the customer's satisfaction — as the full page account. So you will expend many times the effort on the page full of small ads as on the full-page ad of a single advertiser. The higher proportionate rate compensates you for this. The bottom line is that you can make a good deal of money selling the smaller ads. Don't neglect them.

RECRUITING AND MANAGING SALESPEOPLE

Perhaps you're a natural-born salesman and can generate signed contracts almost as fast as you can schedule and make the calls. Perhaps.

My experience, though, has been different. Through sheer necessity I have learned to go out, make a presentation, and ask for the order. But even on my best day I could not hold a candle to real salespeople — those who relish the combat and exult in bringing in the business. So if sales are not your strong suit, find someone to help you out. Management and planning will take the lion's share of your available time in any case. After all, someone's got to come up with the ad idea and the ad copy after the salesperson brings in the contract.

So what do you look for? How do you tell a good salesperson from a mediocre or bad one? There is, of course, a good deal of trial and error. Even the most considered and careful choices can often prove wrong. With salespeople all the old proverbs work: the proof *is* in the pudding; you *can* judge the tree by its fruit.

Can you do better than that? Well, you don't have the budget to go head-hunting, to identify the best salesperson in five states and four provinces and go out and hire him or her, whatever the costs.

So who do you look for? Here are some tips garnered from my own experience, when the budget was limited and the cash flow still nonexistent.

- *Hire people who know the area well and have some personal contacts to prime the sales pump*. In fact, this is one success principle. Hire ten people who can sell an ad to five friends and you've sold fifty ads. It can add up quickly.

- *Hire only those who have had successful sales experience in some field* (retail, over-the-counter sales don't count, unless the personality is there) or who are really confident of success. When candidates for the job say words to the effect of "I just don't know whether I can sell or not . . .," they can't.

- *Look for sales reps who have some income to live on*. You will not be able to provide enough in commissions to buy groceries and pay the rent for Mom, Dad, and five hungry kids.

- *Look for sales reps among two very attractive labor pools*: 1) intelligent, energetic women whose kids are now in school or off at college and who want to become active again — they will love being associated with a high visibility, prestigious business like publishing; and 2) retired persons who are still very capable and who can't stand the boredom of doing nothing.

- *Hire people who are able and willing to schedule their work and work the schedule.* You don't have to have them on full-time. But you do need to know what they are doing and when they are doing it. And you *always* need to check to make sure that, in actuality, it has been done.

- *Hire three times as many people as you need.* Some will fall by the wayside, finding the work more attractive in theory than in practice; some will be discouraged when someone says no; and some just won't like selling. That will leave the one or two or three good people you need to get the project up and going and keep it that way.

You will have to be a careful, meticulous, and supportive sales manager, holding regular meetings, exchanging ideas, encouraging, congratulating, applying balm to the wounds, and checking up. Most of all, checking up. I developed a simple sales guide that I have found useful, a copy of which is reproduced in the appendix. Notice the insistence on regular filing of sales call reports and sales reports.

What should you pay your salespeople? Twenty percent, tops, on sales to new accounts when you do not pay expenses. Fifteen percent is more usual. Ten percent on repeat business is about as low as you can go. *Commissions are due and payable only on submission of a signed contract and all materials necessary to make up the ad.*

EDITORIAL CONTENT

How much editorial space? The answer to this question varies widely from publication to publication. A general consumer magazine *may* be as much as 40% editorial matter against 60% advertising. But most that do have that high percentage of editorial space probably long for the day when their magazine contains a great deal of additional advertising. A successful newspaper may run as high as 75% advertising against 25% editorial.

A first-rate tourism guide should contain at least 80% advertising, if not more. This may seem high to you, but remember that it is the ads that the reader is principally interested in. Unfamiliar with the area, he will pick up one of your guidebooks to shop the restaurants and decide where to go for dinner. If he needs some beach-wear he will browse through the ads looking for a place that he believes will have the kinds and styles of apparel that he wants and needs.

Weekly Sales Report

Name _____ Week of _____

Name of Advertiser/Client	Name of Publication	Amt. of Sale	Contract Attached	Dossier Complete	Comm.	Comm. Paid	Date Comm. Paid

Always keep your magazine design simple. Readability is the primary consideration. Fancy layouts often just confuse the reader and cost the publisher a ton of money that he would be better off spending on something else. You will get full page ads from the ad agencies that will have all the color and extravagant design you need. For the rest of it: SIMPLICITY, the goal to strive for.

All of your editorial matter will feature things to do and places to go. Lists and directories are great (ten top golf courses; public and private campgrounds; state parks and other attractions, etc.).

One paragraph of mini-reviews of advertisers' restaurants certainly ought to be included.

Maps showing the reader how to get there from here will enhance the reader-pulling (and advertiser-pulling) power of your guide.

Articles on history, local color, personalities, and places definitely have a role to play. But these are short (it is better to have ten 500-word articles than five 1000-worders), and they are carefully and professionally written.

How much do you pay writers? Five cents a word will generally be competitive in this market plus, say, $10 per photo. At these prices you'll be dealing with a lot of writers who are just breaking into the magazine field and for whom an acceptance and a check mean far more than the small amount of money involved. You (or someone working with you) will polish and edit, of course.

How Many to Print?

You'll have to face the fact that the first time around, at least, the number of copies you ask your printer to produce for you is not much better than an educated guess. To arrive at this guess, you will want to compile certain basic information.

- How many motel and hotel rooms there are. You will want to keep your magazine available in each of them throughout the life of the current issue.
- How many copies the Chamber of Commerce and the Visitors' Center feel that they can circulate.
- How many retail and other outlets there are.
- How many copies competing publications (including the local newspaper) claim to print.

With this information in hand you can come up with some kind of estimate of what your print run ought to be. And, of course, there is another factor to put at the very top of your list. That is how many magazines you can *afford* to print and circulate and still make the profit that you want and need. Greater circulation brings greater usage and more results for your advertisers . . . but it also generates higher costs. You will have to find a balance.

Since there are certain advantageous "break points" in printing costs, get quotes (not estimates, mind you, but quotes) from several printers on various quantities. For instance, 10,000 books will not cost twice as much as 5000. And since the equipment that individual printers own will vary, some will be able to do longer runs far more economically than others. The chapter on dealing with printers goes into considerable detail on this.

I suggest that you consider the following rough guidelines for determining your print run. You will not be far wrong, and you can fine tune on the second edition. Keep in mind that conditions in various markets differ so widely that firm rules are impossible.

1) Print one book per motel room for each month of the life of your magazine. If there are 3000 rooms and your book comes out monthly, print 3000 for this part of your distribution network. If your book comes out once every two months, print 6000, and so on from there.

2) Now print the same number for distribution at other outlets.

3) Add to this the number that you will leave with the Chamber and the Visitors' Center.

With the sum of these three figures in mind, compare your projected circulation with 1) that claimed by your competition; 2) the cost of producing that many copies of your publication; and 3) your own gut feeling about what circulation ought to be to cover the market adequately.

In general, newcomers to the publishing business tend to overestimate readership and wind up with a lot of leftovers on their hands. But for a first edition it is better to err on the high side than on the low. It won't hurt a thing on the first go-round to have extra books to give away *everywhere*. You need to make a splash. The reputation earned by your first edition is one you will have to live with for a long, long time.

CIRCULATION

As publisher of a tourism guide, you want your magazine to get results for your advertisers. When paying customers come into a motel, retail shop, or restaurant with your magazine in hand, or when a shop owner notes a marked increased in sales after the appearance of the issue containing his ad, you have won a lifetime client. As this base of satisfied advertisers grows from issue to issue, you can spend more and more of your time developing business in fringe areas and secondary markets (perhaps even inventing new things to publish), with your book growing thicker and more profitable year by year. But before any of these good things can happen you have got to get your book into the hands of every possible purchaser of your advertisers' products and services.

There are a number of basics here, but there is one piece of advice at the start. Whatever you do, *make sure that your book is visible, that it is seen in as many places as possible and by as many people as possible.* Not only do you need to circulate your book, but you need to create in the minds of your advertisers the perception that you are circulating the book. These are not, alas, always the same thing.

The Chamber of Commerce or the Visitors' Center may give them away by the dozens, but the shop and restaurant owners who buy space from you do not go in these places and so are not aware of it. The same thing is true of the copies you leave on bedside tables at leading motels. This may be the most effective circulation of all, but it is invisible, insofar as many of your advertisers are concerned. For them, seeing is believing. Remember that you have a twofold purpose. You want to get your magazine into the hands of the people who use it, true. But you also want to convince your advertisers beyond a shadow of a doubt that this is what you are doing.

Since your magazine is free, any number of places will be happy to let you leave copies on a countertop or in other convenient locations. I have found that the tops of cigarette vending machines are perfect for this: just the right height and with plenty of space that is not usually in demand for any other use.

Here is a starter list of circulation possibilities. You will doubtless discover many others of your own:

- Convenience stores
- Grocery stores
- Real estate offices
- Restaurants
- Hotels and motels (leave one for each room and replenish regularly)
- Places of business of your own advertisers
- Banks
- Savings and loan companies

- Airports
- Bus stations
- Service stations
- Gift shops and other retail outlets
- Chambers of Commerce
- Visitors' centers

Circulation vs. Readership

One of the first and most frequent questions your salespeople will hear is the no-nonsense one where the prospect looks them squarely in the eye and asks, "What is your circulation?"

The answer to that question is not as simple as it might seem. You know how many you printed. Let's say that you decided on a press run of 25,000 copies. Is that what you answer? Do you say, "My circulation is 25,000"?

Maybe. Maybe not. What your advertiser really wants is to know is how many people will pick up your magazine, browse through it, and have an opportunity to see his ad. If each magazine stays in a motel room for an average of two weeks before it is filched, worn out, or lost, I think you could say without any exaggeration that ten to fifteen people will have had occasion to read through it.

So, if the half of your press run — 12,500 copies, following the example given above — is read by an average of ten people, then the *readership* of the magazine — as distinct from mere circulation — will be 125,000 for those 12,500 copies. And if the remainder of the press run is read by the one single person who picked the copy up at the corner store, and no more, your total readership is 137,500. This is, of course, a much more impressive figure than the circulation alone, and makes for much easier ad sales. It is also, in its own way, accurate. Your job as publisher is to create a magazine of such interest that each copy attracts as many readers as possible.

If you are in a competitive situation, you must discover what measure your competition (and there will almost always be some competition from some quarter) is using, whether circulation or readership. One of my salespeople reported recently that she had lost a sale to another magazine because, as her prospect said, "it reached so many more people." I managed to get hold of their sales materials and found that they were claiming a "readership" of 50,000. A close look at their rate card, however, revealed that they printed only 12,000 copies of each issue. They simply claimed — on some convenient basis — that more than four people read each copy in circulation.

Our magazine printed 20,000 copies. On that basis our readership would have been over 80,000. Had our salesperson been more experienced and aware of the ratio of circulation to readership, she would have been able to counter the prospect's objection and perhaps overcome it.

The circulation of major national magazines and all paid subscription newspapers is audited, either by the U.S. Postal Service or one of the private audit firms like ABC (Audit Bureau of Circulation). On that level the circulation/readership game cannot be played. The facts are the facts and are there for all to see. Circulation figures are easily and accurately compared. But for regional and local publications like yours my advice is that you should — without ever misrepresenting your actual circulation — *emphasize your readership because that's what the others are doing.*

So that's it — your basic starter kit for a travel and tourism guide. Study the competition. Do what has proven successful elsewhere — you can individualize it later on after you've learned the ropes. Set your ad rates right and generate strong editorial support. You're in business, and in a business that can be quite a winner for you.

NEW CUSTOMER CREATION
TWO WAYS TO GO
EDITORIAL CONTENT
ADVERTORIALS

5.

Publishing a Newcomer's Guide

Every year thousands of new individuals and families move into even relatively small towns. All of them have at least one thing in common. They have left behind them the stores where they bought their clothes, the name of that trusted plumber and other service people, their doctors, their automobile dealers, their insurance salespeople, their favorite restaurants, theaters, schools, nightspots, specialty shops, bookstores ... and hundreds of other places where they were accustomed to go to spend their money to acquire the goods, services, or entertainment that we all require.

Families are constantly moving in and moving out. Even if the total population grows only modestly, the number of new families in town will be very substantial. In some communities, the equivalent of a 75% turnover in population may take place over a ten year period or less.

Furthermore, traveling sales representatives and thousands of other temporary — one night, one week, or one month — residents need and use much of the same information. Such individuals eagerly welcome the kind of information about things to do and places to go that the newcomer guide provides. Every metropolitan area of more than thirty or forty thousand — often even less — is prime territory for such a publication.

The advertising base is much larger than for the tourism guide, since purveyors of all kinds of services — from electricians to interior decorators to specialized medical clinics — can derive great benefit from inclusion. But individuals and families moving into a new metropolitan area for the first time also eagerly welcome the kind of information about things to do and places to go that the more narrowly focused tourism guide provides.

NEW CUSTOMER CREATION

The newcomer's guide is in the business of new customer creation — *permanent* new customer creation. When you arrive in town and need insurance — homeowner's or automobile, say — and you call someone whose name you saw in the newcomer's guide, that insurance rep or agency has a permanent customer, provided that the services he renders are good and customer relations strong and positive. You will not only buy this particular policy from your new agent, but all those that you will need in subsequent years. And you will tell your friends about this excellent insurance person, too. So his ad has purchased not an individual sale but a lifetime of business.

In any town, any business that doesn't go after the newcomers will inevitably wither and die over the long haul. Astute business owners know this and will seize any opportunity to tap into this source of continuing and sustaining business nourishment and vitality.

This is what advertising in a newcomer's guide can do, and what you or your sales force must make your potential clients understand. When you succeed in doing this — and in creating a publication that *will* do this — you will have established a profitable publishing enterprise for yourself.

TWO WAYS TO GO

There are two ways to approach the project of publishing a newcomer's guide. You can come out with a relatively inexpensive magazine, as often as once a month, with moderate advertising space rates; or you can come out annually — perhaps quarterly in a major city — with an expensive, full-color magazine.

Both approaches will work. As a matter of fact, you could possibly do both of them, with the more affordable monthly bringing in a steady flow of cash to do business on and the annual bringing in a one-time infusion of major cash.

OPTION 1:

The Newcomer Monthly

It is theoretically possible to do your newcomer guide weekly, but I do not recommend it. You will see such publications in motel rooms and on tops of restaurant cigarette machines, usually with titles like "This Week."

My experience is that you can do a better job editorially, get better results for your advertisers, and actually increase your take-home profit when you come out monthly. The weekly versions I have seen — because of their super-tight production schedules — usually amount to little more than a restaurant and entertainment guide. You are going after a far wider readership than that.

Keep the format as simple as possible. You do this for several good reasons. First of all, you are on a fairly restrictive production schedule. Much of the layout, design, and pasteup will need to be done in-house. You won't have the luxury or the budget to go to outside color houses or design studios to get your work done. Everything will be done on your own trusty desktop publishing system.

Advertisers — the same the world over, apparently — will all be calling in with last-minute changes. The only way you will be able to accommodate them is to make the changes yourself, in your own offices. If you've sent the materials off to some company half a state away, there's not much chance that customer service of this kind will be possible.

You will want to use a standard size. Your choices are 8½" x 11" or 5½" x 8½". An alternative, if you so choose and if the market is right, is to design your publication in newspaper tabloid format. (The section on tabloids will provide more details on this latter option.)

Color? I would consider it if I had advertisers willing to pay for it. In general, you will be better off in this monthly version limiting the use of color to the front and back covers, and even then spot color is preferable to process color (full color). If competition forces you to it, well and good. If not, stick with the simpler choice.

Use a 70 lb. paper. This will give some body to your magazine. It may be coated or uncoated, slick or matte. It is a question of how much quality your advertisers are willing to pay for. You can't serve them caviar if all they're willing and able to pay for is meatloaf and mashed potatoes.

Much more important is the quality of the content, design, and distribution. A small format magazine has been published for many years in the neighboring town of New Bern, North Carolina. Called *New Bern Magazine*, it is printed on the plainest 60 lb. uncoated offset paper. There is a little spot color — perhaps a background screen on the cover — and nothing more. The ads are modest in design, a little clip art and type and very little more. Yet the magazine stays in circulation year after year. It is making money for the people who publish it. Because it is economical to edit and produce, a large number of copies can be printed. It is seen and picked up everywhere, consulted and used by newcomers and old residents alike.

Remember that you are not in the business of winning literary prizes but of selling advertising benefits to your customers. If your publication is interesting to read, useful to have, and if you get it into the hands of enough people, *your advertisers will get results*. That fact — and that fact alone — is the foundation on which long-term profits will be built. If you can achieve this with an inexpensive, easy-to-produce format you are that much to the good.

Another plus of the monthly, and one that is not at all negligible, is the regular cash flow it generates. With this publication there will be no feast or famine, but a steady influx of funds of the kind that an ongoing, successful publishing business can be built on.

OPTION 2:

The High Dollar Annual

There is much to be said, however, for the opposite approach: The publication of a newcomer's guide that will come out once yearly in a full-color format of the highest possible quality. In spite of the greater cost of production, the advertising rates will be such that your margin of net profit will comprise a greater percentage of gross sales, especially if you do either the sales or the marketing yourself.

I was recently approached by an entrepreneur who had begun a newcomer's guide of this type in a major east coast city of 150,000. He was a real-estate developer and not a publisher. He started his magazine chiefly because he needed a means of advertising his ex- clusive, expensive subdivisions to families moving into the area. His guide was standard magazine size, printed on heavy, coated stock, perfect bound, and lavish in its use of color.

The magazine made a profit but the owner, not being in the publishing business, found it a burden to manage and, in spite of a strong bottom line, not the most profitable use of his time. Would I, he asked, be interested in buying it from him?

I looked at the rate card, counted the pages of advertising, and checked the advertising space contracts to make sure that the ads had indeed been sold at rate card prices. It was a second issue, sold and promoted by someone who had no experience in publishing. Still, it contained at least $80,000 worth of advertising. I estimated that it would have taken about $20,000 to design, typeset, and print it and another $20,000, say, in commissions to the sales force and other sales-related expenses. The gross profit, before overhead, would have been approximately $40,000 — a very substantial sum of money.

Should I buy it from him? Perhaps. But two issues do not, in themselves, convey the guarantee of substantial "goodwill." In addition, one may wonder whether this developer is really interested in staying in the magazine business over the long haul. He may simply abandon his project.

Still, it is an up-and-going concern. I decided that I would not be interested in paying out much cash, since I could always start one myself with adequate capital on hand. I would, however, take the project over and pay the former owner a percentage of the gross over an extended period of time.

The most interesting point to me was the clear way in which this project proved that an annual newcomer's directory, even in the hands of inexperienced people, can generate a substantial profit when there is a need for it in the market and it is well done.

With the annual edition option you do, of course, have a more limited, if more affluent, list of advertising prospects. Every sale will count, and you can't afford to lose any potential prospect. On the other hand even thirty or forty ad contracts at $1500 to $2500 each will quickly add up to a large sum of money.

Since the annual newcomer's guide is expensive to produce, you don't have the luxury of putting it out for free pickup at every restaurant, motel lobby, and convenience store in town, as you did with the monthly guide. Great care will be taken to make every copy count. Ask banks to distribute the guide in their newcomer kits, as well as the Chamber of Commerce and the County Development Commission or Committee of 100.

Sales Effectiveness
You have a finite number of prospects for ad sales in your magazines. Salespersons prepare carefully for each call. You can't afford to burn any lead through inept presentations. Salespeople should be prepared with 1) knowledge of the prospect's business and needs; 2) familiarity with the prospect's advertising to date; and 3) ideas for ads. The purpose of these ideas is to get the prospect thinking about what to put into his ad rather than whether to advertise or not.

A real coup would be to get your magazine placed on the planes of commuter and shuttle-type airlines serving your area. The major airlines will have their own publications. Perhaps the prospect of an advertising tradeout will sweeten the pot enough to attract their favorable attention.

The remainder will be placed *in the rooms* of prestige hotels and motels or placed on sale at newsstands. You won't make any money selling via newsstands, since discounts to wholesale newsrack vendors are large and, in any case, monies owed back to you from copies sold are notoriously hard to collect. But the presence of your magazines on the stands makes them available to others who might desire and need the information they contain.

Being prominently displayed on newsstands also gives your newcomer guide the kind of constant exposure that keeps it in the minds of potential advertisers. It provides that all-important ingredient: highly *visible* circulation.

The Legacy of Landfall: Exquisite Homes in the Most Beautiful of Surroundings.

"We saw the open country rising above the sandy shores...
as pleasant and delectable to behold as is possible to imagine..."
—Giovanni da Verrazano

by Allison E. Baker

Landfall today is known for its excellent golf courses, distinctive homes and panoramic view of the Intracoastal Waterway.

As one of eastern North Carolina's newest planned communities, Landfall holds a future of promise and opportunity. And a history of romance and change.

Landfall's story began in 1524, in another world, when Giovanni da Verrazano sailed westward from Europe in search of riches and fame. After battling the Atlantic for two months, he and his crew made landfall in the New World, at the point nestled along the Intracoastal Waterway near Cape Fear.

Verrazano was so fascinated with the land that he wrote in his journal, "Sailing forward, we found certain small rivers and curves of the sea, washing the shore on both sides. And beyond this, we saw the open country rising in height above the sandy shores with many fair fields and plains, full of mighty great woods...as pleasant and delectable to behold as is possible to imagine... And the land is full of many beasts...and likewise of lakes and pools of fresh water...with good and wholesome air."

Four centuries later, these features enticed one of America's wealthiest men to build his estate on the same piece of land.

EDITORIAL CONTENT

In editorial content the two versions of the newcomer guide are very similar, with this difference: While you can experiment with inexperienced writers and clip art advertising design in the cheaper, monthly guide, the annual magazine must be written and designed by the best people you can afford.

Essential to both versions will be the lists of useful addresses; voter registration information; a guide to school districts, utilities, and governmental services. These make the magazine a useful tool and encourage readers to keep it around for reference use. This is precisely the kind of heavy use that will generate business for your advertisers. When readers consult the magazine for one kind of information they consult it for goods and services as well. It comes across as useful, trusted, and designed and written with the reader's needs in mind. This is the image you want to get across.

Here are some additional kinds of editorial materials that will find a positive response:

- **How-to pieces**: Your imagination is your only limit in this category. Many pieces can be found that can be tied in with advertising, i.e., how to decorate your home, how to buy a home, how to finance a home, how to build a home, how to evaluate subdivisions. Other how-to pieces might be activity related: how to get involved in the arts community, how to get involved in government, how to get involved in community service, how to get involved in sports, how to find a church, and many more.
- **Orientation pieces**: the history, geography, landscape of the area.
- **Recreation pieces**: places to go and things to do.
- **Personality profiles** of outstanding people in local politics, the arts, sports, etc.
- **Guides to the best**: restaurants, golf courses, night clubs, spas, bookstores . . . the possibilities are virtually limitless and all offer good tie-ins with advertising.

ADVERTORIALS

The "advertorial" is important to you in your newcomer guide, and it is discussed at more length in Chapter 6 on city magazines. Sold as regular advertising space, advertorials appear in regular magazine article format with all the elements that make your feature articles readable: characterization, anecdotes, human interest, quotes, etc. You also take care to see that they are every bit as accurate as other articles. There is nothing either in form or quality that sets them off from other articles in the magazine.

Advertorials can be powerful. They work. Suppose, for instance, you had an advertising client who was an interior designer. You *could* run a full-page ad, perhaps with a photograph of the designer, a description of services offered, and an invitation to call for an appointment.

How much more effective would be an advertorial that introduces the designer in article format, giving him personality, showing him in action — solving problems, creating solutions, meeting peoples' needs and expectations.

I have used advertorials many times and often with dramatic results. One young businessman — a financial adviser in a very conservative, cliquish community — credits an advertorial I wrote with overcoming initial resistance to him by making his potential clients feel that they already knew him and could have confidence in him.

Since the entire purpose of your newcomer guide is promotion, there is no need to label these advertorials as "paid advertising." Ethically, your only responsibility, as publisher of a newcomer guide, is to see that the advertorials are accurate in what they say and do not misinform the reader. You are also responsible for seeing to it that the advertorials are strong, readable pieces of writing in their own right. Ideally, they will be so well-written that you would have wanted to publish them whether or not you were paid to do so.

However it is done, monthly or annually, the newcomer's guide represents a very profitable project for the regional publisher, one strong enough to provide the foundation on which a much broader publishing enterprise can comfortably rest.

6.

Publishing a City Magazine

The publication of a city magazine can be a very tempting project, especially to those who derive great pleasure from the editorial and literary side of the business. *Dallas, Atlanta, Cincinnati,* and other top titles are full of good writing, good photography, and good advertising. There is considerable personal reward — not to mention personal status, visibility, and occasional political clout — in being known in the community as the editor or publisher (or both) of such a stylish and dynamic magazine.

City Magazine
Awareness of your new city magazine will grow gradually. It may come as a shock to you, but everyone will not be paying strict attention to your project. If you have a good product and if you are profitable — even marginally — from the beginning, then the outlook for success is very good. Issue after issue, more and more people will see and appreciate the publication. Calls will begin to come in from potential advertisers who contact you on their own to obtain a media kit. When this begins to happen, rejoice! The future is yours to make.

That part of it can be a lot of fun. I have just given in to this temptation myself — or at least to a variation of it. As I write this I am getting a new magazine off the ground. Since I live in a part of my state where there are no cities large enough to support a city magazine as such, mine is a first cousin — a regional magazine for the coastal plains area of North Carolina, called *NCEast.*

The nature of the magazine and the rewards are quite similar to those of the city magazine. The challenges are even greater, since both the editorial coverage and advertising sales are spread over a much wider area. This raises difficulties in two ways. The wide area of coverage makes it harder to create an editorial impact in the marketplace, and the wide area that ad sales reps must cover makes that chore much more expensive. Still, I publish *NCEast* because I want to and because it is a pleasure to see each new issue of the magazine come off the press and go out to the public.

FIRST, THE BAD NEWS

To begin with, let me offer a word of warning — some gentle advice to those bitten by the city magazine bug. The first thing is that you should not bring out a city magazine if the potential for profit is your major or sole motivation. You will work harder for fewer dollars as publisher of a city magazine than in almost any of the other areas discussed in this book. Still, don't let this cautionary advice overwhelm you either. When they are well managed in a trade area that can support them, city magazines can, and usually do, make a profit. It's just a question of how much profit.

The second piece of advice is that you should not go into the city magazine business if that magazine is the only thing your company is going to do. The magazine can give you visibility and act as a magnet to bring in other projects that help create financial stability and staying power. Standing alone as your only source of revenue, a city magazine is fairly vulnerable.

The third word to the wise is that you should not publish a city magazine if too many people intend to derive their entire living wage from it. A magazine fares best with as little fixed overhead as possible. It will be difficult for it to generate more than one "executive level" salary. Instead, you will use freelance writers, editors, and artists, and salespeople paid entirely on commission.

How Too Much Money Can Lead You Astray

When I bought my newspaper I hired an ad sales specialist to come in and give me and my sales staff a seminar. One thing he told us has stuck with me and been a very valuable rule of action for me. "Never," he said, "judge anyone else's pocketbook by your own." I had often done just that, I realized. Since I had always been a writer and a schoolteacher before I got into publishing, I never had much of a nest-egg in my bank account. I lived pretty much month to month. I unconsciously assumed that everyone else was in the same financial shape I was.

Some of those reading this chapter may well have inherited a couple of hundred thousand from old Aunt Emily. Others may have found investors who will pour funds into the business during the start-up months. What such well-financed individuals may not realize, however, is that too much money in the corporate coffers can be a mixed blessing — although too much is *always* better than too little.

If, by some happy circumstance, you have more money on hand than is required by your immediate needs, it may be to your benefit to act as though you don't. Lots of up-front capital will make it easier for you in the beginning but won't guarantee long-term success. In fact, it can even make trouble for you, like an easy remedy that masks a serious illness but doesn't do anything to help cure it. And when you find out that you are sick it may be too late to do anything about it.

This does not *have* to happen, of course, and I am the first to admit that given a choice I would always go for a fat bank account rather than a skinny one. But if you do have money in the bank you will need as much or more discipline than if you do not have it. Because you care about your magazine you will often be tempted to spend a little more for this effect or that, use more color than you can really afford, print on fancier paper than you need to, and so on. This kind of soft-headed management can fritter away even the most substantial cash reserves.

Many a well-heeled publication has made a brilliant debut but, unable to sustain itself with internal cash flow, faded quickly from view. The case of *Southern Magazine* comes to mind. A year ago I heard a talk by the young editor, Linton Weeks. *Southern Magazine* had been financed to the tune of five to ten million dollars. It was editorially brilliant and graphically strong. Yet twelve months later it disappeared from view, fallen on hard times, bought out and renamed.

LEAN AND MEAN

When, as a publisher, you live strictly within your means you are forced to develop strategies to deal creatively with tight money situations. And you can deal with them when you put your mind to it. You find ways to strengthen your magazine without huge cash expenditures. You find writers who will accept lower fees against the day when bigger dollars may roll around. You find photographers anxious for their work to be seen. You do not use that extra page of color that you really cannot afford. Instead you use powerful black and white photos that, in this day of nearly universal color, can have a tremendous impact of their own. You go to printer after printer until you find one who will print your magazine at a price you can afford and set up a payment schedule that you can live with. Built this way a magazine becomes stronger and stronger issue after issue. It pays its own way, and in doing so earns its spot in your company's repertoire of profitable publications.

A POSITION OF STRENGTH

When you develop your magazine from a position of strength, it will grow muscle day after day and issue after issue. Indeed, a city magazine has two of the most important success characteristics going for it: It is focused and it is manageable. It has a concentrated and well-defined market, both for circulation and for advertising sales. And for this very reason it is easier to manage than other publications that might cover a broader and more diverse trade area. You meet your advertisers every day, mingle with your readers morning, noon, and night. You know your magazine's market intimately. Because of these things you can recognize and seize opportunities quickly and react from one day to the next to the challenges that will inevitably confront you.

SURVEYING THE MARKET

As with any other business venture, the first step in planning your magazine is to survey the market to determine the probability for success. You will want to develop answers to preliminary questions such as the following:

How much money — in terms of advertising budgets — is out there to be gotten?

What publications are currently competing for those advertising dollars?

Are any of these publications similar to yours? If so, which ones?

In the light of your competition how will you define a market position for your magazine that will distinguish it from the others and make it an attractive alternative for advertising placement?

There will be three main motives for advertising in a city magazine. These are image enhancement, ego satisfaction, and immediate generation of business. Go through the Yellow Pages and list those businesses that are good candidates for ad sales. Place them in one or more of the three categories. Is this a sufficient inventory of prospects to ensure sufficient ad sales?

Study the rate cards of competing publications. Where will your own rates fit into this pattern of costs? Can you charge enough per page to remain competitive and yet generate a profit?

With detailed answers to these questions in hand you will be in a position to decide whether you should even publish your magazine and, if you decide to do so, to go ahead with your publication plans.

ALLOW FOR NECESSARY TIME

Advertising budgets are set by most businesses at least a year in advance. Since you will be charging premium prices for your space

It was a festive day all day! Mr. Springer's uncle, William Springer, Jr. served on that committee of management. He and Ed Springer's grandfather, Edward Delevan Springer, had bought the lumber mill in South Creek, which had been owned by Isiah Respess and also Shade Harris. It was a very productive mill conveniently

'I've come to admire the land that is so rich with trees, creeks, and rivers and yet still holds mysterious secrets of the past.

located near the water where great piles of lumber were loaded on boats and shipped north.

Speaking of boats, both of the Springer brothers obtained their Captain's licenses and piloted boats regularly out of South Creek.

There were two cotton gins at South Creek in 1878, a brick kiln in 1898, and a barrel factory in 1898. These are all indications that South Creek was a busy, thriving community and larger than Aurora in the 1800's! The advent of the railroad as transportation and later the automobile, changed forever South Creek and Aurora, as they did many other small river towns, from the thriving, bustling communities of earlier days to the quiet and serene atmosphere we see today.

A Continuing Romance
However, by now I am sure you easily understand why my romance with Richland Township continues to strengthen and grow.

A year after I first was introduced to Aurora, I bought a home in Richland Township, ten miles outside of the town. I've come to admire the land that is so rich with trees, creeks, and rivers and yet still holds mysterious secrets of the past that may someday be revealed.

This, for me, has been an adventurous, delightful romance, being able to enjoy Richland Township's bustling past through the generosity of some of the older citizens, and I know that relationship will continue to grow.

It's just the beginning of a great romance!

How the Creeks Got their Names

Durham Creek was named after Richard Durham, who obtained an original grant of 640 acres and which also included Garrison Point at the mouth of Durham's Creek.

Nevil's Creek got its name from James Neville, who had a home at the mouth of the creek. His family of three was massacred by the Indians in the Tuscarora War of 1711.

Leigh Creek or Lee's Creek was named for James Leigh, who obtained a grant of land near the mouth of the creek in 1707. He built a plantation and lived there for a number of years.

Snoode's or Snood's Creek was named for James Snood who obtained a land grant in 1720 which included both sides of the creek.

Maule's Point was originally Smith's Point. This section was the home of the Roulbacs, the Blounts and the Maules and was named after Dr. Patrick Maule, who had a house

there and was a practicing physician in Bath.

Blount's Creek was named after the Blount family but was originally called Tyler's Creek, probably after an early family.

Fresh Pond is located on the farm of Mr. Lawrence Bushousen about three miles from the concrete road at Blount's Creek Crossroads. This pond is about one-fourth mile long and two hundred yards wide. It is fed by underground steams, and the water rises and falls with the tide in Blount's Creek a mile-and-a-half away.

There is an Indian legend about this pond, which has such delightful fresh water. Many, many moons ago, so the legend goes, during the time when the water covered this part of the world, whales were numerous here. Suddenly the water subsided and left a whale in a small depression. This whale, in his effort to seek deep water, wallowed out quite a hole. The whale, however, could not follow his brothers to deep water, and so he died there. Early residents found whale bones to further support the legend, and from an aerial view the pond has the shape of a whale!

11

most businesses will not be able to pull enough out of petty cash or discretionary budgets to place a full year's advertising with you.

Give these larger advertisers as much lead time as you can, so that your magazine can be included in the budget. Even then, as a new publication, you will run into the "it's not in my budget" objection with disheartening frequency.

When this is a genuine objection and not a mere put-off, you may overcome it (as I have often done) by setting up the account on a monthly pay basis. If your magazine appears every other month you divide the advertising price into two payments. If you come out quarterly, it may be divided into three payments — and so on. Small sums of cash, even if required more frequently, are easier for enterprising marketing managers to raise.

SURVEY THE READERSHIP

You will also survey potential readership. Who are the people who will read your magazine? What are their interests? What is the demographic profile of your trade area? You obviously want to create a magazine that will interest the largest number of individuals and families with the most discretionary income. If you are to succeed, your readers must buy your advertisers' products or use their services. To do so they must first *want* to read your magazine, then *read* your magazine, and finally *have the resources* to take action on an advertiser's offer. Without all three of these elements nothing will happen.

One of the magazine success stories of the past decade is that of *Modern Maturity*, the magazine of the American Association of Retired Persons (AARP). If you judged by looking through the pages of this publication you would decide that American retirees are handsome, healthy, and affluent. The editors completely ignore that great segment of the older population that lives close to if not below the poverty level. Why? Because people without money can't buy anything. A readership of food stamp recipients would be hard pressed to attract those full page ads from American Express and the Caribbean cruise ship lines.

The mix of this relatively affluent population who enjoy reading and have money to spend varies from place to place. It will be quite different in St. Augustine and Atlanta. The Dallas profile may vary quite a bit from that of Chicago, San Francisco from Little Rock, or New Orleans from a university town like Ann Arbor. Your survey will tell you what kind of people are out there in your community, people to whom your magazine must appeal.

DEFINE YOUR EDITORIAL SLANT

When you have your readership clearly in mind, you should write out succinctly, in one paragraph, your editorial philosophy.

What kinds of articles will you publish and in what style should they be written?

How long will they be? Will they be heavily or only marginally illustrated with photography?

The editorial policy of *Mother Earth News*, for instance, will differ from that of *Better Homes and Gardens* in many ways and from that of *The National Enquirer* in practically every way.

Do you need to appeal to yuppie types, to the mellow-nostalgia set, to the ultra-wealthy? Each readership would require a different editorial strategy.

When you have determined your policy and written it down, make it even clearer by specifying the contents for your first four issues, even if, at this stage of the game, you are not sure that you will be able to find writers who can handle all the assignments. Let your imagination run free. What magazine would be perfectly configured to capture your target readership? What would the table of contents be? Once you have determined precisely what you want, you can see that it gets done.

KINDS OF FEATURES

Your inventory of possible features is large. Here are some of the staples.

People Articles

All of your articles, no matter what the topic, should be full of people, quotes, characterization, and all the rest. But some of them will be focused more narrowly on individual persons. These can take the form of profiles, interviews (in question and answer form), or narratives that tell the story of the subject of the article and those of his or her accomplishments that you feel will interest your reader.

On magazine writing
People, conversation, case histories,
success stories, examples drawn
from personal experience and the
experience of others — these are the
things that make magazine articles
readable and effective. See that the
articles in your magazines are full
of them.

The interview, in particular, could be a regular feature. These attract considerable attention and are relatively easy to write once the interview is done. The secret is to interview people who are in themselves newsworthy or who are likely to express opinions that are newsworthy. One of the best things that can happen to you is to have quotes from your interview picked up by the news media — with, of course, appropriate credit to your magazine.

Events and Trends

An earthquake, your town's equivalent of the Kentucky Derby or Mardi Gras, or the revitalization of a formerly moribund downtown.

Issues

You can be as political and controversial as you want. *Texas Monthly* can be very rambunctious and stir strong feeling. *Yankee Magazine* almost never is. Controversy attracts notice and readers so long as it does not alienate large groups of your subscribers. Present controversial personalities and let them tell their own stories. It is not the magazine's stand, but that of the individual. *Public interest controversy* is always good, since it can be at once strong, good for the community at large, and fairly safe. Uncovering unrecognized sources of pollution of your water supply, for instance, could generate an article that would fall into the realm of public interest controversy. In these articles you take the side of the public at large against the special interests. This kind of piece also lends itself to some strong investigative reporting.

Round-Up Articles

Round-up articles tell what is going on in certain broadly defined areas. Typically, a large number of individuals involved in the activity may be interviewed. A piece on development trends in the suburbs, for instance, is a round-up piece, with information solicited from a variety of sources.

Service Articles

Service articles are always very attractive to readers when they are on topics of strong and general interest. Service articles tell people how to do something or get something that they want. I once published an article in *Esquire* magazine called "A Year in France on $1000." It was a service article. I am currently writing an article for *NCEast* magazine on "Little-Known Sources of Financing for Your

New Business Enterprise." This, too, is a service piece. Popular service articles include those that tell how to get a lot for a little, how to lose weight, how to make money in business, and dozens of other "how-to" pieces.

Nostalgia Articles

These are surefire crowd pleasers, and they can be adapted to any editorial policy guidelines. A nostalgia piece tells and, more important, shows, how things used to be. An "album" of old photographs of your city, if they are fresh and little known, can keep a magazine alive for years and increase pass-along readership substantially. Old maps, reproduced pages from old newspapers and other periodicals can be a strong draw, too. In general the accompanying article can be fairly brief. The cutlines will tell the story.

The Departments

Unsure of your ability to write readable magazine articles or judge the readability of articles that others may write for you? You can get help from many available books on magazine writing. One of the best of these, and one that I highly recommend, is the Magazine Writer's Handbook, by Franklynn Peterson and Judi Keffelman-Turkel (Dodd-Mead & Co., 1987). Read through this book. It will open your eyes.

A magazine's departments are those old friends that you meet issue after issue. Often they are the first articles that a reader turns to. Some departments can be slanted to fit your magazine's editorial policy. Others may not be appropriate for some magazines and just right for others. Here are some departments that are often seen:

The "**editor's notebook**," in which the editor chats with his readers, introduces his issue and his writers. It is personal, one-on-one in tone, and it can be important in developing reader identification with the magazine.

A **book review** column is generally appreciated by readers. The books chosen for review pull the column into conformity with editorial policy.

Restaurant reviews are always a good draw. Perhaps your magazine will offer a directory of night spots and restaurants and a system of rating them. Your restaurant review must be factual, honest, and fair. If the service is bad and the bread day-old, you have to say so. If you feel that you can't be this forthright, then don't do a restaurant column. In some magazines I have solved this problem by trying restaurants until I found one I liked, and then I wrote about that one.

Activities departments, like cooking or gardening, are appropriate for some magazines, but not for others.

Theater and art reviews are appropriate for upscale magazines in rich cultural environments.

With the **editorial pages** I have found that a full page editorial (I like to put it on the page opposite the inside back cover, but it can go anywhere) is a strong reader pull and generates an active letters to the editor column. It enhances the feeling in the reader's mind that your magazine is one of substance and has a point of view that must be taken into consideration.

Stimulate these letters to the editor shamelessly. A strong editorial content will generate considerable correspondence. In the beginning you might consider imitating the technique of Henry Luce in the first days of *Time* magazine. He wrote both the letters and the answers himself, and in doing so jump-started what has since become one of the most lively and readable "Letters" columns in any American magazine.

THE FORMAT OF YOUR MAGAZINE

The idea is to make your magazine look like other successful magazines. It should be standard in size, 8½ (or 8¼) by 11 inches. It should be self-covered for reasons of economy. The first eight and the last eight pages should be in full color. Add additional color as ad sales permit. If you sell a full color advertisement for the center spread, for instance, this will open the center signature to you for color.

You should print your magazine on 70 lb. coated stock if it is seventy-two pages or fewer. You may use 60 lb. stock if you run eighty pages or more. If you print a magazine that has ninety-six pages or more you may use a 60 lb. signature on the outside and print the remainder of the book on lighter stock, even 50 lb. The 60 lb. stock on the outside will give the entire magazine the feel of this heavier paper. (But it is also possible to go in an entirely different direction, if you feel that the market is right. Your product will not be what is usually thought of as a city magazine, but it can still be quite profitable. Read Chapter 11 on "The Tabloid Alternative" and see if such a publication might serve your market. A tabloid is effective in some trade areas. You will come out more frequently, spend less on layout and art, and sell more ads for less money to a wider range of clients.)

CREATE AN IMAGE

A city magazine is usually a slick, sophisticated publication, whatever

Night Stories

On country porches at nightfall the stories they told would curl your hair.

by Tom Williams

THERE WAS A SPECIAL time in the tobacco country when families gathered on long front porches to sit quietly in whatever coolness might be stirring in the twilight and talk their way slowly into the deep, rural night.

The world seemed unnaturally still on these long summer evenings, its quiet broken only by the deep rumble of a distant storm or the spine-chilling shriek of a far-away freight. There were few automobiles to speak of, and even those few seldom ventured out on the deserted country roads at night. You could glimpse the faint glow of a headlight or hear the straining of a motor as some lonely driver strained up a distant and nameless hill.

Then even that would disappear, leaving the evening undisturbed except for the ceaseless chirruping of the crickets or the chronic, dry squeak of the old swing's chain. Back in the house you would hear a final brief clatter from the kitchen as the last of supper's dishes were put in their places on the shelf. Then the women would come out on the porch, too.

I can remember those moments from my boyhood, sitting on the steps and watching in wonder and apprehension as the last light faded from the yard, the fields and the distant woods. The whole world seemed to my young imagination to merge into a formless and somehow threatening mass of fearful shapes and shadows.

Anything could happen out in that darkness, I knew beyond a doubt, and I was glad to be safe on my porch.

If I had to leave it to go to the woodpile or the barn or to perform some other duty or errand, I did so with pounding heart and in full expectation of disaster. Columbus' reluctant sailors, terrified of falling over the edge of the world, could have been no more fearful than I was as I stepped off that porch into the foreboding circle of night, or as unspeakably relieved as when I finally rushed back into its protective bound.

It was not so much the night itself that caused my flesh to prickle, my face to pale and my wide eyes to see far more in that darkness than may, in truth, have been there. It was the talk that did it, talk that regularly scared me almost beyond endurance, but which I would not have missed for anything.

As the grown-ups rocked, or swung gently, or propped their feet up on the porch rail and took out a smoke, the talk would begin. Someone would tell of the strange ball of lightning that balanced so unaccountably on the front fence post before moving into the house to burn the pattern of cousin Harold's steel-rimmed spectacles onto his astonished face. Someone else would tell of fierce misdeeds of chain-gang convicts or of a woman's body found floating deep in the river swamp, a gaping wound across her throat.

Then all would join in, telling and retelling tale after tale of evil,

THE ORIGINAL WASHINGTON AND

BEAUFORT COUNTY
MAGAZINE

Volume IV

Table of Contents

35

its target readership. You will want to create the same upscale image for yourself, your sales reps, and your magazine as you approach the market for the first time.

Media Kits

A very carefully prepared media kit will pay off. As a start-up magazine going after high ticket advertisers you will want it to contain some items in the beginning that you will not need later on, after you have previous issues to show. These items include a sample cover bound around enough inside pages − including types of projected advertising − to give the client a feel for the kind of magazine you will publish. I have found that no amount of purely verbal description, even by the most silver-tongued of sales reps, can conjure up an adequate image in the customer's mind. Only the printed product can do that.

This is a fairly substantial expense but it is necessary, serving the same purpose as the "credibility brochure" discussed earlier. This piece can, however, do double duty for you. You can print your rate card and mechanical information within it. I would recommend the center spread for this material.

This packet of information will be your public visage. When the account executive at an ad agency or the director of marketing at any retail firm opens it, he or she must be immediately struck by the quality of your product. First impressions *are* lasting impressions.

Your Sales Reps' Image

Your sales people, too, to the degree that it is possible, must possess personality traits and a level of professionalism consistent with the quality of your product. They must be very well informed in the product knowledge needed to sell ad pages costing many hundreds − even thousands − of dollars. The same old-boy type salesperson who can be very successful selling $150 ads to a carpet cleaning or muffler repair service for a weekly newspaper may not fill the bill for other kinds of client.

News Releases

You also need to keep a steady flow of news releases going out to all media that could be at all interested in your activities. Start these as early as possible and continue them as long as possible. Call the local TV stations and land a spot on local talk shows. This is almost always possible, especially if you are willing to go on at short notice when someone else cancels or fails to show up.

PUTTING TOGETHER THE TEAM

As publisher of a city magazine you will want to be certain that you have available the talent you need in five distinct areas of activity: management, editorial, design and production, advertising sales, and circulation.

This does not mean that you will put a separate person on the payroll to fulfill each of these functions. A single individual can often perform two or more of them, especially in the beginning when cash is scarce.

You as publisher will provide the management. Beyond that, the work you do depends on your skills. My own skills, for instance, lie in the areas of writing and, secondarily, in layout and design. In magazine start-ups that I have done I have generally assumed the burden of writing (or obtaining the work of free-lance writers) and of layout and design.

Others come to their publications with a different set of talents. The person with a background in sales, marketing and promotion can be just as competant and successful in the publishing field as the person whose editorial skills come first. Such a person might concentrate with his magazines on management, sales, and circulation, leaving the editorial and design components to freelance writers, editors, artists, and graphic designers. Each function is different from the others and has different requirements.

Management

Management will fall to your lot, as publisher. You tell others what to do and when, you collect revenues and pay bills and see to it that the former is greater than the latter — at least most of the time.

Editorial

The editorial responsibility may present the most difficult problem to solve for the publisher who is not also a good writer. It takes a good writer or editor to recognize another good one. This was not so much a problem for me because I knew writing. Even the most brilliant sales-oriented publishers, however, may have great difficulty distinguishing between the passable, the good, and the excellent — and a city magazine wants to stick to the excellent. That extra quality is, after all, what sets it apart from the lifestyle pages of the local newspaper.

The non-writer publisher has two ways, it seems to me, to solve his problem in this area. He may locate an experienced writer to act as his editor on a part-time basis. This writer must have been published by magazines of a quality equal to that of the magazine the publisher is bringing out and have good recommendations from others in the writing field. Just remember that there is no substitute for the practical experience, the credits and credentials. You may meet some candidates for the job who say, "Yes, I can do this. I studied journalism at the state university." Without the clips and credentials the education means nothing. I have met journalism graduates who could not write a complete sentence.

In your search for an editor, you have this going for you: Opportunities for writers are few and the opportunity to serve as editor of a city magazine is very tempting. You may find someone willing to do the job for a very low fee in return for a promise of future reward when the magazine catches on. I took on my first job as magazine editor of a regional publication for a few hundred dollars an issue. I was teaching on a college faculty at the time, so I did not need the money to live on. The pay was puny, but the things I learned were very valuable. It was my apprenticeship in the publishing business. I believe that there are others like me who will take on the job at even the most modest fees.

The second way to solve the problem is to take on a partner who is an editor. In this scenario the partner would own a piece of the magazine and thus be reinforced in his willingness to contribute the requisite sweat equity. You would still, however, have the problem of choosing a partner/editor who really possessed the necessary skills.

Design

You will need someone to do some ad design, cover design, department headings, etc. A great deal of this can be done on your computer using page make-up and graphic arts programs. Much of the odds and ends of art can be obtained from the best clip art collections that you can find on disk. Other clip art can be obtained from the services discussed in the section on the weekly newspaper.

Nevertheless, some graphic design will be required beyond this. I have found it best to use the work of young designers who come in on a part-time basis. The art school at the university in my town provides a rich source of such people. There are usually very few entry level jobs for commercial artists. Many are virtual sweat shop environments. The companies specializing in the silk screening of T-shirts are an example. In order to build their portfolios in search of something better, these young artists will come in and work ten to twenty hours a week, as needed.

You will find that you will need these people less than you might think, although when you are in need there is simply no substitute for their talent. You will need them less because many of your ads will come in to you not only camera ready (already made up and ready for the printer to photograph) but even film ready (already in composite film form). This will be true for almost all of your advertisers who use the services of an advertising agency. In addition, the magazine will develop its own regular formats and layout style. Once designed, the heading of the restaurant review column does not need to be redone. In fact, it *should* not be redone, since repeated design elements give a feeling of continuity. In addition, your column widths, gutters, margins, headings, subheadings, etc., can be fairly rigid, varying little from issue to issue. Every article does not need to be introduced by a prize-winning piece of design. Successful magazines like *Esquire*, *Time*, *Smithsonian*, and many, many others look very much the same from issue to issue. Go to the newsstand or the library and study the magazines that seem to use a more or less fixed format. Adapt one or more of these formats for your own use. I have sometimes done almost all of the in-house generated art for a magazine I was publishing. I stuck to very symmetrical patterns and balanced presentations. Such designs, while less adventurous than some you might find, can be classy and create just the effect you are after.

Sales Reps

I will refer you to the section on finding and hiring good part-time salespeople in the chapter on tourism guides. The same things are true in the case of city magazines.

With a salesperson the proof is in the pudding. It is hard to know which ones will work best before you give them a try. A strategy I like is to give a list of prospects to each of three or four reps. Some will make the calls and some won't. Of those who make the calls, some will sell ads and some won't. I then eliminate those who can't do the job, retain the one who will, and hire a new batch of trainees.

But if you can't be sure of good performance before sending your salesperson out to make calls, you can improve the odds of finding a good one by looking for a person who is personally attractive and outgoing, well-read and personally likes magazines and other print media products, has some successful sales experience in the past and knows the city well, is active in many groups, and can meet the most ego-driven executive on a one-to-one basis without feeling second best.

And let me add that sometimes the strangest, most unlikely, and least charismatic man or woman can go out and, day after day, sell more ads than anyone else. Always be alert for this special salesperson who doesn't fit your fancy profile but sells ads like mad. I wish I had a dozen of them.

SELLING THE ADS

Your ad rates will be high — perhaps higher than those of any other publication in the community. You will be selling fewer ads for a great deal more money. This means that you can't afford to lose many sales through lack of preparation or poor salesmanship. You also must work to create a positive awareness of your magazine before the call is ever made (see the discussion of image above).

Virtually every chapter in this book contains tips on selling advertising and/or services. But there are some special problems and opportunities in city magazine ad sales that you should be aware of.

Rate Card Deals

Your rate card should be etched in stone. What you say you are going to charge for an ad is what you will actually charge. You do not stray from it easily or often. Still, there are some deals you can negotiate without creating problems for yourself in the marketplace.

If your rate is "gross," that is, if it includes a 15% commission that will be paid to an ad agency, you can negotiate that same percentage to any customer who does what an ad agency would do — furnish a completely camera-ready ad.

When, at the last minute, a premium position has not been sold, you can call around and offer it to clients at a discount rate for last minute insertion. This kind of deal is similar in nature to cheapie air fares that are sold on a last minute, space available basis.

You can offer price incentives to customers in your first issue, or to first time customers in any issue. You should be willing to make the same offer to any advertiser who goes in the book. I have found it useful to tie the new advertiser incentive to a long term contract. To get it the advertiser has to agree to appear in three successive issues or in three issues over a twelve month period. Advertisers who fail to meet their end of the bargain would be charged the difference

The Many Faces of Carteret.

In tourism, jobs and county infrastructure, Carteret leaders are moving ahead.

by Thomas A. Williams
and Kim Bennett

North Carolina's coastal Carteret County is a region of many faces.

There are the fishing villages of that long and solitary coast reaching northeastward from Beaufort, through Sea Level to the tiny town of Atlantic.

There is Harker's Island, so rich in pride and tradition, and with a keen sense of place and its own identity. Harker's Island people, those who live there will tell you, are special.

There is the attraction of Old Beaufort, both a historic town of great beauty and a trendy stop in the annual migrations of the species *yachtsman* from New England to Florida and back.

There is staunchly middle-class Morehead City, home of the balanced budget and the county courthouse—the administrative hub of the county. Among Morehead's other claims to fame may be that of being the narrowest county seat in North Carolina. Built on a slender spit of land between Bogue Sound and Calico Creek, Morehead is just five blocks wide, with a population—according to the 1980 census—of 6,000. (According to mayor Bud Dixon, this number may increase to the 10,000 range when inhabitants are counted anew in this year.)

And then, of course, there is the Carteret most North Carolinians know best: the great Bogue Banks beach resort areas tagged by marketing specialists as the "Crystal Coast" sometime during the 1970s. With its pleasing alliteration and implications of an environmental purity that are not always easy to guarantee, the name "Crystal Coast" seems to be sticking and the marketing working.

And there is the town of Newport, nestled in the green grass and pine woods that stretch westward from Morehead to the Craven County line and invites, among

SAMPLE RATE CARD

Back and Front of Rate Card

Advertisers Guide to Graphic Design, Art, Production and Photography

Graphic Design: Williams & Simpson, Inc., publisher of *NCEast*, operates a full-service advertising agency with a complete art department. The services of this agency are made available to advertisers on a discounted basis. Please ask for rates.

Color Separations: Williams & Simpson provides color separations to advertisers at our wholesale rate. These rates are as follows: Up to 5 x 7, $85; 6 x 10, $110; 9 x 12, $152. These prices are for separations made from color slides. Add $10 for separations made from color prints.

Duplicate Separations: Ads which we design for our customers are at their disposal for other uses. Duplicate separations or composites are available at our cost of $30.

Color Tints: Background colors of various kinds are achieved by using tints of the primary colors. Some colors – a light blue, for instance – can be made with a single screen tint. Others – including most PMS matches – require the superposition of tints of two or more colors. There is a $10 charge for each necessary screen tint.

Photography: Williams & Simpson has working arrangements with experienced commercial photographers in most market areas. We can provide any photographic services which our advertisers may need. We will be happy to quote our discounted rates for you.

Williams & Simpson, Inc., is a full-service communications and publications firm serving North Carolina and located at 2409 South Charles Street, and at 201 West Main Street, Washington, NC. Williams & Simpson designs edits and publishes books, magazines, catalogues, direct-mail pieces, newspaper inserts, employee handbooks and manuals and other print media items. The corporate offices may be reached by calling 919-756-8617.

NCEast

The Magazine of
Eastern North Carolina's Heartland

RATE CARD 2

*The Voice of
Eastern North Carolina's
Heartland*

Williams & Simpson, Inc.
ADVERTISING   PUBLISHING   DESIGN
2409 South Charles Street
Greenville, North Carolina 27858
919-756-8617

Middle two pages

The Voice of Eastern North Carolina's Heartland

NCEast serves residents, newcomers, present and prospective businesses and industries in the Eight City area -- *your* area. *NCEast* is the only authoritative, comprehensive and vital source of information on the region's best features, lifestyle, culture and economic advantages. The emphasis of *NCEast* is on you and your business and includes stories of interest and use to present residents as well as future prospects and businesses.

NCEast is circulated to the general public through newsstand sales; to newcomers, business, industrial and professional recruitment prospects through Chambers of commerce; to banks and real estate companies; to political members of Chambers of Commerce; to other decision makers in business; to political decision makers, regional and national; through the NC Dept. of Commerce and to universities and schools, libraries and other public institutions; to prestige hotels and motels.

NCEast is the Showcase of the Eight City region.

Advertising Rates* and Specifications

AD SIZE	B/W	4 COLOR
Full page	1895.00	2495.00
2/3 page	1400.00	1870.00
1/2 page	1170.00	1475.00
1/3 page	750.00	1050.00
1/6 page	450.00	N/A
Cover 2, premium pages		2895.00
Cover 3		2895.00
Cover 4		2995.00
Center Spread		4995.00

*Rates are for space only.

Showcase of Business

NCEast offers businesses an unusual opportunity to tell their story through dramatic, professionally written articles appearing in the pages of *NCEast*. Our sales representative will, at your request, show you samples and provide rates.

Creative Services

Many clients will have their own advertising agencies. For those who do not and wish to use such services, Williams & Simpson can furnish complete art, design, typographical and camera services.

Williams & Simpson, Inc. does not warrant the accuracy of advertising copy submitted by advertisers. In case of typographical errors which are the responsibility of Williams & Simpson liability is limited to a negotiated percentage of the cost of the space occupied by the advertisement.

Other Charges

Advertisers will be charged for halftones provided by the publisher at the rate of $10 each. The cost of color separations furnished by the publisher will be charged to the customer at cost plus 20%. Typography will be charged to the customer at the rate of $45.00 per hour.

Ad Sizes

Publication trim size is 8 1/2 by 11 inches. Page format consists of three 13 pica columns, ten inches deep. Full page ads may go to page size limits (full bleed): 2/3 page vertical, 4 7/16 by 10; 1/2 page horizontal, 8 by 13/16; 1/3 page vertical, 2 1/8 by 10; 1/3 page horizontal, 4 15/16 by 5; 1/6 page vertical, 2 1/8 by 4 15/16.

Mechanical Requirements

Advertiser is to furnish stripping negative or camera ready art. The publisher, Williams & Simpson, Inc., will furnish creative services at the advertiser's expense if assistance is needed. Advertiser furnishes color separations. 133 line screens required.

Cancellations

If copy is not received by closing date and insertion order has not been cancelled, the previous advertisement of the advertiser or a house prepared ad will be inserted. Cancellation of any portion of a contract voids rate and position guarantees.

between the negotiated rate and the one-time ("short") rate on the cancellation of their contractual agreement.

The Importance of the Little Ads

Your salespeople will always prefer to go for the big ticket, full page ads. This is natural. It takes no more time, and sometimes considerably less, to call on the bank that is going to take the back cover as to call on the one-person interior design shop that may take a sixth or a twelfth of a page.

But the small ads are important to you for several reasons. The first is that they build credibility. The greater the number and the more varied the types of businesses included among your advertisers, the more believable your publication becomes. The big clients you approach, including ad agency execs, will search your pages for evidence of broad-based support as part of their evaluation process. "A publication full of small ads must be working for someone," they will decide. "Maybe it will work for me." Small businesses do not buy ads, time after time, in publications that do not work for them.

Small ads are also repeat ads. They are inexpensive and can be factored into modest ad budgets. Intelligently designed, with the kind of know-how displayed in the back pages of *Better Homes and Gardens* or *Southern Living*, they can create real traffic for the businesses that buy them. Once you convince the advertiser that his ad is profitable for him, he will continue it issue after issue. The small ads thus become the sustaining advertising that you can always count on. Then comes the good part. Because, inch for inch, small ads cost more than the full pagers; twelve one-twelfth page ads bring in a lot more cash than one full page ad.

The Dreaded Coupon

Advertisers usually do not have any accurate way to judge the response to their advertising. If the grocery store down at the mall advertises country hams for fifty cents a pound in the Wednesday newspaper and sells out by noon on Thursday, they know that their ad worked for them.

Magazine advertising is more difficult to evaluate. Often it is a question of image building and name recognition. A small businessperson does not need a new bank every day or even every year, but he may think first of the bank he saw advertised — somewhere, at sometime or other — as being friendly to the financial needs of smaller enterprises. When an interior design firm advertises its services, it may or may not receive immediate calls that can be attributed to its magazine ad. After all, it advertises elsewhere, too — in the Yellow Pages, for instance. The person taking the call is more interested in selling design services than in conducting an inquiry into the source of the call, and the caller is just not going to say, "I saw your ad in X magazine and decided to give you a ring."

Occasionally someone will come up with a device which he considers foolproof in evaluating response to advertising: the coupon. Try to avoid these, for several reasons. In the first place coupon return is a low to middle income habit and will not be much practiced by upper income readers. Second, people typically do not like to cut up a handsome city magazine. They want to save it. As a matter of fact this long shelf life (or coffee table life) is one of the strengths of the magazine. It has a very high pass-along readership — as many as three additional readers for everyone who initially purchases or is sent a copy. That's why you will stress readership rather than circulation.

Third, coupons bring a significant response only when mailed in huge quantities, far beyond that reached by your magazine's circulation. Fourth, coupons work most successfully when linked with products that most people use most days: cigarettes, soap, cereal. These are precisely the kinds of things you will not be advertising in your high priced city magazine.

So what do you do when the customer insists on coupons? How do you design a coupon that has a chance to do well for you?

First of all, coupons should be relatively large. Those the size of a dollar bill or larger do best. Second, the coupon should offer specific benefits: "This coupon worth $10 on your next $30 purchase" will pull better than "Get one-third off with this coupon on your next purchase of $30." The benefit to the customer must be a substantial one. Would you cut out a coupon, drive across town, and go in an unfamiliar store, to save $2 on your next pair of shoes? Not very likely, for you or for anyone else.

The best results of all, in my experience, are obtained by loose, postpaid business reply cards inserted ("blown in," in the terms of the trade) into each of your magazines. But these are more expensive too, since the advertiser incurs a printing charge as well as an advertising space charge.

Editorial Integrity

Editorial integrity is important to your city magazine. You determine who and what will be featured. Suggestions are welcomed, but you do not slant your stories to fit requirements of any person or organization outside the editorial staff of the magazine itself. Most of all, you do not trade off stories for advertising. A quality of life magazine or a tourism guide is not as sensitive in this respect. It is all paid advertising in one sense or another. But your city magazine must be trusted by its readers, who need to feel certain that the facts they read in your features and departments are objective and unbiased. You do not trade off a good restaurant review for a full page ad, no matter what the temptation. You do not praise a second rate hospital that buys the center spread. You do not praise unscrupulous developers as noble, community-minded citizens merely because the company has signed a yearly contract for the back cover.

That said, and understanding that without advertising there would be no magazine, I have found that there is much one can do editorially to stimulate ad sales.

Develop an editorial calendar in cooperation with your sales department. Your editorial schedule should be blocked out six issues in advance. Although you will not be able to specify each article precisely, you can determine subject matter areas. A legitimate question would be, "What kinds of article will stimulate advertising sales?" If you want to sell the center spread to a construction company and you see other opportunities in the same area you can plan a piece on "builders and building" in your trade area. Key advertisers can be interviewed along with all other major players in the building game. No promises are made about content, and no advertiser is ever, ever allowed to approve or even read copy before it goes into print. You can also plan features in other key areas of business activity, including entertainment, art, and cultural activities. As long as you choose each feature *because it is a good story and not merely to sell ads*, you are on solid ground.

Although your magazine must have a broad readership, it should clearly appeal to the business and financial communities. To the degree that it is possible, choose articles of interest both to your advertising constituency and to the general reader. This is not difficult, if you focus on *interesting people doing interesting things*.

Select interviews with highly visible, interesting indviduals. You can do a lot of good for yourself by carefully selecting a series of interviews with individuals *from many different segments of the community*. This builds broad awareness of the magazine and identification with it among the different groups who make up your potential readership.

Up-and-coming interviews are a feature I developed for my *NCEast* magazine. In each I do a mini-profile of four people who had

It is hard to overestimate the pleasure that most people derive from seeing their names in print. You would do well to keep it constantly in mind and pepper you pages with names, names, names. In a weekly newspaper you will have a glorious opportunity to do this. But magazines and county histories offer golden opportunities as well. And, whenever possible, add a photograph to the name. This strategy will build a very loyal base of readers and a fine reputation for you as a strong supporter of you community.

an idea, put all their energy and know-how behind it, and single-handedly achieved success. These "featurettes" cover everyone from rare book dealers to art gallery owners, to founders of dance companies, to more traditional builders, merchants, and service providers. These people often reciprocate by buying a small ad, and when they grow larger, they buy bigger ads. They appreciate what you have done for them and, as long as they are getting results, they will continue to do business with you. While you do not trade editorial for advertising there is nothing to prevent your sales rep from approaching a client about whom you intend to do an article anyway. These featurettes, in addition, have strong reader interest.

ADVERTORIALS

What about advertorials? The fact remains that advertisers want to be "written up" in your magazine and they are willing to pay you for the privilege. The same is true for every major magazine on the market. To take advantage of these available and badly needed dollars, the industry is turning more and more to the "advertorial." It looks like an article and reads like an article, but it is clearly labeled "special advertising supplement."

We have been talking about builders and developers. To attract their dollars you can design a special section, perhaps the center signature in the magazine, that will include editorial matter and photographs of each of those who advertise at a certain level. This paid advertising supplement can then be reprinted — or overprinted — as a separate piece and furnished to the advertisers for promotional use. The same approach will work for any segment of the business community that has sufficient dollars to afford to buy the space.

Showcase

There are many approaches to advertorials. One that I have used very successfully is the "Showcase of Business." This is a one-page featurette introducing a business, its owner, and its personality, service, or product to the readership. I write these showcases myself, giving them all the care I would give to a feature article in the most prestigious magazine. I want them to be ultra-readable, with anecdotes, quotes, and characterization — as much fun to peruse as any article in *Reader's Digest*.

The showcase stands alone, not in a special advertising section.

On the masthead of the magazine it is identified as paid advertising. But the piece is so carefully done that it attracts and holds readers.

The showcase works. If anyone really wants to test the pulling power of your pages suggest a showcase rather than a coupon. After it appears, the advertiser's phone will begin to ring with messages of congratulations from customers and friends. It can really be quite impressive. Many clients who would not normally buy more that a sixth or a twelfth page ad will often buy a showcase and be very proud of it.

"As Seen In . . ."

Once an ad appears in your magazine cut it out, affix it to a piece of illustration board on which you have printed the legend, "As seen in X magazine," or perhaps, as I done from time to time, "X magazine seal of approval." Have this board laminated and affix a cardboard fold-out easel stand to the back. Take these ad boards to your advertisers. I promise you that you will please the advertiser and that he will proudly display the laminated ad in a prominent place, thus building awareness not only of the advertiser's business but of your magazine as well.

Advertising Rates

As far as your advertising rates, your city magazine will be fairly expensive, certainly more expensive than the newspaper or assorted tabloid publications that are on the market. Read the discussion on setting ad rates in Chapter 8 on newcomer guides. That same material will be relevant here. Let me remind you that in magazines, unlike newspapers, the cost of the ad covers space only. Any art, design, or color separations, etc., should be billed back to the client. You can offer to provide these services free as an incentive to get a firm commitment to place an ad if you so desire.

An example of acceptable ad rates? In a city-type magazine that I currently publish the black and white page rate is $1895. A full page color costs $2495. Circulation is 22,000 per issue. The magazine is used by the largest commuter, short-hop airline in this area as its seat-back publication in addition to the regular circulation.

Ad budgets are generally modest in North Carolina. This is

about the maximum advertisers can afford. At these rates, this new magazine generates a modest profit for the company. Later, as the ratio of ad pages to editorial builds more favorably in favor of ads, profits will grow to levels that are acceptable over the long term.

ASSURING GOOD CIRCULATION

A good, effective circulation system is an absolute necessity for continuing success. Sell it, mail it, give it away . . . but get it into the hands of the people for whom you designed it and whom your advertisers want to reach.

Your advertisers are not really hard to please. As long as a modest number of people do let them know that they saw the ad and liked it, you are safe. If no one mentions it at all, selling the next edition can be tough. In other words, the work is not over when the ads are all sold, the articles all written, and the books all printed. The job of getting them to the readers remains to be done. Here are some guidelines.

Controlled vs. Paid Circulation

Controlled circulation goes to a list of individuals whom you have identified as likely to enjoy your magazine and patronize your advertisers. They do not pay for the magazine that they receive. Paid circulation goes to subscribers who have paid their money to get the magazine.

While it might seem to be financially advantageous to mail magazines only to people who pay for the privilege of receiving them, this may not in fact be the case. It takes considerable money to do the direct mail campaigns that will get the subscriptions in the first place. Second, you would be hard put to develop your list of subscribers to the desired level before the first issue of your magazine actually comes out. Add these things to the fact that your advertisers want guaranteed circulation from the very first, and you begin to see the difficulties with the paid circulation route.

Combined Controlled and Paid Circulation

The usual route is to combine both paid and controlled circulation. Each issue contains tear-out subscription reply cards. Many people not on your original list may take advantage of these to ensure that they get the magazine, as will readers who pick up their copies at the newsstand.

You may also program your computer so that the mailing label prints out the words "complimentary issue" above the name of the recipient. These words serve to alert the reader to the fact that he must send in the subscription card to be sure to get his issue regularly. To reinforce this, you vary your controlled list so that the same people, within possible limits, do not get each and every issue free of charge. Gradually your ratio of paid to controlled readers will increase in your favor.

Newsstand Sales

Newsstand sales are not a great source of revenue, although they can be brisk if your cover is well-designed and carries very strong sell-lines. It is important for your magazine to be seen on newsstands, however, to build name recognition and to reassure your advertisers that it is indeed being circulated.

OTHER PROFIT CENTERS

As publisher of a city magazine you will gain the expertise necessary to carry out a variety of other publishing projects, many of which will be very profitable. I refer you to Chapter 14 on secondary profit centers.

It is amazing how many times I have overlooked the opportunity to advertise my own company's other services in the pages of the magazines I publish. Keep in mind that you can always afford space advertising in the most prestigious publication in your market area. You can afford it because *you* are the publisher.

SELLING OUT FOR PROFIT

In many businesses the real profit comes in the form of capital gains. You sell the enterprise you have built through the sweat of your brow and the reach of your mind to someone else who has neither the time, the inclination, nor the know-how to start from scratch as you did.

Always keep in mind that publications are valued differently from other businesses. When you sell you can expect to be well-compensated for all those eighteen hour days and seven day weeks you put in during the start-up process.

In general, a publication will be valued for purposes of sale on the basis of a multiple of the previous twelve months' gross revenues. One times gross is the bottom line, with that amount going up from 1.5 times gross to two, three, and even higher multiples depending on the characteristics of the market and the market position you occupy within it. A young, vigorous, growing magazine will generally demand a higher multiple than one that shows evidence of having passed maturity and fallen into decline.

When you name your magazine keep in mind that the name is a valuable property. A fabulously catchy and marketable name has a value of its own and can greatly enhance the attractiveness of your magazine when you put it on the market.

A "WIN-WIN-WIN" PROJECT
A WELL-DEFINED PROJECT
A SUCCESSFUL DIRECTORY PROJECT
PROSPECTING FOR DIRECTORIES
HOW TO GET LEADS
SELLING THE ADVERTISING
GOING THE EXTRA MILE

7. Publishing Association and Membership Directories

Opportunities to publish association directories and membership directories may not abound, but they do exist if you know where to look for them. If the chance to publish such a directory comes your way, latch onto it. They are relatively easy to sell and produce, and once in place a directory can be quite profitable over an extended period of time. Indeed, there are publishing companies whose entire business is built on their publication.

The concept is simple. An organization of professionals, a trade organization, or some other organization wishes to provide its members — and those who do business with its members — with a quality membership directory. The directory will list the membership in alphabetical order, by order of specialty, and in other useful ways. It will also contain other useful contact names and addresses.

The organization itself has neither the know-how nor the cash on hand to undertake such a project. You, as publisher, agree to design, edit, and publish their directory absolutely free of charge. You deliver to the association, on an agreed date, the specified number of copies.

A "WIN-WIN-WIN" PROJECT

The appeal to the association is very strong. In return for their endorsement of your advertising sales, they receive, at no cost to them, a shipment of impressive, full color membership directories that you publish. These they distribute to their membership.

The appeal to the company to which you sell advertising is powerful as well. A company in the business of selling fire engines, for example, will jump at the opportunity to display its wares in the membership directory of a national or statewide association of firefighters. It is the ultimate in targeted advertising.

The appeal to you as publisher is equally strong. You sell advertising at premium prices and retain as profit all proceeds beyond the cost of typography, design, and printing. Occasionally, but not always, there may be an additional 5 to 10% of gross sales to be paid into the treasury of the sponsoring organization. This is discussed more fully below.

A WELL-DEFINED PROJECT

Like other publishing projects that I have found to be successful for small companies, the publication of an association directory is quite well-defined and manageable. The membership list is finite and will be furnished to you, complete and up-to-date, by the administrative officers of the association. Beyond this list, you will have to generate a very modest amount of editorial copy — say two or three 2000 word articles.

You have no circulation responsibilities, since you deliver the entire printing to the association to do with as it wishes. And since a business or professional association has, by definition, a community of interests, potential advertisers are easy to identify and reach.

A SUCCESSFUL DIRECTORY PROJECT

Several years ago, in response to declining domestic markets for textiles and other manufactured goods, a number of business leaders in a southern state formed an organization to gather information, ideas, and resources to market these and other locally made goods abroad.

This led to the formation of a World Trade Association for that state. Numbered among its members were many of the leading manufacturing firms in the state, as well as shipping lines, international freight forwarders, law firms specializing in that branch of the law, insurers, and many others.

For the first two years of its existence the fledgling association distributed a rather primitive membership list. It was prepared on a typewriter, duplicated on someone's office copier, folded, stapled, and mailed out. It was obvious that if the organization was going to develop the prestigious, leadership image it desired and needed, something much more impressive would be required. An associate of mine, on receiving a copy of the first membership list, recognized the organization's need for something far better and the opportunity, for our company, to supply it.

We set up a meeting with the president of the association and worked out an agreement to produce a membership directory. When he discovered that the entire project would not cost him a single penny he was happy to go along with us.

We established a sales and production schedule and went to work on the project. My associate noted the banks, service organizations,

MEMBERSHIP BY SERVICE

Neill J. Hines
Weyerhaeuser Co.
P.O. Box 1391
New Bern, NC 28560
919/633-7476

Carolyn L. Holsclaw
Shuford Mills, Inc.
P.O. Box 1530
Hickory, NC 28603
704/322-2700

James E. Holt
Celwave Technologies, Inc.
P.O. Box 39
Claremont, NC 28610-0039
704/459-9787

J. S. Kiziah
Siecor
489 Siecor Park
Hickory, NC 28603
704/327-5988

William L. Mabe, Jr.
Cone Mills, Corp.
1201 Maple St.
Greensboro, NC 27405
919/379-6465

John M. Mims
General Electric Co.
P.O. Box 780
Wilmington, NC 28401
919/343-5625

Jimmy Mitchell
Omark Industries, Inc.
P.O. Box 946
Zebulon, NC 27597
919/269-7421

Sherry S. Mullen
Omark Industries, Inc.
P.O. Box 946
Zebulon, NC 27597
919/269-7421

Frank M. Rich
Rico Suction Labs, Inc.
P.O. Drawer 2508
Burlington, NC 27216
919/584-1826

John E. Signet
Rexham/Laminex
1313 Renflow Ln.
Matthews, NC 28105

David F. Taylor
Shuford Mills, Inc.
P.O. Box 1530
Hickory, NC 28603
704/322-2700

Larry G. Teague
Carolina Mills, Inc.
P.O. Box 157
Maiden, NC 28650
704/428-9911

Patricia Thompson
Shuford Mills, Inc., Tape Div.
P.O. Box 1530
Hickory, NC 28601
704/322-2700

W. Torchinsky
Ciba-Geigy Corporation
P.O. Box 18300
Greensboro, NC 27419
919/292-7100

John E. Varela
Byron Jackson Pump Division
P.O. Box 7482
Charlotte, NC 28217
704/588-1950

N. Warren Wilkerson, Jr.
Privateer Manufacturing Co., Inc.
P.O. Box 69
Chocowinity, NC 27817
919/946-7772

Lillian S. Wilson
Concrete Machinery Co., Inc.
P.O. Box 99
Hickory, NC 28603-0099
704/322-7710

T. V. Yount
Siecor
489 Siecor Park
Hickory, NC 28603
704/327-5988

Kurt G. Waldthausen
Hettich America Corp.
P.O. Box 7664
Charlotte, NC 28217
704/588-6666

William Houston Miller
Mars Manufacturing Co.
P.O. Box 6874
Asheville, NC 28816
704/254-0741

Barbara N. Wilhelm
Arrow International, Inc.
200 Commerce Place
Randleman, NC 27317
919/498-4153

1985 DIRECTORY $25.00

NCWTA
NORTH CAROLINA WORLD TRADE ASSOCIATION

_____ *Sales and Marketing, Inc.*

ars of sales, marketing and managment
xperience, specializing in:

ng complete programs for maximum
use of a company logo
s and promotion consultancy
valuation, planning and placement
• **Special projects**

Let us go to work for you!

1003 Crosstimbers Parkway
P.O. Box 437
Morrisville, NC 27560
(919) 469-5561

51

and others interested in doing business with association members and got the ad sales underway. He was able to close this out in just a few weeks.

Meanwhile I had designed a handsome magazine-style format, with a fabulous cover featuring one of the "blue planet" photos of Earth against the deep black background of outer space. I had assembled the membership lists and written the introductory articles on the association and its activities. From that point on it was just a matter of typesetting and printing.

We continued the project for three successive years. By the fourth year the association had hired a full-time executive director, who decided to convert our directory to an in-house publication and so divert total advertising revenues to the treasury of the organization.

Such a move is not infrequent. It always seems easier than it really is to sell advertising and publish quality products. I do not know how successful the directory became under association editorship. I do know that there was a two-year gap in publication. Normally, when handled by those who do not know the business, things do not work smoothly and the cost of doing the project increases dramatically. Printing costs alone will probably triple or quadruple, and without professional editing, the written portion of the directory will deteriorate.

In any case, my company had the project for three years and profited considerably thereby. If we had worked harder to cultivate multi-level contacts within the association — as we certainly should have done — we might still be doing the job. More about this later.

PROSPECTING FOR DIRECTORIES

Prospects who may offer opportunities in the membership directory field fall into two categories. The first is associations who need a directory but don't have one. These may be brand new organizations — spawned by some new technology or economic reality, for instance — or older organizations that have recently grown to a size that makes a first-class directory desirable.

In the second category are organizations whose members may be paying for their directories out of their own pockets and will be delighted to learn that you will do it for them at no cost. Also in this category are organizations whose members are dissatisfied with their current product. Perhaps the publisher has been careless about correcting typos in names, addresses, and telephone numbers — the fastest way to lose a client in the directory business — or has not met promised publication schedules. Perhaps they want to share in the gross revenues and the current publisher will not agree to such an arrangement. Perhaps there has been a simple falling out or personality clash between the publisher and the executive director. Whatever the reason, a certain number of those organizations that currently have directories will be in the market for a new publisher.

How to Get Leads

How to develop leads? The bad news is that the market for association membership directories is necessarily limited. The good news is that opportunities are fairly easy to identify and locate. Here are the major sources.

Newspapers and Periodicals

As a publisher you will be reading the newspapers — local, state, and national. You will be looking for items that tell of the formation of a new trade or professional association or mention one that you have not heard of and that may offer an opportunity for you. You will also be looking for news stories concerning new products, processes, or technologies that have already generated new associations or are likely to do so in the near future.

An example? Is there a newly-formed "National Association of Desktop Publishers"? Is there a state association? Would a membership directory be in order? There would clearly be a very strong advertising base to support such a publication. Everyone from printers to paper manufacturers to computer companies and graphic arts equipment firms would head the list of prospects, which would also include dozens of lesser advertising markets.

The Yellow Pages

There is a heading in the Yellow Pages of most telephone books for "Associations." Check your local listings for associations which have their headquarters in your own town. Check the telephone book for your state capital city, especially. Associations, one of whose main functions is lobbying legislatures, will cluster around the center of political power. Your telephone company will send you directories for any city in the U.S. for just a few dollars each.

Other Associations

Check the *Encyclopedia of Associations* (Gale Research Company) in the reference room of your library. You'll find listings of more associations than you ever dreamed possible. You will be dealing with these on two levels, national and state. If the national office of a large organization is difficult for you, as a small publisher, to reach and do business with, there is usually a state branch that is much more accessible. There is the National Education Association, for instance, but there is also the North Carolina Association of Educators. The same national/state split occurs in many other organizations.

In the Yellow Pages of my local directory I find a listing for a state association of volunteer fire departments. Preliminary fact-finding tells me that this organization is a good prospect. They do have a directory of sorts, so I know that they want one. Examining it, I find it primitive in design and marginal in quality. I can easily do much, much better. Further, they are currently *paying* a local printer several thousand dollars a year to produce it for them.

I can show them how they can get it done free, get it done better (thus enhancing their professional image), and maybe even develop a small positive cash flow from the project by helping us target advertising sales in return for a small percentage of gross sales.

SELLING THE ADVERTISING

In selling the advertising for your membership directory you will, of course, first prepare the same kind of rate card and media kit materials that are needed for any publication sales campaign.

In general there will be fewer advertising clients than for a publication of more general readership, but those that you do identify will be stronger prospects and willing to foot the bill for more expensive advertising. Remember, your readership is very clearly *targeted*, including virtually every person, company, or corporation of importance within any specialty or trade related to the interests or activities of the association.

How do you identify good advertising prospects? Remember that certain firms — banks, for instance — will want to reach any financially strong base of possible customers.

Others will be in the business of serving specific needs of those listed in the directory. In my World Trade Association directory I had pages from the biggest banks and from a major national accounting firm. I also had pages from state port authorities in my state and adjacent states, shippers, freight forwarders, attorneys specializing in international business, translators, and specialists in international marketing.

Pore over the Yellow Pages, not only for specific advertising prospect names but also to trigger in your mind whole categories of advertisers whom you then locate individually and contact. You will also read the trade press to see who is already trying to reach the market your directory serves. This source will reveal some of your most likely prospects.

The majority of your sales will be made by telephone. You call, introduce the project, and send along a media kit. This is reviewed, fresh contact is made, and an insertion order is sent off for a signature.

The executive offices of the association with which you are working will also be interested in seeing the project succeed to the fullest extent possible. Strong advertising support for the directory will convey the desired message that the organization is vital, doing business, and making money — a real image builder. You can add to this initial and very real incentive an arrangement whereby the organization will receive a percentage — never more that 10% and sometimes less — of sales resulting from good leads that it furnishes.

Relatively few sales at fairly high prices will make an association directory a profitable venture. In the World Trade Association project we sold only ten pages of advertising. This brought in $28,000. The cost of writing, printing, distribution, and sales commissions totaled less than $10,000. This is an excellent profit margin.

This was a small project, easily handled in a short period of time. Regional or national directories will take longer to do and be more expensive to produce and distribute, but in return for the extra effort they will bring in proportionately more money.

GOING THE EXTRA MILE

The idea, of course, is to repeat your directory project year after year. Some advertisers will drop out and new ones will come on board, but in general you will soon establish a base of advertisers who will simply renew time and time again. You can publish your directory many times *if you pay attention to the needs of the organization (and the individual executive director or president) for which you are working.*

As a business person you will doubtless recognize many opportunities to cement a positive, long-term relationship with your client. Never miss one of them. They put money in the bank — your bank. I especially recommend the following:

- **Cultivate the president-elect as well as the president.** This tip alone can preserve a lucrative contract for you over many years. Most organizations, in any given year, will have a president and a president-elect. The president-elect won't have a lot to do with this year's directory, but he'll be the man in charge of next year's. Generally he will be a business executive who has little free time. He will not be aware of you, personally, and the good service that you and your company have provided to his association unless you make it your business, in every subtle and inventive way possible, to *make* him aware.

- **Invite his input and ask for his opinions.** Just be careful to phrase your questions in such a way as to elicit responses you can live with no matter what they may be.

- **Go the extra mile in the quality of the product.** Always give service above and beyond what is required or even paid for. What costs a little more now may pay off handsomely in future profits.

- **Use the finest affordable paper.** In most short-run directories the cost of the paper is a very small part of overall production costs and enhances appearance tremendously. Also use heavier stock. Eighty pound coated paper is much handsomer and more impressive than sixty. Of course, if you have a run of thousands the cost of paper can become a more important factor, but this is not usually the case.

- **Spend whatever it takes to design a powerful cover.** The cover is all most people will ever see of your directory, and it must be top drawer. Self-covered publications are less expensive, but separate covers on heavier stock are desirable. In any case be certain to order liquid lamination of the cover or some equivalent process to give the cover bulk and gloss.

- **Proofread with great diligence.** If you are not an experienced proofreader, then hire someone who is. There will be thousands of names, addresses, and telephone numbers in your directory. You must do everything you can to see that not a single one of them is wrong. Often the association office itself will be sloppy in getting materials to you. Make certain that all lists that come in are accurate and up to date. You can't satisfy an irate member whose name or number is wrong by telling him that it was not your mistake. All he knows is that it *is* wrong, that it is wrong in the association directory, and that you are the publisher of that directory. The buck always stops with you.

- **Offer extra services whenever possible**. Photograph the annual convention. Offer your design and creative services for an association brochure. Take a 35mm camera to the annual convention and take several hundred snapshots — which you then make available to the association. Every positive contact with your client makes the relationship with your company more secure and long lasting.

- **Meet your deadlines, no matter what**. If you have agreed to have a directory available in time for the annual convention or some other important occasion, do so. Schedule your work to allow for unavoidable delays. Remember that the overworked secretary in the association office has nothing to gain from working overtime to get you the materials you need at the precise time you need them. Remember, too, that presses break down and that even Federal Express sometimes loses or misroutes shipments. Allow in your planning for all such delays.

- **Make a splash at the annual convention**. Set up a display. Give away something useful — perhaps something as simple as imprinted pen and pad sets for taking notes during sessions. Set up a hospitality room in your suite or, better yet, offer to sponsor or co-sponsor a before-dinner cocktail hour. Be everywhere, talk to everyone, exhibit your interest in the welfare of the organization in unmistakable terms.

Association membership directories are neat, well-defined projects. Advertising prospects are easily identified and sold. Typical profit margins are very attractive. Such a project is a worthwhile addition to your desktop publisher's repertoire.

8.

Publishing a City or County History

A local or county history will make money, if carefully planned and executed. Indeed, at the right time and in the right place it can make a great deal of money. Such a book is not difficult to compile and publish, even though it may be very heavy with detail and require considerable time and attention.

In general, local histories are published in signed and numbered "collector's editions," with all of the extra attention to binding and the general appearance of the book that such an approach implies. This runs production costs up slightly but allows you to charge considerably more for the finished book. A minimum might be $30 a copy, with $40 to $50 not at all unusual. What's more, many of these copies can be sold prior to publication, guaranteeing break-even or better before you even go to press. There are secondary profit opportunities, too, that can considerably enhance revenues.

A local or county history takes a while to do. You will probably be involved in other projects while this one is going on, keeping it moving forward with a day a week, say, of your personal attention. There may be special circumstances that will permit or require you to move much faster, such as the approach of a historic date that the publication is tied to. I once brought out a town history in ninety days in order to meet such a deadline. I don't, however, recommend such haste. It is usually not necessary and, for sure, the tight calendar does not give you time to take advantage of the secondary sources of profit that I mentioned above.

SURVEYING THE MARKET

There are as many opportunities to do local or county histories as there are towns and counties. The first step in identifying those that are good bets for you is to survey the market. Here is what you do.

Visit the local library and even contact whatever department is in charge of historical matters at the state level. In North Carolina it's called the Department of Archives and History. Every state has one of these, whatever its name.

You will want to draw up a bibliography of every book — assuming there are some — written about the town or county in question.

And be alert here. You may well turn up an out-of-print classic that you can bring out at a later date in a reprint edition with a new introduction and index.

If your research reveals that a book such as the one you plan has been done within the past few years, then you probably need to move on to greener pastures and come back another time. The market is probably saturated. You could possibly come up with a new slant that might justify another book, but unless you have a sponsor (see below) willing to underwrite your efforts you are much better off moving on to a locale where a book has *not* been done. One of these books a generation is about all the traffic will bear.

If you discover that there is indeed an opportunity to do your history, then you will, through your research, already have established a basic list of all your sources. From them you draw not only historical facts for your narrative, but maps and photographs as well. These materials will also give you leads as to where other such items can be found.

Check the Calendar

Is there an anniversary, a historic commemoration, a centennial, sesquicentennial, or bicentennial to celebrate? Such events are perfect occasions for the publication of a book of history. The entire community will be in a frame of mind that will lead them to buy it, and sales will be far stronger than might otherwise be the case.

Analyze the Market

You can expect to sell a number of copies equal to 1 to 2% of the population in your initial sales campaign. After that sales will trail off although, over time, you will sell out any reasonable run of your first edition.

Is this number of initial sales sufficient for you to recoup expenses and make a profit? I currently live in a small town of 12,000 inhabitants. In the entire county there are fewer than 50,000 men, women, and children of every age and educational level. I might break even doing a history of my town and county, but I surely wouldn't make a significant profit.

Twenty miles away is another city. It has a population of 50,000 and the county adds another 150,000. I could expect to sell at least 2000 books there. Even at a bargain basement price of $29.95 each I would gross $59,900. Out of that I could pay printing costs and overhead and still keep a sizeable profit for myself. At worst-case sales levels of 1000 copies I would still do all right. It takes little imagination to understand what the profit potential could be in a major metropolitan area.

GETTING STARTED

So, after your market survey you decide that your book is a saleable idea. What next? How do you get started?

The first step may be to find a sponsor who can put an organizational or institutional seal of approval on your project. Though you can well succeed without such sponsorship, there are some real advantages to you in such a deal. The right sponsor could relieve you of all financial risk through arrangements like a guaranteed fee or through guaranteed pre-publication sales. Where do you look for such a sponsor? Check out these possibilities first.

Financial institutions, especially, like to position themselves in the market as "hometown folks." One of the largest banks in the United States, North Carolina National Bank, is currently running a series of television spots touting itself as "the best bank in the neighborhood."

A new mega-buck bank start-up in my area is being promoted as the "return to the hometown bank." This institution, The New East Bank, is going head-to-head with an older, but expanding, institution, the East Carolina Bank.

All three of these banks would be prime candidates to sponsor a city or county history, although the latter two, having a more accessible, regional headquarters might be more likely to take the bait you offer.

Savings and loans, too, are good prospects as are homegrown industries that have made it big or other industries which are new to the area but are seeking to develop local roots and identify themselves as "good corporate citizens." Strong prospects at any time, such companies are especially interesting targets for your efforts when they are about to celebrate an anniversary of some kind.

Your Presentation

Prospects such as these will be accustomed to dealing with advertising agencies and marketing persons who exhibit some degree of professionalism. At least they give all the outward signs of it. In this environment your presentation should be as well prepared as you can make it. You should understand and prepare for the fact that your idea will have to be taken to a variety of committees and departments for discussion and approval. Since you will certainly not be present at all of these discussions to make your case, your presentation will have to speak for you. This presentation will have two parts.

First, you should prepare a brief written narrative describing the project: the physical appearance of the book; a summary of how the book fits into the bank's marketing plans; your credentials for undertaking the project, including all past successes; accounts of other such projects elsewhere that have worked well, if you know of any; and the way you suggest that the deal be structured.

This written portion should be straightforward and easy to read. It should be classy without being fancy. (Your desktop equipment is perfect for this.) It should be easily read and digested in no more than five minutes. In no case should it take an attentive reader more than ten minutes to get the meat out of it.

It should be duplicated and spiral bound in at least ten copies. When you discuss the proposal with your client or when the client takes it into conference, you want everyone present to have a copy in his or her hands.

Along with your written narrative you will prepare some exhibits; a picture is indeed worth a thousand words. Many very successful and very busy people rely almost entirely on image and ear to make decisions in preference to the written word. Your visual exhibits will include the following items.

You will prepare a title page just as it would appear in the finished book, prominently displaying the name of your client as sponsor; a dummy foreword signed by the CEO of your client organization; a typical two-page layout, a photo spread with cutlines, a cover concept, etc. These will be affixed to artboard that will easily stand up on an easel during your presentation.

Each board will have a cover of tracing paper held neatly in place with white art tape.

Make sure that every item on your visual presentation is clearly labeled so that it can all be as easily understood in your absence as when you are present to explain it.

When you want to convey the idea of the physical appearance of the finished book take along some samples of other books that are similar to the one you have in mind. Most people — even intelligent people — will be unable to visualize the book that you are describing in words.

Work hard to see that the ultimate decision maker is present at the presentation. In banks especially, those who have "marketing" positions as a rule have no authority to make decisions or sign contracts. They often have little advertising or public relations experience. They can say no, but they can't say yes. Such people can be dangerous to your success.

FRIENDS AND ENEMIES

Deeply embedded in human nature is the drive toward asserting and preserving one's own self-interest. Recognizing this fact and having strategies in place to deal with it will smooth the way in many a business deal.

You should be prepared to face two such problems in your effort to reach an agreement with your financial or industrial client. The first may come from the client's on-staff marketing person. The second may come from the client's advertising agency.

You have to remember that these people see you as competition, and the less self confident among them, consciously or unconsciously, may not want you to succeed. They may throw obstacles in your path, obstacles that will be hard for you to overcome. The better and more capable you are, the more formidable your perceived competitive threat becomes.

It is a question of money as well as ego. One of my early projects was for a book called *Sunday Drives*. It focused on family excursions within easy reach of the city I was living in at that time. It featured places of intrinsic interest; places that were free or virtually free; and places that could be reached before the children began to ask, "How much farther is it?" It was illustrated with excellent photography and some very fine cartoon-style maps by an artist friend of mine.

I prepared a presentation just as I have described it here and succeeded in attracting the very favorable attention of the president of the largest savings and loan in the city. Just as we were about to sign the agreement he called his advertising agency in for advice. From that point on it was all downhill. I did not get the project.

What happened? I realize now that the money the S&L was going to put into my book idea came from the same advertising budget that the ad agency drew its own funds from. More money for me meant less of it for them.

Ad agencies live, in part, on the 15% commission they make in placing advertising for their clients. Had I been more knowledgeable I would have made it clear to the agency that the project was "commissionable," that is, that they would receive their 15% in return for their "consultation" on the project. I feel certain today that this approach would have worked and that I would have left the room with the project in the bag.

With ad agencies, money — in the form of standard commissions — talks. But what about the staff marketing people? You can't pay off the staff with cash, but you can stroke them in other and very effective ways. Although some staff marketers may be highly qualified and skilled people, some — or so my experience has been — are not. They are somewhat insecure in their positions and do not relish the idea of being shown up.

You will have to tailor your approach to the personality of the individual in question, of course. What works for one may not work for another. But in general you want to create the feeling that you are colleagues working together on a joint project. Ask if the marketer would like to have a credit on the title page as co-editor or co-author. Compliment the marketing person in his or her presence and in the presence of the boss. Let the marketer know that your main aim is to put together a project that will bring recognition to the institution and to the marketing department of the institution.

STRUCTURING THE DEAL

How do you structure the agreement with your institutional sponsor? There are several ways.

The institution agrees to buy the first edition of your book at a discount. It can then use it as a public relations tool, give the books to new depositors (in the case of a bank), sell them or use them in any other way it chooses. This first edition contains a foreword by the CEO of the institution and a credit on the title page. The institution may or may not wish to have an option on succeeding editions.

If your book had a retail price set at $39.95, you might sell the first edition to the bank at a 20% discount, or $32 per copy. On a first edition of 2000 copies that would give you gross revenues of $64,000. You would want a portion of this sum (say, one-fifth) on the signing of your agreement, a second installment (adequate to pay the printing bill) on approval of page proofs, and the balance on delivery. I used this approach in the sale of the first edition of my book, *Tales of the Tobacco Country*, to Philip Morris.

If the institution declines to exercise its option to buy the second printing, you could keep the book on sale on your own, should you choose to do so.

The institution could buy all rights to the book, to the first and all future editions. It would, essentially, own the book. This generally would involve a somewhat larger payment to you. In principle, the institution could handle printing and production itself, although it is unlikely that they would wish to do so.

A NON-INSTITUTIONAL SPONSOR: THE HISTORICAL SOCIETY

Virtually every town or county has a historical society. The more active of these organizations are prime candidates for sponsoring a city or county history and, in fact, you see such books appearing quite frequently. The strength of an agreement with a local historical society is twofold: its membership is likely to include some of the most prestigious families in the area, and its members also constitute a primary pool of book buyers, both before and after publication. In addition the society can provide many of the key sources you will need in compiling your book.

Collaboration with the historical society can also open up a source of important additional profits derived from the inclusion of a section devoted to family histories and photographs, for which individuals pay in advance. More about this later.

TERMS OF THE AGREEMENT

Your presentation to the historical society can be as substantial and impressive as the one you prepared for the institutional sponsor candidates. You need to impress the members with your professionalism and ability to carry the project through to conclusion. Remember that once you strike a deal you have to remain firmly in control of the project, so it is important to establish your role as expert in the very beginning.

What form will an agreement between your publishing company and a historical society take? Here are the areas in which you will wish to work out specific terms.

The society will need to be reassured that *it cannot lose any money and that, no matter what happens, it will not be obligated to pay out any funds.* Unlike the institutional sponsor, the society will have no advertising and marketing funds. It is run by collecting dues of just a few dollars a year from each member.

On the other hand, it does want to see the book come out. So you offer to underwrite all the costs of editing and printing the book in return for the help of the society in gathering materials for your book and selling it.

- You might, for instance, ask the society to solicit its members to order a certain number of paid-in-advance pre-publication copies.

- You might include the enticement of a discount when payment accompanies the order, thus securing some working capital.

- You may ask the society to sponsor a publication reception and autograph party at which books will be sold.

- You may ask the society to provide working space and telephone access if you are working away from home.

- You may ask the society to assist in the sale of family histories (see below).

- You may ask the society to gather materials and submit them to you on a mutually agreed-to schedule. (You will work this schedule out and get them to agree to it. Remember that it is essential that you remain in complete charge.)

- You may offer to share revenues with the society, establishing a "commission" on the pre-publication copies sold, or on all copies sold either to or by members. Commissions will be payable, however, only after the project reaches a safe level of profitability.

OTHER SPONSORS

Another sponsor could be the temporary commission or committee established to coordinate the celebration of an important date in local history — an anniversary of the founding of a town or county, for instance.

Such a commission will be glad to hear from you. They will have been thinking about doing a commemorative publication, but they will not know how to go about writing and publishing one. I have seen many such books that were very badly done and at very great expense — all through lack of know-how.

And since the organization is temporary and will be disbanded once the celebration is over, its members will be reluctant to incur any debt that they are not sure they can easily retire. Indeed, they are mostly looking for activities that will *raise* money to help finance parades, displays, dinners, and other activities.

You will, therefore, have two things going for you. First, you know how to do the book and can take the entire burden off of the commission's shoulders; and you can structure an agreement in such a way as to guarantee a positive financial return to the commission. It was with precisely such a project that I first got into the publishing business (see Chapter 1). You simply agree to compile and produce the book. The commission agrees to give you all support, endorsement, and press coverage that it can. It sets up publication parties and autograph parties. It aggressively markets its book through every possible outlet, using its contacts to get the book not only in bookstores, but on drugstore counters, in clothing stores, and in other retail outlets. It sets up a sales force of volunteers that will attempt to meet quotas of sales in every segment of the community. In return, the commission gets a negotiated percentage of the retail price of each book sold.

The historical society or commission has everything to gain and nothing to lose.

DOING IT YOURSELF

Sponsors are great for business, since they lower the risks you are taking as publisher. But when everything else is right — you have a good market in which no such book has been done for a long while — they are certainly not necessary to success. You can just as well do the project yourself, on a wholly speculative basis. In the right market, the profits on a spec book can be even higher than with the sponsored version.

PLANNING YOUR BOOK

In any case, sponsored or not, let's be clear about the book we are planning. We are *not* talking about a formal history, laboriously researched from original sources. Such a book would take years rather than months to write and might not make much money when it did come out.

Our book will grow out of what is already known. Rather than a long, uninterrupted prose narrative, it will be feature-oriented, much like a good magazine. And it will be heavily illustrated by photographs, drawings, maps, and other graphic items culled from the pages of old newspapers or other publications. As a matter of fact it could be compiled from photographs and graphic items alone.

So there are two choices. The first is a combination of written and photographic history, with about equal amounts of each. I used this technique in my book, *A Greenville Album.* It allowed me to tell a good deal about the history of the town but did not tie me down to the "history-book" feel of a densely-packed text. I opened with a 4000 word history of the town, which I wrote myself. It was gleaned from two or three published sources as well as my own knowledge of the most recent two decades. Even this narrative was in a magazine style, editorially. I developed a miniature line drawing of the first Pitt County courthouse to divide sections of the narrative into easily digestible "fact-bites" of history.

I then assigned certain other topics for article-style treatment to writers whom I knew. Dr. Stan Riggs, a geologist, did a piece on the Tar River, on whose banks the city was founded. There was a piece on the Civil War days, another on the great fire of the 1890s, and still another on the days of the riverboats. Other articles were on local folklore themes, the coming of the railroads, the founding of the university.

There was an extensive bibliography of genealogical and historical documents and records. And there were dozens of old photographs, many seen in my book for the first time. Since I gave all my writers a thirty day deadline — including myself — I was able to generate the entire text in one month's time.

This half-and-half approach works very well, and the breaking of the written portion into easily manageable segments made the gathering of the text very simple. I have since decided that the text could have been drastically reduced, making the project even simpler. An introductory narrative of 4000 words would have been adequate, with the space saved devoted to more and larger photographs.

You can easily substitute photographs with fully-developed cutlines for the articles. For my piece on the riverboat days along the Tar River I could have used a two page spread of the James Adams Floating Theater (the original for Edna Ferber's *Showboat*) moored along the Tar and included a two or three paragraph description of it. Most other eras could have been treated in the same way.

I believe that an even higher readership and more widespread knowledge of historical facts would have resulted from this technique. Publishers, writers, and others who love books generally overestimate the number of people who read anything at all. But people *will* look at pictures and read the words printed below or beside them. The Sears-Roebuck catalog — if nothing else — proves this to be true.

GATHERING YOUR RESOURCES

You will want to organize a public relations blitz at two stages: when you are just starting out to gather materials and later on, when the book is ready to go on sale.

The local media will find your project newsworthy. Your job is to help them report it in a way that is helpful to you. Your goal is to become, as nearly as possible, a "household name." When you call on someone in your search for old photographs, many of which may be family heirlooms, you will get far more cooperation if your name is a familiar one.

Write News Releases

Deliver them in person to the daily and weekly newspapers in your trade area. Make yourself available for interviews. Send press kits to TV stations. Let talk show hosts know that you are available for interviews. Call program chairpersons for civic clubs, book clubs, and other organizations. Give as many talks as you can fit into your schedule. And, in everything you say or do, *emphasize the fact that you are asking for assistance and that those with documents, information, or photographs should call you so that their materials can be included in this important book.*

And make no mistake about it, the publication of your book *will* be an important event in the life of the town.

THE WRITERS YOU NEED

You will need the assistance of writers who know local history. Every town has at least one and sometimes two or three persons who have taken on the role of local historian. You will want to identify these people and get to know them. They will be invaluable to you.

The more extensive the written material you decide to include, the more valuable to you they will be. Even in preparing cutlines for photographs you will want someone available who knows the subject thoroughly and can add the depth of information that might otherwise be missing, as well as the odd tidbit of information that enlivens the book. Some of them may know the whole subject; others will specialize in certain areas. All can be very useful to you.

SET TIGHT SCHEDULES

Many of the people you will be dealing with will have little notion of the value of your time or the necessity of getting things done on schedule. In dealing with them it is essential to set up deadlines. A general statement such as, "I've got to have this just as soon as you can get to it," or "Let me have your article as soon as possible" leads to troubles and disaster. "As soon as possible" may be six months from now. If you need your material by next Friday, say so. If your source can have it done, he'll agree to the timetable. If he can't, he'll tell you that too, and you can go to someone else or do it yourself. Above all, you must remain in control. You are the editor and, in the last analysis, your decisions are the ones that stand.

Contacting these source people is important in another way, too. By consulting them and giving them the chance to get involved, you acknowledge the years of work that they have devoted to their task. Failure to do so can — and probably will — result in hurt feelings and perhaps in making an enemy. The smaller the town, the more important this kind of personal contact becomes.

THE GREAT PHOTOGRAPH HUNT

The time you spend digging up fabulous old photographs will be time very well spent. How do you begin? You will have asked those with photograph collections to contact you in the course of your initial PR campaign and you will call on these people. But this is just the beginning.

The trail will lead from one person, by referral, to two others and from them to four of their best friends. Soon you will have called on scores of prospects.

Always ask to see the photo collection for yourself. Many people will have no idea that, while the persons gathered in the foreground may be of no particular historical importance, the street scene all around them may be particularly valuable. The photos on old post-cards are a valuable source for street scenes. Ask about these, too. And never leave one home without asking for referrals to others.

Many people will be reluctant to let you borrow their old photographs, and understandably so. You can allay their fears to some extent by the professionalism of your approach. Always carry large catalog envelopes with you. Slip each picture into a separate envelope. Number the envelope and on its face write clearly and distinctly the name and address of the person from whom the photograph is borrowed. On the outside of the envelope you will carefully note, for future reference, all the information you can gather about the photograph: where it was taken, by whom, what it shows, the names of individuals appearing in it, etc. Then, on another sheet of paper, give the individual who owns the photographs a receipt enumerating all the items that you are borrowing.

A photographic copy board will be a good investment. This is a simple device which allows you to take a photograph of another photograph. It has a stand to which a 35mm camera is attached. There are bulb holders for even artificial lighting and a base for holding the original photograph in place. In all, a decent copy board will cost $40 or $50. In addition, you will probably need a closeup lens for your camera.

The copy board is quite portable and, if necessary, can be set up in the home of anyone who simply will not let the photographs out of his possession. You can easily copy photographs for those who insist on having the originals back in short order. When no demand is made that photos be returned quickly, it is better to keep the originals and send them to the printer along with your pasted-up pages. His camera should do a better job with the original than with your copy.

Although you will lose something in quality, you can also scout through earlier books and magazines for photos that you can pick up from them. At one time, traveling photographers used to scour the countryside and put together illustrated brochures for Chambers of Commerce. Many of these little publications contain complete sets of photographs of the business district as it existed at the time they were taken. You will want to give these booklets to the printer so that he can pick up the photos you want to use in the most effective way.

In addition to photographs, you will be looking for drawings of scenes from earlier times, as well as maps and other documents. Period ads reproduced from old newspapers can also be used to good effect.

HOW TO DESIGN YOUR BOOK

You want to sell your book at the high end of the price range. Expensive books sell quite well, but to do so they must *look* expensive. It could be that you are a fine book designer. After all, as I pointed out in the introduction to this book, people get into publishing from varied backgrounds. But you may also be a salesman (or even a writer) with limited design experience.

Text is easy. After all, a page of type is a page of type. But with hundreds of pictures to handle it gets more complicated.

If I lacked the necessary know-how, I would do two things. First, I would find a competent graphic designer who wanted to do a little moonlighting, someone I could get for ten or fifteen dollars an hour. Second, I would put into this designer's hands a copy of a book I liked that used lots of photographs, if possible another local picture history book. And I would tell the designer, "Make me a book like this one. Here is the manuscript of the text and here are the photographs and other graphic elements we will be using." It is possible that your printer can recommend someone to provide these services or even provide them himself.

You will work very closely with your designer. Bear in mind that he will not know the subject nearly as well as you and will need your constant input to stay on track. Have him rough out ten or fifteen pages. See how you like it. Eliminate any trouble spots, then rough out the remainder of the book. Fine-tune this rough, and then do your pasteup.

Here are some other things to remember:

• **Use the finest paper you can afford**. This is going to be a short run book and it will contain a great deal of photography. You will need a good grade of paper anyway. Moving up to the best grade will not cost much more. Coated paper is highly recommended, though it need not be glossy.

• **Create a limited edition**. In the front of the book, print a page as follows:

> This first edition of _(name of your book)_ is limited to _1000_ (or whatever number you have chosen) copies of which this is copy number _____.

- When the book comes off the press have the finest penman you can find **inscribe the number of the copy** on the bottom line. This way you create an instant collector's item.

- Be sure to **include the names of all collaborators, contributors, and others involved in the project** on a page of acknowledgments. Those who have made significant editorial contributions may be listed on the title page. Such listings sell books.

- **Go the extra mile in binding your book.** Ask your printer to show you samples of his best bindings. You might consider going to a printer who also prints college annuals (such as the Delmar Printing Co. in Charlotte, NC). They will be able to furnish simulated leather bindings, richly embossed, at a reasonable cost. If you are in an area where a true custom bookbinder is located you could pre-sell some full-leather bound copies, perhaps signed as well as numbered, for several hundred dollars each. But, of course, these should be sold _before_ they are produced.

- **Do not consider bringing out a paperbound edition.** It will merely siphon off sales from the more profitable hardcover version. Those who want this book will buy it in hardcover. The one exception to this rule might come in the case where you are publishing a book for a public event under the auspices of a bicentennial, centennial, or other such commission. The commission may feel that it has to make the book available in a less expensive edition for those who can't afford the deluxe edition. In any case, keep the cost of the paperback version as close to that of the hardcover as possible. Or at least keep the profit margins on the two versions as close together as possible.

PROFIT FROM FAMILY HISTORIES

A section of family histories will produce considerable additional revenue and also help generate significant additional sales. If you have an institutional sponsor, a section devoted to individual families may not be acceptable. But in any of the other options — historical society, special event commission, or outright entrepreneurial publication — such a section will work. Here's what you do.

Get the word out that family histories will be included in your book. You can do this through interviews, news releases, mailings to the membership lists of sponsoring and other organizations, talks and speeches, classified advertising . . . through every means possible.

Design a brief flyer describing the histories. A simple 8½" x 11" sheet, folded once, will suffice. In your flyer tell your prospects the following things:

- ❏ They will be responsible for researching and writing the family history.
- ❏ You will retain editorial control and may edit the text for style and appropriateness.
- ❏ A minimum charge for a family history will be a certain number of dollars — $100, say, for a basic one column write-up on a three column, large format page. You can alter this figure to fit your own market, client list, cost of production, and page size.
- ❏ Additional space may be purchased at the rate of so much per column inch. This rate will be slightly higher, on a space-proportioned basis, than the minimum charge.
- ❏ You will include a photograph at an additional charge. You will devise a list of two or three standard sizes that fit your format. The client will purchase the space that the photograph occupies, plus a charge of $25 for processing the photograph for printing (making a halftone screen).
- ❏ This fee must be paid in advance (you will take credit cards, of course).
- ❏ Each person whose family history is included must place an advance order for at least one copy of your book, along with a deposit of, say, $10, to reserve the copy for them. It is a limited edition, remember, and copies will be numbered.

The inclusion of family histories will permit you to generate some advance income for use as working capital and to pre-sell books. Most families who submit a history will purchase more than a single copy. To encourage this you may offer a discount for multiple-copy sales. You should also consider offering a discount for all pre-publication sales paid in advance.

Business and Organizational Histories

In additional to individual family histories you can offer to include the histories of churches, civic clubs, and other organizations at the same per column rate. These usually prove to be quite popular and are easy to sell.

HOW TO SELL YOUR BOOK

So now you've done all the work. The book is written, designed, and printed. Cartons of the finished copies, recently arrived from the printer, are stacked in every available spot throughout your home or office.

So what do you do next? How do you sell them? If you have succeeded in acquiring a bank or major industry as a sponsor, of course, this problem doesn't exist. You just deliver the books to your sponsor, bask in the warm glow of community recognition for a job well done, and . . . cash your check.

Usually, though, there will be a sales job to be done. With a book of this kind it is not difficult to do, but there are certain steps that you will want to take.

Select the Optimum Publication Date

Almost half the books sold in the United States over a twelve month period are sold in October, November, and December. Let this lesson not be lost on you. Many more people give books as gifts than ever read them. And your limited, collector's edition is unique – the perfect gift. It is expensive, yet affordable, and it will become an heirloom. So schedule publication for the period from October 15 to November 1 if at all possible.

If your book is linked to some historic date or celebration, then link your publication date to the opening festivities. See that your book is available *everywhere*.

Pre-Publication Sales

You will have sold a fairly substantial number of books before the official publication day rolls around, if you have planned a careful campaign of pre-publication sales. You will have solicited sales to the members of sponsoring organizations, to members of families who have included their family histories, and to other prime prospects whom you have reached by telephone or mail. Remember to provide the incentive of a pre-publication discount and offer to accept credit cards. Stress that your book is a limited edition and a collector's item. Its value will increase over the years. Make it clear that an advance purchase assures that a copy or copies will be reserved for the purchaser. Implement a profit-sharing arrangement, if this seems likely to produce orders, through your sponsoring organization. There is nothing quite so comforting as bringing a book to market with enough copies pre-sold to pay the printing bill.

Start the Second Movement of Your Public Relations Blitz

You got the work out effectively when you began your project, and this was valuable to you. Now you will redouble your efforts, building a crescendo of publicity to climax on publication day.

The first step is to prepare the basic *press kit* that you will distribute to all newspapers, radio stations, magazines, television stations, program chairpersons, and all others likely to take an interest in your project and publicize it. Try to make the project sound as newsworthy as possible. Remember that the media people you will be dealing with are interested in putting items of strong local interest on the air, on the screen, or on the printed page. Your press kit needs to let them know that your book is just such an item.

An effective press kit will be packaged in an attractive presentation folder and contain, at a minimum, the following items:

☐ **A news release for your local newspapers** — dailies and weeklies, as well as shoppers and all other periodicals. This release should be written in two versions, one a straight news story announcing the publication of your book and the other a full-fledged human interest feature story on it.

☐ **Photographs** of any editor and writers you may have hired and of yourself as editor and publisher.

☐ **A photograph of the book itself.** Your bindery can furnish you a book cover (called a "case") even before the final binding is done. In this way you can have the kit complete and out before the books actually arrive for distribution.

☐ **Quotes** that you will have collected by circulating galley proofs to notable persons. Such quotes and endorsements are an important part of the promotion campaign. The more quotes you have and the better known the persons who give them to you, the better they will work.

☐ **A fact sheet,** giving data on the book, names of all collaborators, quotes of colorful or especially interesting passages, price, availability, and all other information a news department might need to put together their own article. Many newspapers, for instance, will not want to run the canned release verbatim.

After you have mailed your press kit to all available sources of publicity, begin calling the hosts of talk shows on radio and television. If there is no talk show, call and talk to the program director or the news director. Time may be available for you in some other program spot or on the news.

Remember that the publication date itself is straight news copy. Be sure that the press is alerted and present as you sell your first copy, present your first copy to the mayor, autograph the first copy, etc.

Contact program chairpersons of organizations, civic clubs, etc., just as you did when you were cranking up the project. Work up a standard twenty minute talk on the adventure of getting the book together and publishing it. Always have a supply of books available for sale on a table in the rear of the room after the talk is over. Your audience will also have been able to inspect the book before the meeting starts. This often stimulates a very useful question and answer period.

Your books are expensive, so you will not want to waste copies. But it is a good investment to send review copies with a cover letter and press kit to book editors and feature editors of local and regional publications. An alternative is to send a press kit and invite the recipient to send for a review copy if he or she wishes to publish a review.

Use Direct Mail Promotion

It will be relatively easy to gather a mailing list of members of the historical society, Rotary and other civic clubs, and the members of other likely organizations. Prepare a one-page flyer on your book, with a reply coupon on the bottom. Mail this to each person on the list. Emphasize that telephone orders are encouraged. Be sure to indicate that charge cards (and which ones) are acceptable.

You may also include space for gift copies that the recipient wishes to purchase for others, especially family members who live out of town. You can offer to do the mailing yourself along with a gift card. You may also offer a discount for such multi-copy orders.

You will also send your flyer to libraries in your state. A one page flyer with a simple order form on the bottom seems to work better than more elaborate brochures. The front of the flyer, with the address on it, should carry a blurb of some kind indicating to the acquisitions librarian that the material inside concerns a new book about the state, along with favorable comments from reviewers. Most such books are automatic orders.

Do a little research to determine which librarian in the large metropolitan system does the buying. Such persons may purchase up to several dozen copies, one for each branch in the system.

School libraries are another good source for sales. Address your flyers to the "Teacher in Charge: (Your State) History Program." In North Carolina, state history is taught at grammar school levels and in the higher grades. The blurb on the front of these flyers should announce "An Important New Resource Book for (Your State) History."

Evaluate the Pull of Paid Advertising

In general, paid advertising will not be necessary to your success in this kind of project, but it can be helpful in keeping your book's name in the reader's mind. After your burst of PR and promotional activities has died down you might consider placing a one or two column inch ad in the newspaper to run each day for a month. This ad will bring your book to mind again and again and it will end up generating some visits to the bookstore or telephone orders directly to you. If you place your ad and it doesn't seem to be working, simply cancel it.

You can get a great deal of material in a small ad, and readers seem to love them. Study the ads in the back pages of *Southern Living* or *Better Homes and Gardens* for some ideas on great utilization of a very small space.

Sell Your Books in Bookstores

Having seen you talk about your book on TV or read a review of it in the paper, many people will go to the local bookstore(s) to buy a copy. You need to be sure that the book is there when they arrive.

Bookstores will be glad to stock your book. They will, of course, expect to make a profit on the books they sell. Here's how the system works.

Bookstores normally purchase books for resale at a 40% discount from list price. Thus, if a book retails for $20 the bookstore will be able to buy it for $12. However, with local titles given to them on consignment you can usually do better than a 40% discount. The bookstore doesn't pay the publisher for a consignment book until it is sold, nor do they incur the expense of ordering and the freight charge for shipping. They have no cash tied up in the book, so they can operate on a narrower margin. Consignment discounts at hometown outlets range from a low of 20% to about 30%, tops. Out of town bookstores will want the full 40%, no matter what.

Other Retail Outlets

Your goal is to sell the largest number of your books over the shortest possible period of time. Since the book is a great gift item, you can place copies in gift shops and other retail outlets. Upscale clothing stores and even furniture stores have worked for me. Hallmark card shops and similar establishments are also good bets, as is your town's classiest jewelry store. Books will be left on consignment and discounts will be the same as with bookstores.

Organize a Publication Gala and Autograph Party

A great many books can be sold at a well-organized publication reception and gala. Send out good, classy invitations. If you have collaborators and contributors, list them as guests of honor. Be sure to include as guests of honor as prominent a group of people as you can put together. Include all of those even remotely connected with the project. If at all possible have the Chamber of Commerce (which you will have joined) or the county historical society sponsor and host the reception. Otherwise you must organize it yourself. In this case you present it as given by your publishing company to honor the new book and the people who made it possible.

Have *high stacks of books* available on tables for inspection and purchase. Have on hand those whose names appear on the title page to autograph copies. Be sure to have an assistant or two to do the actual selling of the books. The persons doing the autographing will be at another table. Be sure to have on hand the equipment necessary to accept charge cards.

You will serve drinks and hors d'oeuvres and, about forty-five minutes into the reception, make your speech to the assembled guests.

If you do all these things, you will sell a considerable number of books. Sales of your city or county history will have a predictable sales curve. There will be a gratifying number of pre-publication sales. At the time of publication there will be a sharp peak, then a slow but steady decline in sales volume over the next six to eight weeks. After that time your book will continue to sell a few copies each month until the edition is exhausted.

9. Publishing a Weekly Newspaper or Shoppers' Guide

A weekly newspaper can be a tempting business enterprise. Such a publication has a lot going for it. It easily meets our three criteria for success in regional and local publishing: it has a clearly defined and limited trade area; it targets a finite list of advertising prospects, all of whom are easily reached; and, because it is free to the consumer and cheap to produce, it easily achieves saturation circulation.

There are some modest start-up costs, mainly for office space and initial supplies. You could avoid the space cost if you have a large basement, attic, or double garage that could be converted to use for your business. Most needed equipment, chiefly your desktop publishing computer and laser printer and an enlarging/reducing copy machine, can be leased by paying a couple of monthly installments up front. Production tables, light tables, files, and other paraphernalia are generally very simple to design and can be homemade.

These up-front costs are more than balanced by the short weekly billing cycle you will be working on. By the time your next month's lease payments come due you will already have four or five (yes, some months will have five Wednesdays in them!) week's accounts receivable to pay them. If, in the beginning, you do not need to draw out great amounts of cash for your own living expenses, it really is quite possible to start a newspaper of your own and pay for it as you go, wholly out of current revenues.

This is precisely what I did with the *Mecklenburg Gazette*, a weekly newspaper that I owned in Davidson, North Carolina. When I got hold of the newspaper it was literally a week away from bankruptcy. I had no cash to speak of — just a few thousand dollars in savings to live on until advertising revenues started coming in. I borrowed funds from the bank to pay the former owner a modest sum to cover the cost of the equipment he was transferring to me.

I did decide to buy the building the newspaper was housed in, mainly because it was a good deal. It was not a necessary part of the transaction. When the first monthly payment for the equipment and the building came due some six weeks later, I was easily able to meet it. Thereafter, month after month, I was solidly in the black. After three years I sold the paper to one of the larger chains and made a handsome profit.

I accomplished all this without a single cent of cash outlay on my part. My only investment was the three months' sweat equity I put in before beginning to draw my own salary as editor.

SURVEYING THE MARKET

Does such an opportunity exist in your area? Odds are the answer is yes — if you commit to running a tightly organized, reader friendly, and customer-oriented publication that takes account of the realities of the marketplace. Even quite small towns offer great opportunities.

Just across the Pamlico River from where I live there is a small town of 1800 residents. It has no newspaper. I believe that a weekly would survive and thrive there. And since it is clearly a growth area, the paper would grow with it.

How do you evaluate the chances for success? Mainly by studying the base of ready and willing advertisers. I once gave a talk on community newspapering to a class of journalism students at a nearby university. "What is the secret of success?" one young woman asked me. "What makes one weekly paper do well when another might fail?"

Now, I am sure she wanted me to talk about fine writing, investigative reporting, and an editorial page that gets nominated for a Pulitzer Prize. My answer was in a quite different vein. "Success in the weekly newspaper business require six things," I replied. "Four grocery stores, a K-Mart, and at least one large discount drugstore." The point, of course, is that if the advertising base is not there will be no paper to publish all that fine reporting in.

Success is a word that has different meanings for different people. One publisher may be content with a newspaper which provides thirty-five or forty thousand dollars a year in take-home compensation while another wants much more. Forty thousand is not much in Washington, New York, or San Francisco, but it can be a living wage in the South and many other regions of the country. Especially for those happy souls who, like Epicurus, understand that happiness lies, after all, in the limitation of desire.

The population of the town where I published my weekly was only 2800 and, as a matter of fact, there was only one discount drug store, and not a very big one at that. There were also two big city dailies competing for market share (the *Charlotte Observer and News*, published just eighteen miles away) as well as a free circulation shopper. Yet my paper was successful, and my family of five derived a comfortable income from it.

The major advertisers provide your sustaining cash flow. You need them for the long-term financial health of your paper. Once they decide to go with your paper, they will do so for an extended length of time. If you serve them well, they will stay with you. You do not have to resell them week in and week out, as you must do with some small retailers.

When you see a weekly newsprint publication that tries to get by without such advertisers, you are looking at a publication that has created needless obstacles for itself through a misunderstanding of the market, or one that is catering to a special market. Except in very unusual circumstances — and with some notable exceptions — this latter option is almost always a mistake.

THE JOYS OF COMPETITION

So you say there's another publication already in place. That's good. It means that the market is lively and advertising-active. Once when I was doing research for a direct response business I was building, I came across a valuable piece of advice in the great book by Julian L. Simon, *How to Start and Operate a Mail-Order Business*. Contrary to my expectations, Simon advises direct mail entrepreneurs not to seek out a new, untried product. Find out what is already selling, Simon advises, and sell it better.

The same lesson holds true in the publishing business. The presence of competition can be a good sign. It proves that the trade area can and will support an advertising medium such as yours. You just have to find a means (and a market position) that creates the impression in the minds of your clients that you are doing the job better, or more affordably, or both.

Competition is not to be feared. It is to be overcome. With your weekly schedule you can give competing small town dailies a real run for their money. There is a typical pattern in the growth of these dailies, exemplified in my neighborhood by the experience of the Greenville (NC) *Daily Reflector* and the Washington (NC) *Daily News*. These dailies exist within twenty miles of one another. The trade areas they cover are also served by the Raleigh *News and Observer*, a large metropolitan daily published in the state capital and, of course, by the three major television networks, a public television network, and a full range of cable services.

Both the *Daily Reflector* and the *Daily News* started out around the turn of the century as weeklies, reporting local news exclusively. As the populations they served grew (Washington to 12,000 and Greenville to 50,000) these newspapers expanded their publication schedules and eventually became dailies, reporting both local and national news.

Perhaps in the '20s and '30s there was a niche for such small dailies with world-class headlines emblazoned across the front page. Transportation was quite difficult. Few people traveled very far. Radio, as a news medium, was in its infancy. But today virtually no one depends on these local newsrooms to keep up with the latest dispatches from Washington and the world. Television and the metropolitan daily circulating from the state capital do that.

Small town dailies find themselves in a bind. They still have to report the national news, since there are simply not enough local stories to fill up its pages six or seven days a week or enough reporters to write the stories, in any case. They are dependent on the wire services for much of their copy.

Because they have to report the national news, no matter how incompletely or inadequately, they do not focus on local stories fully and completely. This leaves the market wide open for a competing weekly that will regularly print front-page local stories and features, so long as the space rates and circulation are attractive enough to result in signed contracts for advertising space.

THE PERSONALITY OF YOUR PUBLICATION

The more well-defined the personality of your publication is, the better reader identification with it will be. The look and feel you give it will depend on the market position you stake out for yourself and, to a large extent, on your personal interests. You will be deeply involved with your project on a day-to-day basis, and you will want it to be something that you like and take pride in.

There is a wide range of possibilities. At one extreme is the full-fledged weekly newspaper, with strong editorial content covering all aspects of local news: town council meetings, business developments, social news, and sports — everything. At the other is the free circulation shopper, which includes no news at all — beyond the news of the wonderful bargains to be had at local places of business that week.

Between these two extremes are a number of very viable market positions. It is these middle of the road publications that I recommend most highly from a business point of view.

THE READER APPEAL OF ADVERTISING

Before I go over your options in detail, let me mention a few basic facts about the appeal to readers of your advertising. Whatever format you choose for your paper, you can go a long way to making it a solid hit with readers if you go the extra mile in advertising design and copywriting. Here are two facts that you never want to lose sight of.

From the point of view of the average reader, the advertising has very high reader interest. The people who pick up your paper *want* to read the advertisements; they *want* to know where the bargains are. Television commercials are often more entertaining and more professionally produced than the programs on which they appear. Your newspaper ad should have this same exceptional quality.

The most read pages in any newspaper, research shows, are the classified pages. More people read the classifieds than read the editorial page, the sports pages, or even the comics. Yet there is not a single news "story" to be found in this section of the paper. For this reason, space rates in the classified pages are higher than elsewhere in the newspaper.

People love to browse through advertisements looking for that special bargain, that nugget of consumer information that will save them big bucks on some purchase they are planning to make during the weekend. When my wife's copy of *Better Homes and Gardens* comes in each month, she immediately turns to the small twelfth and eighth page ads in the back of the book, looking for new products, bargains, or sources for unusual items. I do the same with the trade publications that come to me. Each issue has an article or two that catches my attention and that I may or may not read through. But I scan *every page* looking for new product information or product offerings that will make my business more efficient, more profitable, more fun — or all of these.

When ads are well-designed and interesting to the eye, readers will pore over every column inch of them with much the same spirit that a grizzled prospector might have pored over an ancient map purporting to show the best spots to dig for that long sought-after treasure.

The point I am making, and it is often misunderstood by beginners, is that the quality of your advertising has as much to do with the readability of your newspaper as the stories themselves. The same care should be taken with ad design as with the writing of a front page story. Both have powerful appeal for the reader.

WHAT KIND OF NEWSPAPER?

With this background in mind, let's go over your main options in choosing the type of newspaper you will develop.

Full-Fledged Weekly

There are many good reasons for establishing a full-fledged weekly newspaper, but they are almost all of a personal, and not a business, nature. You may simply *want* to have such a paper. Well and good. It will work, although the ratio of time spent to profit earned will not normally be as favorable to you as another of the options. I would consider it myself only if no other newspaper existed in the community and I had a virtual monopoly.

You may feel that the community needs such a publication, or there may be political reasons (and these are the shakiest foundation of all). You might feel that the editorial policy of the established daily regularly takes an *anti* stance on issues where you favor the *pro* side. And people have told you that they would "like to see" such an alternative newspaper. Just remember that advertisers, not readers, support your endeavor, and advertisers spend money. Money, for the most part, is definitely not sentimental. It does not take sides. Talk is cheap. It seeks only to sell products. You may consider these hard truths, but there they are. *Advertisers spend money to increase sales, not to "support" one side of an argument over another.* When you make a presentation to a major food store chain, their questions will almost surely center around circulation and price and not whether your editorial page is liberal or conservative in the stands it takes on the issues.

The full-fledged weekly option works best for writers and editors who expect to hire salespeople to flesh out the staff and, in fact, such persons are the only ones likely to choose this option.

This kind of weekly is less feasible for sales-oriented entrepreneurs who expect to hire writers. Those who specialize in sales may or may not have a sense of what constitutes good writing and what does not, and of what readers want to read. Generally speaking they may feel understandably reluctant to make such decisions.

On the positive side is the fact that when the time comes to find a buyer for your paper, the full-fledged weekly will command a higher price than any of its easier-to-manage cousins.

Modified (or Modular) Weekly Newspaper

The modified weekly works well for those who want local news coverage and yet do not want the full editorial burden of a traditional weekly newspaper. It is a winner in a market where small town daily competition exists. You give the feeling of covering local happenings far more fully than you in fact do. A weekly that was in competition with my own *Mecklenburg Gazette* used this modular format quite successfully.

In this format you establish up front certain fixed types of story that you want to do in each issue, and then you simply fill in the blanks. You leave fast-breaking news up to others (TV, dailies, etc.) to cover. You do feature stories only, people-centered whenever possible. You use as much photography as possible. You establish a few regular columns by well-known local personalities, editing or rewriting these as necessary.

This is the route I would take if I were going to do a start-up here in my hometown — a project which I have, in fact, seriously considered lately. For my paper I would generate the following features, or modules, each week:

- A **profile of some interesting person**, with generous use of pictures: an award-winning gardener, the volunteer of the week at the local hospital, a civic leader, a church leader, an artist — anyone at all who stands out from the ordinary in some special way.

- A **profile of a new business start-up**: the idea, the people involved, obstacles overcome, prospects, etc. Such stories not only give much needed and deserved recognition to individuals who are putting themselves on the line to make an idea into a reality but, in the long run, create a loyal base of advertisers for you. Your local daily probably has a policy *against* doing such stories and often even charges businesses for running the standard ribbon-cutting photo with its brief cutline. Never forget that behind every business start-up there is a strong human interest story.

- A **local history column** written by the established (there is always at least one) specialist in the history of your town. Old photos, maps, etc. will do much to heighten reader interest. Such a column is a real winner and will help to establish a loyal readership.

- **All You Ever Wanted to Know about ...** These background articles on items high on the local political agenda will attract readership. Are there environmental questions?

Decisions concerning annexation and expansion? Complaints about utility rates? Without taking sides just gather and publish all available facts. This feature could be called the "Citizen's Notebook," or something similar.

- If **local sports** is an important subject, publish a column by the high school football coach. You can't cover the weekend games; these would be old news by the time you got to them nearly a week later. But the coach's reflections will draw strong reader interest. A column on golfing by the local pro could be a strong feature as well.

- An **editorial page** with your own editorial and the comments of others. Devise ways to solicit letters to the editor.

- Flesh these regular features out with columns purchased from the syndicates (more about these later) on how-to subjects of wide reader interest: *How to Supply Your Own Vegetables from a Backyard Garden; Treasures in the Attic: A Guide to Antique Hunting; Saving Money with Coupons; Furniture Refinishing; How to Write a Family History; Cash in with Free Government Publications; How to Start Your Own Business; How to Supplement Your Income with Your Own Home Business.* The possibilities are endless.

Syndicated How-to and Service Articles Only

You can decide not to cover local news at all, and rely on the excellent supply of columns — humorous, how-to, and others — supplied by the national feature syndicates. You then fill the space around your ads with columns, puzzles, crosswords, etc.

No Editorial Copy at All

Finally, in some markets successful weekly shoppers have appeared with no editorial copy at all. These will use design principles to hype the money-saving, bargain-hunting aspect of the advertising. I have established two such publications, one called *Dollarsworth* and one called *Bucksworth*. Both relied heavily on the use of discount coupons to generate reader interest.

CIRCULATION

Make no mistake about it: *effective circulation*, no matter what your editorial format, is the key to success. Your goal is to get your paper into the hands of every person in the trade area who buys anything at all — from turkey necks and fatback to new cars and homes with swimming pools.

In achieving this you have a certain advantage over any competing, paid circulation publication. Since you give yours away free, you can see that it goes to every single household. Indeed, you *must* see to it.

Until recent years newspapers and other publications were delivered almost exclusively to paid subscribers or to those who put a quarter in the rack before pulling out a paper. There are still some built-in advantages to this way of doing business. First of all, the U.S. Postal Service gives preferential rates to paid circulation newspapers, making them very inexpensive to mail. And most states specify that "newspapers of record" — that is, newspapers in which legal notices can appear — have predominantly paid circulation.

In the past twenty years this picture has been rapidly changing. It has become clear that it is far more profitable to guarantee saturation distribution to the entire market and reap your rewards in advertising dollars than to collect the very small sums that paid circulation brings in — often not even enough to defray costs of record keeping and subscription renewal campaigns. My mail regularly brings in such full color magazines as *American Printer*, *Southern Graphics*, and *Target Marketing*. I do not subscribe to or pay for any one of these. They are sent to me by virtue of my position as president of a publishing company. And for good reason. When their ad sales reps fan out into the marketplace they are able to say without hesitation that, yes, their publication goes to 90% or more of the heads of enterprise and decision makers in the relevant trade field.

Weekly newspapers have come under especially strong economic pressure to adopt free circulation strategies, and some have abandoned their paid circulation status to compete more effectively with saturation circulation shoppers.

The *Mecklenburg Gazette* was a paid circulation newspaper. Had I kept it I would almost certainly have gone to a free circulation system. I would have had to to meet the competition.

Advertisers buy prospects for their services and goods. The more prospects you can deliver to them, the more results they will get. And when they get results they are willing to spend more money on advertising. It is a circular relationship from which everyone profits.

Circulation Techniques

How do you get your paper to the public? The job of circulation will naturally divide itself into two parts. Each of them is handled differently.

There is in-town circulation and out-of-town circulation. Your out-of-town readers will be those who live along the rural delivery postal routes that surround your town. Your first job is to go by the post office and ask to see a diagram of the rural routes themselves — where they go, how long they are, and how many boxes each of them includes. Perhaps you can eliminate some of those that trail off into another trade area or whose residents, for some reason, do not meet your demographic requirement. Some routes may be conveniently included in your in-town distribution setup.

Usually the rural routes will be reached by third class mail (for free circulation newspapers) or by second class mail for paid circulation. You will bundle and bag your papers according to instructions that the Postal Service will gladly furnish. If you deliver them to the Post Office on time, week after week, they will be worked into the normal schedule, and you can be confident that they will be delivered in the next available mail.

An alternative is to have a route man of your own attend to this rural delivery chore. This is certainly possible if the routes are not too long, and thus too time consuming, for one person to handle. A disadvantage to this method is that it is illegal to put anything in a mail box other than official U.S. mail. You would have to toss your paper onto the lawn wrapped in a weatherproof polyethylene bag or purchase a carload of those round paper boxes and install them at each home on the route. This is expensive, although the bright-colored bins with the name of your newspaper on them are very strong advertising for your own product.

It is also possible from time to time to find route men for other papers who will piggyback yours onto their delivery schedule. There are usually rules against their doing this — set up by their main employer — but such rules are seldom enforced.

The strength of having the post office do your delivery for you is that the papers go right into the mail box and are much more likely to be taken into the house and consulted.

IN-TOWN DELIVERY

In-town delivery is more complicated, and will have to be done by carriers. The larger the metropolitan area you cover, the more complex this job becomes. For small towns perhaps you can supervise this yourself, but you will quickly reach the stage where this responsibility will require someone to give it his or her full attention.

Since it is a one day a week chore, it is perfect for the retired person who wants to remain active yet not earn so much as to jeopardize social security checks. Such people are competent, loyal, and hard working. The job does not overtax them, since it is limited in the number of hours it requires them to work and is mostly supervisory.

Your circulation manager will divide your town into territories, each of which can be handled by one delivery boy or girl. Locations will also be designated for distribution from racks, which can be serviced by the manager. In the main you will want a free circulation rack outside the entrance of each grocery store — advertisers and non-advertisers alike. Patrons like to consult the ads for specials as they walk up and down the aisles. Racks will also be salted liberally through major shopping centers and shopping areas.

In a town of 10,000, a dozen or so racks is perfectly adequate. These can be bought at prices ranging from $15 for indoor racks to $75 or more for reconditioned weather-proof racks. I order mine from Sho-Rack, a supplier to the trade.

The function of the racks is twofold: They make your papers available to the public in high traffic locations, since they are very visible and imprinted with your paper's logo, and they convey to the advertiser the fact that the paper is out there and working to bring in customers.

I suggest that you pay your circulation manager on a contract basis — a flat fee for doing the one or two day a week job. Your newspaper carriers should be paid on a per-copy delivered basis. As little as one to two cents a copy works in most markets.

A word of warning: Close supervision of these carriers is necessary and frequent spot checks are mandatory. When this is not done many bundles of bought and paid for papers may be thrown behind bushes and down storm sewers.

YOUR PUBLICATION SCHEDULE

Your newspaper will come out weekly, on Tuesday afternoon or early evening, in plenty of time to make the third class mail deliveries to your rural routes on Wednesday morning. The racks — especially those in front of grocery stores — you will fill up on Tuesday evening.

I have seen publishers of some small newspapers experiment with a once every two weeks schedule. This is always a mistake, whatever the reasoning behind it. It is a mistake because the retail cycle of sales and special dollars-off promotions occurs weekly. The advertising needs of these retailers change from week to week, not every other week.

Your most important clients, the discount and grocery stores, unlike the owner-operated boutiques, do not make advertising decisions on an issue-by-issue basis. They will decide to go with you for a period of time, then evaluate. But if you do not come out weekly, they will not try you at all. You simply will not fit their merchandising program.

No Delays, Please

Never allow yourself to put off publication by even a single *hour* to accommodate the needs of a particular client. You have a deadline and you must stick to it. Once you give a little on your deadline, the word gets around that there is some slippage available for late insertions. You will then have this problem to contend with week after week. I guarantee it. You just can't operate on this basis. You will lose your deadline credibility.

It is almost always the smaller, more disorganized advertisers who will not get materials in on time. If you delay publication to benefit them you risk alienating your bigger, bread-and-butter advertisers. On the Wednesday to Saturday food shopping days the grocery stores rightly consider every single hour of shopping of great importance. For them, it is make or break time.

Further, you will have arrangements with some nearby daily to print your paper on their presses. Press schedules are rigid. Once you establish it, you must be there, ready to go, when the bell rings. Otherwise one of two things will happen. The daily will tell you that they cannot accommodate you and that you must go elsewhere to get your work done. Or they will put you on the press at the next convenient time — convenient to them. This may be twenty-four or more hours later, a ruinous delay for you. And, into the bargain, their prices will go up, since you will have become an unpredictably troublesome account.

Newspapers, all of them, work on rigid deadline schedules. Yours will be no exception. Space should be reserved by 10 a.m. Monday. All copy should be in by Monday noon, with the exception of camera-ready copy, which you can allow to come in up to a few hours before press time.

You will work as late as necessary on Monday to paste up ads and paste up pages. On Tuesday morning you will drop in the camera-ready ads from your larger clients. You will set aside two hours for careful proofing of the ads you have typeset and designed yourself. At the appointed hour you will put your pages together and deliver them to the facility that will print them. An hour or two later you load up your freshly printed papers and set the distribution process in motion. You have told your advertisers when you expect to be on the street. Be there, rain or shine, holiday or no, whatever the circumstances. The professionalism and credibility of your enterprise are on the line.

SELLING ADS

Secrets of successful ad sales? There are many, and you will have your own long list before you have been in business for more than a few weeks. What I furnish you here is a starter kit of bedrock basics.

I learned these things the hard way. When I bought the *Mecklenburg Gazette*, I had never worked for a newspaper, never sold a newspaper ad, never written a newspaper story. Yet I closed the deal one Thursday afternoon and brought out my first issue the following Wednesday — right on schedule. It wasn't the most beautiful paper in the world, but it was mine, it was on time, and it contained enough advertising to break even.

I sold many of the ads myself, although I had inherited one part-time salesperson from the previous owner. What I didn't know about ad sales would have filled a book much longer than this one. I set about learning all I could.

I went to seminars whenever and wherever I could afford it. I never came away from any of these without an idea or two that I was able to turn into real profits as I began to build my paper. I went to the director of advertising of a very successful weekly in a nearby town. He agreed, for a modest fee, to come down and give us a day's training in sales-building methods. I took his very helpful tips and tried to put them into practice, winning a few and losing a few.

You, of course, will go through the same trial and error learning process. It is inevitable, since no two trade areas or advertising clients are identical. Still there are some fundamentals which, when implemented, will give you a head start.

Retail merchants are going to advertise . . . somewhere. It is not a question of whether to advertise or not, but of where to place their ads and how big to make them. The important thing, therefore, is to develop a long-term relationship with each client based on *professionalism, customer service, and delivering on your promises.* As you learn more you can become an unpaid (except for the price of the ad) consultant to the small businessperson. Analyzing results week after week, you will soon develop a pretty accurate feel for what works and what does not. Relate success stories to your clients. Make recommendations. Research out-of-town papers for advertising ideas that are likely to bring customers in the front door for businesses that advertise with you. Become a storehouse of information and a source of positive, business-building ideas. *Show* your customer, week after week and issue after issue, that you have his best interests at heart.

Make your calls on individual businesses at the *same time on the same day of the week for each issue.* If you call on a client at 10 a.m. on Thursday this week, you should be back in his shop at 10 a.m. on Thursday of the next week. And the week after that. You or your sales rep should show up as regularly as clockwork. You will be expected. If you are consistently well prepared to serve your client, if you are upbeat and positive, your visit will be looked forward to.

When dealing with key accounts, find out when the salesperson for any competing publication comes to call. Make sure that you get to the customer first.

Reduce this schedule of client calls to written form. Make it into a weekly checklist with every actual and potential client represented on the appropriate day at the appropriate time. Check each of them off as the call is made. If you supervise the work of other salespeople, prepare this list for them and require them to check off the calls as they are made.

Always have something in your hands to show the prospect. Sales increase measurably (some consultants estimate by as much as 25%) when you have an advertising idea sketched out and in hand to show the client.

This technique enables you to control the sales call and to begin right away to discuss the strengths and benefits of the idea you have presented. You listen carefully, of course, and begin to make changes and adjustments as your client suggests them. Note that you are now discussing the details of the advertisement that will run and how to design it for maximum effect. You are now at the more basic question of whether or not the client will run an ad at all.

At a minimum you need last week's ad neatly cut out and affixed to an art board. A lift cover of tracing paper dresses this up and reinforces the professional effect you want to get. Along with — or in place of — last week's advertisement, you may show an ad pulled from another source, but with the customers' name and logo pasted in. Your ad service (which we will discuss later) will be a good source for such materials.

Product Knowledge Sells

Your product, as far as the advertiser is concerned, is skillfully designed advertising that works. Spend the time necessary to study every book you can get your hands on about the design of effective advertising. *Know* this material. Read *The Wall Street Journal* and *Adweek*. Memorize relevant statistics, and increase your store of them week by week. Look for and talk about success stories involving advertising that seemed to do a super job.

Absolutely essential is the book of John Caples, *Tested Advertising Methods*, available in paperback. Also study carefully the hard, practical information on creating successful print media advertising in David Ogilvy's *Confessions of an Advertising Man*. Ogilvy is talking about the rarified atmosphere of national, big-money campaigns, but the lessons he teaches will bear rich dividends across the board — even at the relatively unglamorous level of the local weekly. The other books that I will recommend later also contain chapters on advertising design. Study all of these; make the information your own. *Teach it again and again to everyone who works for you.*

You customer expects you to know what you are doing. He is trusting you with his money and the future of his business. You want him to consider you or your representative the most knowledgeable source of advertising ideas, strategies, and information available in the market.

In the beginning you will be walking a thin line. You will not know as much as you will even a few short weeks later. But the things you *do* know need to be made use of with confidence and authority.

Every effective ad contains these four elements: 1) the offer; 2) the benefits to the consumer; 3) the first two items represented in both written and graphic form; and 4) the name, address, telephone number, and logo of the merchant who is doing the advertising.

Finally, in this quick survey of ad sales techniques, there is the simple advice given to me by the out-of-town ad director I hired to come in to give us a seminar: "Never," he told us, "judge another man's pocketbook by your own." Always go for the big sale. You will be surprised how often you get it.

BROADSHEET OR TABLOID

There are two basic newspaper formats to choose between: the tabloid (more like a magazine and the size of *The Christian Science Monitor* or *The National Enquirer*) and the broadsheet, or standard, full-sized newspaper.

Which should you choose? There are many things to consider, and some of them may be unique to your editorial philosophy or your market position. If your area is flooded with tabs (short for tabloid) then you may want to set yourself apart by publishing a broadsheet paper. If all the competition is broadsheet then you may want to go tabloid. Writers with magazine or literary backgrounds may also be attracted to the tabloid format simply because it looks more familiar to them.

There is no denying that a tabloid can be very attractive, with a large (virtually full page) photograph on the cover to draw the reader in. A great success story of recent years here in North Carolina is the development from simple idea to multi-million dollar publication of the *Carolina Farmer*, a tabloid distributed free to the agricultural community throughout North and South Carolina. The front page of each issue of the *Farmer* is devoted to a oversized photograph of the individual about whom the cover story has been written.

There are, however, very serious financial components in the decision-making process about which format to choose. Newspaper advertising is normally sold by the "column inch." A column inch is one inch of vertical space in the column as it appears on the newspaper page. A broadsheet page, because it is twice as large, will contain twice the number of column inches as a tabloid.

This fact has important consequences for your bottom line. Grocery stores typically think of buying full pages, two-thirds pages or, rarely, half pages. They are not thinking of the cost, so much as the proportional space on the page, which they want to dominate. When such a store buys a full page in a broadsheet paper they are buying twice the space, at twice the cost, that they would be buying in a tabloid.

When I bought the *Mecklenburg Gazette* it was losing money in a tabloid format. Three months later I took the bull by the horns and converted it into a broadsheet paper. The result was that my income from my grocery store advertisers virtually doubled overnight, and the paper was established on a firm basis.

I was emboldened in my decision by a contact I made at an ad sales seminar. I met the publisher of the *Winston-Salem Chronicle*. The *Chronicle*, he told me, had been a weekly tabloid that had recently gone broadsheet.

What had happened to his advertising revenues, I asked.

"They doubled!" he immediately replied.

In addition, if you're going to include a good deal of editorial matter, the broadsheet, especially in the smaller communities, may be more likely to be thought of as a "real" newspaper.

So, though I personally like the look and feel of the tabloid — it is much easier to hold in your hands and read — I would, in most cases, recommend a broadsheet format.

The case for the tabloid format? If I had to summarize some of the most viable reasons for choosing it I would be sure to include the following.

You like it, are comfortable with it, and that's that. You believe in your publication and can communicate strong, positive feelings about it to your staff and your customers.

You may believe that you can circumvent the financial disadvantages of the tabloid format by selling ads on a modular, percentage of page basis rather than by the column inch, thereby raising the cost per page. More about this in our discussion of ad rates, below.

You may have developed a market position where grocery store advertising is not your chief source of revenue. *The Spectator*, a tabloid published in the highly educated, Research Triangle area of North Carolina, has been quite successful without this kind of advertising. Because its trade area includes three major universities and the corporate offices of some of the largest research-oriented corporations in the United States, it exploits the broad readership of highly educated, culturally-oriented individuals.

It is essentially a newspaper of culture and the arts. People do not read *The Spectator* to find out where to buy chicken this week at a few cents less a pound. They want to know what books to read, what plays to see, and which restaurants to eat in. Gourmet, natural, and other up-scale food ads might catch their attention, but in general they will expect to look elsewhere for run-of-the-mill grocery shopping information. In this market the tabloid may well be the format of choice.

WHAT DO YOU CHARGE?

How do you set your rates? There's no substitute for research here. Assemble rate cards from other newspapers and shoppers in your market and from papers out of your market in towns of similar size. Study these carefully. They will tell you what the market will bear.

You do not necessarily have to set your prices below the level of the competition, but you should not set them higher — unless you have double the circulation or some other concrete, easily understood reason for doing so. The statement "We're a little more expensive, but worth it," can, in the right circumstances, be a strong selling point. *But the statement must be true.*

The rates you can live with will be a function, too, of the total advertising you think you can sell. If there is an established daily in your market, count the number of ad inches in it on its skinniest day and on its best day. The number of inches you can expect to sell on a regular basis will fall somewhere between these two numbers.

If you calculate that you can sell advertising at an average of $500 a page and you sell sixteen pages of ads, then you will gross sixteen times $500, or $8000 per week. Plug this figure into your business plan. Can you live with it? Is it competitive? Perhaps you will find that you must charge more, or sell more, or both.

You want your initial rate card to list rates that you can live with over the long haul. You will not be able to "adjust your rates" upward more frequently than once a year. Rather than attracting advertisers with low initial rates — and then finding yourself stuck with them — you might work out some incentives that will make it easy for a business owner to give you a try — say, a free ad for every two he buys for the first six weeks. This, in effect, is a discount of 33%, but *you have not lowered the price for the ads he actually pays for* — an important psychological point. You will then have six full weeks to convince the customer that it is in his best interest to continue to advertise. If your circulation plan is carefully implemented, your advertising design good, and the other aspects of your paper attractive to the reader, the results will be there.

THE COMPARATIVE PRICING GAME

People, being human, do make comparisons — and not always in the most intelligent and analytical way. Some newspapers, for instance, employ a six column format and some an eight column format.

Each column on the standard broadsheet page is 21½ inches high. When you multiply the number of inches in each column by the number of columns you discover that the six column format contains 129 inches per page while the eight column format contains 172. (Some classified pages are based on a nine or ten column format, with even more inches per page.)

If two competing newspapers had exactly the same full page rate — say $500 — the column inch rate for the six column paper would be $500 divided by 129 inches: roughly $3.75 per column inch. The eight column paper would divide $500 by 172 to fix its inch rate at roughly $3.30 per column inch. The second paper appears to be cheaper but, in fact, its rates are exactly the same. As a matter of fact, it could charge $3.50 per column inch, be more expensive, and *still* appear to many advertisers to be cheaper.

Another strategy for minimizing apparent costs in your paper is to employ the modular ad sales technique. This is especially useful for tabloids. Instead of selling ads by the column inch, you sell them on a percentage of page basis. If your tabloid has a four column page, your ads would be divided and priced on the basis of full page, half page, quarter page, eighth page, twelfth page, and sixteenth page. The number of column inches is not mentioned. Thus, when an advertiser compares the cost of a "full page" in your newspaper, a tabloid, with that of a full page in the competing broadsheet, you can appear to be less expensive though, on a strict column inch basis, you will be more expensive. "A full page in the Daily Blah costs $500," your ad rep can say. "In our paper it is only $375." What he fails to mention, but what is indeed not at all hidden and quite apparent to everyone concerned, is that there is twice as much space in the broadsheet full page. For some reason, this mode of reasoning is perfectly acceptable to many merchants.

A nice thing about modular sales approach is that your ads, being sold in standard sizes, facilitate page layout and eliminate many pesky problems brought on by running ads of many irregular sizes.

EARNED RATES

While the larger dailies will usually peg ad rates to annual contract commitments from their clients, smaller publications will generally employ "earned rates" to reward frequent, large advertisers.

You will bill monthly, and the billing will be pegged to the amount of advertising placed during that month. On a column inch basis, for instance, the "open" (or non-discount) rate may be set at $4.00. If, at the end of the month, the advertiser has placed 100 inches, then the rate charged is, say, $3.90; 200 inches brings a rate of $2.80, and so on.

PLUS LINAGE

I learned about plus linage at one of the earliest seminars I attended, and it was a profitable lesson indeed. In newspaper jargon, plus linage refers to advertising space bought by the customer *above and beyond what that customer would ordinarily buy on a weekly basis.* Here are some tried and true ways of generating plus linage.

Special Interest Supplements

The holidays and special occasions that you are accustomed to may appear to be scattered randomly through the year. When you look more closely, you discover that they are spaced rather evenly through the calendar and that they are merchandising tools. In recent years we have seen National Secretaries' Day, National Grandparents' Day, and even National Bosses' Day — all sponsored by the American Florists' Association, much to the profit and benefit of its membership.

At regular intervals you will want to distribute, along with your weekly paper, special sections relevant to the time of year. In March, for instance, there will be a lawn, yard, and garden supplement; in April a bridal and wedding supplement; in the summer a home improvement and an outdoor fun supplement. August brings the back to school supplement and November the gift ideas supplement.

These supplements usually have a magazine feel to them. They are typically designed in tabloid format and include articles appropriate to the special subject matter that they focus on. These articles are furnished by the advertising services such as Metro. Often your ad service will send you a completely designed and laid out publication with only the ad spaces to fill in.

Remember, you haven't gained anything if your advertisers simply shift their ads from the regular sections into the special supplement. The technique is to sell the supplement six to eight weeks in advance. Then, the week before it appears, you can still make a call for your regular pages. So, when the supplement appears the client will have ads in two places, in the regular pages and in the supplement.

Plus linage can, however, result when advertising is shifted over, as long as the supplement itself is a strong enough sell to encourage larger placements.

Sponsorship of Special Features

Plus linage can also result from the sponsorship of special features. These will vary from section to section of the country. A favorite in the town where I now live is the illustrated Bible story. This is done quite well in comic book style in a space covering the greater part of a page. At the bottom of the story there appears the list of the names of the firms "sponsoring" — that is, paying for at normal advertising rates — the Bible lesson. Many of these firms, such as industrial or service concerns, would not normally be prospects for the usual advertising sales.

The Bible story appears every week, as do the names of the sponsoring firms. The result: an additional page of paid space in each issue of your paper.

Variations on this theme include special pages for the United Way solicitation, the American Cancer Society solicitations, back to school safety campaigns, and many others. Most small, community newspapers utilize these special promotions, though they are rarely seen in big city dailies.

Other plus linage strategies that work include ads designed like Christmas greeting cards in sizes ranging from twelve to twenty-four column inches. These are an easy sell around Christmas. Business is good, and merchants wish to thank their faithful clients. You will come upon other plus linage ideas in the books recommended for further reading and in the pages of the ad service to which you subscribe.

YOUR AD SERVICE

I have mentioned the reliance you place on your ad service. There are several such services and each of them does essentially the same thing: furnish books of advertising layouts and ideas, often complete except for prices and logos, and keyed to the month and season. A good ad service is very valuable to you and quite affordable. It would be almost unthinkable to attempt to publish a newspaper without one.

All such services do the same thing, but one of them does it much, much better, in my opinion, than any of the others. This is the *Metro* service. It even has a special service edition for weekly papers like yours. You can contact them by writing Metro Associated Services, Inc., 80 Madison Avenue, New York, NY 10016. Ask them for details and samples. Once you see what they offer you will have no question about their usefulness to you.

EDITORIAL CONTENT

Your editorial content will come from two sources: that which you generate locally and that which you purchase from the syndicates. As I pointed out above, it is possible to publish a readable paper based entirely on syndicated copy if you wish to do so. But most editors will want to include many local stories as well, because local stories create reader interest and identification with your publication.

The Syndicates

Readers just love to be given a list of ways to achieve some goal that is important to them. This kind of service article always has high reader interest. Some examples?
• Thirteen Ways to Save on Vacation Hotel Bills
• Ten Ways to Improve Your Love Life
• Twenty Ways to Increase You Profits as a Desktop Publisher
. . . Get the idea?

The surprising thing about the syndicates is that they are so inexpensive. You can get the work of top columnists, the classiest feature stories, how-to pieces, and others for just a few dollars a week — much less, in fact, than you would have to pay a local writer for the same work. Fifty dollars a week ought to buy all the first rate syndicated copy you will need.

Write the syndicates and ask for lists of availabilities. Describe the kinds of features that you are interested in running. They will be back to you quickly with samples of their wares.

You might also subscribe to a news service like that of *The New York Times* or *The Christian Science Monitor*. These include a great variety of features, including top of the line crosswords, among which you can choose.

Check the latest edition of *Literary Market Place* for a complete list of current addresses. For starters, try the following: United Features Syndicate; King Features Syndicate; Christian Science Monitor Service; New York Times Service.

Local Writers

Local writers are always available. Word of mouth, spurred on by a classified ad or two, should bring in enough inquiries from writers eager to see their work published to get you up and going.

Remember that newspapers are considered a "break-in" market for beginning free-lancers. Pay rates are quite modest and are usually determined on a price per inch of published copy basis. When you find a good, reliable writer, pay him as much as you can afford to keep him writing for you, but remember that for the new writer the money's not really the thing: It's the by-line that counts. And you can take comfort from the fact that no newspaper in your neighborhood is likely to be paying writers more than a fraction of what they are truly worth. The wonderfully low cost of syndicated materials keeps local pay scales for writers at very depressed levels.

THE EQUIPMENT YOU NEED

There are a few items of basic equipment that you will need to set up shop as a weekly newspaper publisher, not including the normal array of desks, chairs, and file cabinets that go along with any business operation.

You will need a computer, a graphic arts program, and a laser printer capable of turning out work of at least 300 dots per inch resolution. There was a time when the bulky, expensive dedicated typesetters marketed by Merganthaler, Compugraphic, and Varityper ruled the day, but no more. Microcomputers do the job today, especially for weeklies.

Although the MS/DOS systems now have typesetting, page layout, and graphic arts capabilities, I do not hesitate to recommend the Apple Macintosh, in its latest, most powerful version, and the Apple Laserwriter as your ad design and typesetting workhorses. These machines are, in my opinion, the most flexible and most useful for general newspaper purposes. Programs like MacDraw, MacPaint, Pagemaker, MicroSoft Word and others simplify nearly every procedure required to lay out and design an ad or a page or to type straight matter to specifications. A bonus — and not a negligible one at that — is that this same computer can run an accounting and billing program to do all your bookkeeping. Classified ad maintenance and billing programs are also available and highly recommended.

To someone like me, who had to do all these things by hand, in a much more time- and labor-intensive way just a few short years ago, these advances are little short of miraculous.

A scanner is desirable, but not essential. A good scanner can read typed articles and transfer them directly to the memory of your computer. It does, however, occasionally commit typographical errors of its own. See the discussion of scanners in Chapter 2 on setting up shop.

You will need a waxer. In newspaper pasteup a thin coat of liquified wax, applied to the back of the item to be placed on the page, is used to hold everything in place. It is quite easy to use and allows for great ease in changing the position of items that you have laid down and perhaps changed your mind about. Nothing else — rubber cement or spray adhesives, for instance — works nearly as well. An economical waxer that I have used and recommend is the Art Waxer.

A light table is a handy item used to affix items on a page relative to a grid pattern placed beneath the page. It consists of a light source, a translucent top, and a frame. You can easily build one of these items for yourself, but the table-top models I use in my business now are dirt cheap (just over $100 each), adjustable, and very reliable.

You will need drafting tables and production work tables, with inclined adjustable tops. These can be purchased or built in any home workshop. I built mine. You must be able to use a T-square with them.

A copier that gives good, solid coverage to black tones is essential. Your copier should enlarge and reduce originals in one percentage point increments — down to 50% and up to 150%, or as close to these figures as possible.

Beyond these major items you will need a variety of single-edged razor blades, X-acto knives, printers' rulers, layout sheets, etc.

SEEING HOW IT'S DONE

Even the best recipe book is no substitute for a visit to the kitchen. Similarly, after having read through these pages you will benefit greatly by visiting the offices of as many small newspaper publishers as you can.

A competitor in your trade area may not look with approval on having you snoop around his shop and sniff out his secrets, but out-of-town publishers in non-competing markets will surely be cordial. Newspaper people are a friendly lot.

Time your visits for Thursday or Friday, which are generally the quietest days in the weekly business shop. The action is taking place out in the field where the ads are being sold. Monday through Wednesday are generally so action-packed with production and distribution that no one will have time to talk to you, no matter how willing to do so they might be otherwise.

Look around. Ask questions. Get names of suppliers. Who gives the best deal on layout paper? Where can you buy news racks at an affordable price? Which supplements seem most successful? What deadline and production schedules does your local printer favor? If he has a large, web press, can he print your paper as well as his own? For how much?

The more visits you make, the more you will add to your inventory of ideas and strategies to make your own paper the success you want it to be and that it certainly can be.

10.

How to Sell Information by Mail

In the late 1970's I bought a weekly newspaper in the small college town of Davidson, North Carolina. I had edited a magazine and published books out of my office at the university where I was then teaching. At the university, publishing was a breeze. It was easy because I did not really have to make a living at it. My full professor's salary was generous. Anything beyond that was pure gravy.

The weekly newspaper business, I quickly discovered, was another matter altogether. In buying the *Gazette* I had burnt all my bridges, resigning my teaching position and the wonderfully regular salary it provided. I had to make it week by week on the cash that ad sales generated. The financial safety net was gone forever.

I was immediately confronted with the task of meeting a weekly payroll, with my own name at the top of the list of those who needed a check. It was, I learned, a simple proposition: no profit, no pay.

I scoured every nook and cranny of my little journalistic kingdom for possible secondary profit centers. There was a temporary reprieve from the cash-flow terrors when, a month after becoming a newspaper editor and publisher, I cleaned out the storeroom and discovered a treasure trove of lead bars left behind from the days when the previous publisher set his type with an old-fashioned Linotype machine. I sold the lead to a metal salvage firm for $3000.

But what else could I do to bring in more money? I took inventory of the possibilities. Along with the newspaper I had acquired a darkroom, a decent graphic arts camera, and an ancient Multilith 1250 duplicator press. These I decided that I would put to work doing job printing — turning out letterheads, envelopes, brochures, and advertising flyers when I wasn't busy meeting the deadlines of my weekly newspaper.

But how would I market my printing services? Davidson, after all, had fewer than 3000 inhabitants. The nearby towns of Huntersville and Cornelius, also in my trade area, were even smaller.

I was puzzling over this problem when the postman brought the morning's mail. On the top of the stack of the day's assortment of catalogs and brochures was a newsprint publication called *The Printer's Shopper*. It was a wish book, full of the odds and ends that printers require to do business: glues, racks, light tables, clamps, pica rules, T-squares, business forms, encyclopedias — thousands of prosaic but fascinating and useful items for the small print shop.

Idly thumbing through, I stopped cold when, at the top of page 63, I saw an advertisement for a book that promised to solve the problem of building an income in the printing business. Written by Owen C. Brantley, it was entitled *144 Ways to Sell Printing by Mail*. The book did not promise you *some* ways, mind you, nor a few ways, but a full 144 separate and distinct ways to get people to pay you money to do their printing for them no matter where they lived.

The offer was irresistible. It was precisely the information I needed. The price ($29.50) was relatively steep for those days, but if the book lived up to expectation I felt certain that it would make me money. As cash poor as I was, I wrote out a check and sent in my order.

The book was delivered two weeks later. It was not much to look at — just a sheaf of mimeographed pages held together in one of those binders that you buy in business supply stores with two brass clamps that you stick through holes in the paper and fold over to hold the pages in. I did not care. It was the information I was interested in, not the design of the book.

And the information was there. I applied Brantley's techniques and found that they worked. I was a satisfied customer. I had just bought information I needed by mail.

STILL GOING STRONG

Today, twelve years later, I am in an entirely different business in an entirely different town. The most recent edition of *The Printer's Shopper* arrived in this morning's mail. On page 41? You guessed it, an ad for *144 Ways to Sell Printing by Mail*, by Owen C. Brantley. For twelve years (that I know of) Brantley has been steadily selling his book to printers nationwide. All this time he has been bringing in a steady profit. (Nobody continues to advertise a product that people don't buy.)

How did he do it? Simple. He created an advertisement that promises *information that a well-defined and targeted group of buyers want, need, and can expect to profit from* — an unbeatable combination of qualities. He sold information by mail.

AN EXTRA $500 (OR $5000) A MONTH

In his book *Guerilla Marketing* (Houghton-Mifflin, $8.95) free-lance writer Jay Conrad Levinson tells how he made a profit of "about $500 a month for the past nine years" from a little self-published booklet called *Secrets of Successful Free-Lancing.* (Turn on your calculator. This comes to $54,000.) *Secrets of Successful Free-Lancing* was just forty-three pages long, but it promised to reveal little-known tips that every aspiring writer — and there are many thousands of them — longs to know. "After I had been working a few years as a free-lance writer, I'd learned quite a few important things about free-lance writing, things that nobody ever told me, things that weren't written in books. So I wrote a book and published it myself." Levinson's book was priced at a very modest $10.

Each copy of *Secrets of Successful Free-Lancing* cost a dollar to print and, on an average, about $3.00 in advertising for each copy sold. With a retail price of $10, that left a very satisfactory 60% margin of net profit. Today, with the current inflated prices on the covers of all books, I believe that a price of $19.95 might pull just as well. It would certainly deserve testing.

Jay Conrad Levinson was doing other writing, so he limited himself to this one project in selling information by mail. But he could as easily have done ten of these information-packed booklet/manuals and brought in an income of $5000 a month rather than $500. And, indeed, why not twenty titles and $10,000 a month?

If you can zero in on what people want to know, need to know, and can profit or otherwise benefit from knowing you can do just that.

A friend of mine is successfully targeting those bigger bucks. Carole Marsh, founder of the Gallopade Publishing Group, and her husband Bob Longmeyer have published hundreds of information-based titles, the majority of which are marketed by direct mail. She sends simple one-page laser-printer flyers to buyers for school and other libraries and also sells through wholesalers like Baker and Taylor.

A recent big seller to school libraries is her *Sex Stuff for Kids.* Carole Marsh, a prolific writer, used to generate virtually all of her titles herself, but has now begun to contract with free-lancers to do manuscripts for her on a "work for hire" basis.

All of this, I might add, is accomplished in a converted garage attached to her home in the small North Carolina village of Bath, population 300. In the workroom are two Mac Pluses, an Apple II, a laser printer, a spiral binder, and an inexpensive laminating machine.

Ninety percent of all Carole Marsh Books are produced right there, as orders are received. There is no inventory.

WHAT INFORMATION DO YOU SELL?

The next question, naturally, is this: What information can *you* sell and where do you get it? You will become quite proficient in recognizing good, saleable ideas as you become more involved in the business. But to help prime the creative pump, you can use these guidelines that have worked for me. The best ideas, I have found, have two essential ingredients:

The best ideas pull orders from a small percentage of a very large potential readership, or from a large percentage of a smaller but well-targeted readership.

Here's what you are dealing with. Only a certain percentage of those who read about your book will want it; of those who want it, only a certain percentage will have the money to buy it; of those who want it and can afford it, only a certain percentage will take the time and trouble to order it. By this time you have whittled your pool of potential buyers down considerably. The larger the number of prospects you start with, the greater the number of books you will sell.

For instance, you may have some very hot information on "How to Invest in Real Estate on the Island of Martinique." No matter how good the book, the number of people who can see themselves engaging in that activity is relatively small. The topic, "How to Make $100,000 a Year Selling Information by Mail," will appeal to a far greater number of people. Joe Karbo's famous mail order book, *The Lazy Man's Way to Wealth* appealed to even more. That's why Joe Karbo is a millionaire today.

The best ideas are related to basic human desires. Four of the most powerful of these are: money and how to get it; sex, and how to enjoy it more; self-fulfillment, or how to be the person you want to be; and good health and good looks, and how to get them.

Sources of Ideas

Begin with yourself. What do you know how to do that others would want to know about? Since I am a writer and a successful desktop publisher, I write on that subject. There is a virtually endless supply of information that I can impart and be paid for. I expect to sell this very book, by mail, to those who want, need, and can profit from the information it contains.

There are other topics, too, in my personal inventory that I can muster for sale. Some years ago I did a lot of reading in the field of psychical research. Today, with very little effort, I could put together a manual on what has become known as "channeling" — a current name given to the old phenomenon of mediumship. A book called "How Anyone Can Channel Information from Higher Worlds" might be profitable. To find out whether people will buy it or not, I can place a test ad before I ever put a word on paper. If the ad pulls an adequate response I can quickly write the piece and send it out to my customers. Another of my topics might be "How to Interpret Your Dreams: Latest Scientific Discoveries Give Key to Dream Meanings." Another book might be "How the U.S. Government Will Finance Your Business Idea."

These are all subjects that I know about and have researched at one time or another. You may find that you have accumulated information that is saleable, too, if you will just take the time to dig for it.

YOUR IDEA NEED NOT BE UNIQUE

And here is an important note: *your idea does not have to be unique to be profitable.* We all bring a different slant, a different perspective to our information, and this difference can be valuable. So where can you find ideas that work for you?

One sure technique for success in selling by mail is to look at what is making money for other people and let it make money for you, too. Look at the subject of weight control, for instance. Is there just one successful book on the market? On the contrary, dozens are published every year. The same thing is true of books that fall into any of the three basic categories listed above. *The key to success is not so much in the uniqueness of your product as it is in the skill and persistence with which you market it.*

In addition, utilize and build on the ideas and know-how of others. Look at your friends and acquaintances with a new eye. What do they know that others would pay to know? I have a friend — a retired naval officer — who is setting himself up as a specialized nurseryman, growing and marketing a rare and much sought-after variety of holly to landscapers nationwide. Another friend just completed a course of study at the local community college and now has his electrician's license and a three-truck business.

A third acquaintance, retired from colder climes to North Carolina — a former high-level school administrator — has established a successful bed and breakfast hotel. Another friend, a more literary type, now has a search service for rare books.

Would others want, need, and be able to profit from a handbook on how to do these things themselves? Could you gather more success stories and combine them into a manual on home businesses for retired persons? I am confident that if I looked deeply enough into the work that these friends are doing I could, with the proper slanting and generalizing, come up with some saleable titles.

Research Newspapers and Magazines

Browse through four newspapers daily: your local paper, the newspaper of your state capital (or closest major metropolitan area), a national paper such as *The New York Times* or *The Washington Post*, and *The Wall Street Journal*. Look for trends, needs, products, research. I promise that once you start searching it will be a rare day that goes by without adding a couple of really strong book ideas to your inventory. Your only problem will be picking and choosing among them.

Do you see articles on a new (real) cure for baldness? An aid to male sexual potency? A hot business idea for retired persons? A piece on how to save money when buying a new car?

These and many more could be packaged for mail-order information selling. You (or the writer to whom you assign the project) will simply write your source for more information, do some interviews, consult local specialists, read through other literature in the field, and put it all together in handbook form.

The Government Printing Office is a gold mine of information for mail-order sellers of information. For a catalog of government publications, write the Superintendent of Documents, Government Printing Office, Washington, DC 20402.

Browse through the list and order the books that interest you. These are usually in the public domain (without protection of copyright), so you can use the information they contain in writing your own for-sale publications.

Some examples? Opening the most recent Government Printing Office catalog to page 1, my eye falls on the title, *Fast Facts and Figures about Social Security*. Combine this with information on Medicare and Medicaid (*Medicare Handbook*, page 8), other government programs for older Americans, plus additional tidbits derived from your own imagination and experience, and you can easily come up with a *Financial Fact Book for Retired Americans* that could promise "everything you need to know about living well and getting all the benefits to which you are entitled" during the retirement years. I think it would sell, though I might work on the title a little.

On page 20 of the catalog is a blurb for a book called *Summary of Existing Legislation for Persons with Disabilities*. On page 26 is *Wise Home Buying* and on page 11, *Starting and Managing a Business from Your Home*. All such subjects can provide rich rewards to the desktop publisher selling information by mail.

WHO DOES THE WRITING?

You do not have to be a writer to sell information by mail. Indeed, even if you are a writer you will soon find it necessary to farm out many projects to others. You will simply not have time to do it all yourself.

The principles contained in this chapter will work for any entrepreneur, whatever his or her background and special talents, as long as he can obtain the specialized services which he himself lacks and therefore needs. A later chapter tells how to do this. A writer, for instance, may wish to seek an associate to help with marketing. A sales-oriented individual will come up with ideas and find a writer to put them into words. A 100 word-per-minute typist with desktop equipment and a flair for organization could set up as a publisher and hire both writers and salespeople.

Finding Writers

When you need writers how do you find them? It is not difficult, and once you touch base with two or three, word of mouth will do the rest. Begin with a classified ad in the largest newspaper near you, stating "Free-lance writers wanted for non-fiction, how-to assignments. We buy all rights. Contact . . ."

You might also attend meetings of writers' clubs in your area. They will be delighted to see you and hear about your projects. In North Carolina there is a statewide organization called the North Carolina Writer's Network. If there are is such an organization nearby, you would do well to inform the editor of their newsletter of your needs. This will generate the inquiries you need.

Once you are approached by a writer ask to see a résumé and some clips of previously published work. Study these clips carefully for readability and writing skill. Applicants will surely submit the very best pieces that they have.

If you know writing, you can hire energetic beginners who will do the spade work and whose prose you can edit and improve. If you are not a writer then you should, if at all possible, work with people who have a track record of some kind, however limited.

HOW TO PRODUCE YOUR PUBLICATIONS

When you sell information in bookstores you spend a lot of money making your books look right. When every other book on the shelf has a liquid-laminated, super-shiny cover printed in every imaginable color, yours has to have one, too. If other books are perfect bound, yours must be too.

But when you sell information by mail, these rules do not apply. It is the information that is important, not the appearance of the cover or the binding. So long as the content is as advertised you will have very few returns from dissatisfied customers. Jay Conrad Levinson offered an $11 refund on the $10 purchase price for his book on free-lancing to anyone who thought the book not worth the price. He reports that he had very few takers. And remember, he spent only $1 each to produce each forty page book. He clearly did not spend heavily on appearance.

Your text will be keyed in on your computer and stored on disk. That way you can update it as needed. As you sell books you will create a steady flow of feedback (tips, clarifications, questions) from your readers. Some of these you will wish to incorporate into the text. This can be done easily if the text is disk-stored.

FREEDOM FROM INVENTORY

Using your computer you can work on an inventory-free basis. You do not have to tie up thousands of dollars printing books that may or may not sell as expected. Instead you create the books as you need them. If the week's orders total thirty copies of a given title, simply print out the required amount of the latest version on your laser printer, spiral bind it, and mail it out.

The pages may be printed on one side only to give the book more bulk and to simplify the task of reproduction. After you have printed and collated the pages you can bind them. You can side stitch them with special staples — any printer will show you samples — or you can spiral bind them. Most quick print establishments can do this for you, though you will want to invest in a spiral binding machine as soon as you become convinced that your project is a winner. These devices are inexpensive and will soon pay for themselves many times over.

Even though the information is more important than the packaging, you can devote some attention to page design, borders, running heads, page numbers, wide margins with motivational quotes, illustrations, tips, and other "extra-text" items. You should also include appropriate photographs. In the *Self-publisher's Handbook* that I brought out some time ago I included a shot of myself autographing copies of my self-published books. The crowd of buyers around the desk and the stack of books on the table told the reader more about the success potential of self-publication than words alone could ever have done.

Are these small manuals really books? They sure are. Your product will be copyrighted like a book, sold like a book, recorded in *Books in Print* like any other book, and have its own ISBN number and Library of Congress number. In short, it *is* a book, and you should think of it as such.

FINDING BUYERS: SECRETS OF SUCCESSFUL MARKETING

To get people to buy your book you must let them know 1) that it exists; 2) that it will solve their problems for them or make them money; and 3) that it can be theirs very easily when they place their order.

In addition, you must inform them that they risk nothing in placing an order since, if they are not satisfied with your book, you will cheerfully give them their money back.

There are a number of ways to get this message across, some of which are quite affordable. In North Carolina, for instance, the state press association offers a statewide classified advertising buy. For just $200 you can get a 25-word classified ad inserted into newspapers whose circulation totals 1,600,000. Such deals are available in most other states as well. Check with your state's press association.

Marketing your books can be expensive, and it will be if you do not proceed intelligently. The trick is to start slowly, testing your idea while risking the smallest possible amount of money. After you are satisfied that there is a demand for your product, you may then expand your advertising so as to generate every possible order.

And never forget this: the most costly advertising is advertising that doesn't work. Inexpensive advertising is advertising that creates profit, no matter what the cost.

Before beginning to advertise, you should set up a toll-free 800 service so that your customers can reach for the telephone and buy on impulse. This kind of telephone service has become very affordable. Just today a flyer came to me from AT&T offering an 800 service "ready line" on my home telephone. After a small installation fee, there is a $20 a month service charge, after which you are billed only for the time spent actually taking orders. These small costs can be factored back into the selling price of the book.

Mail order selling can work without an 800 service, but you may put yourself at a needless and costly disadvantage if you are without one. Try it for several months. If it works, well and good. You're that much better off. If it doesn't, you have lost very, very little money. But most mail order pros agree that the 800 number boosts sales many times over.

After you have satisfied yourself that there is a demand for your book, you can expand your advertising gradually, financing the expansion with the income generated by ongoing sales.

BEGIN WITH THE CLASSIFIEDS

Classified advertising is, without a doubt, the best buy in print media advertising today. Classified pages consistently pull more readers than any other section of the publication in which they appear. They are perfect for testing the salability of a new book idea and for testing alternate approaches and sales pitches to determine which pulls best.

Many of the very best magazines have classified sections, and almost all trade magazines — those with specialized readerships — do. There is affordable mass media classified advertising in publications like *The National Enquirer*, read by millions of people each week. There is specialized mass media advertising in such newspapers as *The Wall Street Journal*, which even has regional buys available. And there are the magazines that go to reasonably well-defined and targeted readerships, such as *Writer's Digest*, *Personal Publishing, Inc.* magazine, and scores of others.

Check Your Library

Read through likely publications. Determine whether their classified sections seem to be fertile ground for projects like yours. Are other ads selling information in evidence? Do they appear issue after issue? If the answer to these questions is yes, then that newspaper or magazine may be worth a try for you.

Inventory the publications that seem likely to reach your market. In the reference rooms of most libraries you will find standard references such as *Gebbie's Press All-in-One Directory* (Birkline Publications). *Gebbie* lists by subject all U.S. publications, including obscure trade magazines, niche publications, and internal house pubs.

Advertising in specialized magazines can be valuable to the direct mail seller of information, since there is no waste circulation. You can carefully target the reader interest group or groups that you want to reach. Those who get the magazines are pre-qualified. Everyone who would read *Publishers Weekly*, for instance, is likely to be interested in books and publishing. Readers of *American Firefighter* are surely interested in fire fighting equipment and supplies and the personal welfare of firemen.

In addition you will want to consider general circulation publications like *National Enquirer*. Its hundreds of thousands of readers will respond to ads for books on making money, losing weight, and other topics of more general interest.

CHECK THE DEMOGRAPHICS

When you single out a publication that you are interested in, study the demographic profile of its readership as carefully as possible. Are these the people you want to reach? Check out the advertising rates and measure investment against probable and possible return.

You can get the telephone number and address of advertising sales offices by looking at the information given on the masthead. Or you can obtain it from *Gebbie's* directory or from a reference publication like *Standard Rate and Data Service*. Write or call requesting that you be sent a media kit containing all rates, specifically classified (words only) and classified display (words and design) rates, and demographic information on the readership. You will have these in hand quite quickly. The media kit will also contain a sample copy of the publication for your files.

Standard Rate and Data Service (SRDS), available at most large libraries, contains circulation and advertising rate information, but usually not in as much detail as the media kit. On the other hand it will be far more objective in the presentation of its data, whereas the media kit is essentially a sales piece.

Once you have assembled this information choose two or three publications as test markets for your book. In the process of making this decision you will be looking closely at the cost. You have to live within the budget you have set for yourself. But within this limitation always choose the publication that promises to work best for you, not the one that is cheapest.

HOW TO WRITE A CLASSIFIED AD THAT WORKS

This is a subject that you will give considerable attention to as you become more and more experienced in selling information by mail. You will test your ad wordings extensively, noting what works and how well it works.

Sometimes a simple change in a headline can improve response beyond anything you might imagine. Titles, too, can be important. If one title doesn't work well enough, try another. Emanuel Haldeman-Julius, a marketing genius and the founding father of the mail-order book business, tells us that when one of his "Little Blue Books" did not sell as well as expected, he retired it to his "book hospital," where a new name was found for it. With this new name, the book often took on new life, going on to become a very profitable item on his list.

Entire books have been written on the subject of copywriting for mail order ads, and I am going to refer you to the best of them here. Study these books closely and use the tips that they contain. They are derived from years of experience and are worthy of your confidence.

The first book I will recommend is possibly the finest book on advertising copywriting ever written, *Tested Advertising Methods*, by John Caples. Caples learned his trade in the mail order business, so his advice is right on target.

Another book that can help you achieve your goals of writing effective ad copy to sell books is Melvin Powers' *How I Made $1,000,000 in Mail Order*. Powers' book is especially interesting because his background is in mail order book selling, specifically books that package information. He includes many reproductions of ads that have worked for him (and some that didn't work).

The third book is probably the best and most complete treatment of the mail order business in general — including print media classified and display advertising — that is in print today. It is *How to Start and Operate a Mail-Order Business*, by Julian L. Simon.

There are many other such books on the market, and doubtless many of them contain much valuable information. But when you own these three you will have the heart of the matter on your bookshelf. Study them carefully.

Basically, effective advertising is constructed according to the "AIDA" formula: attention, interest, desire, action. Put the main benefit of your offer ("Make $100,00 a Year Selling Information by Mail," "Lose 30 Pounds a Month without Dieting") in the headline. Such promises will get the attention of the readers you are interested in reaching, opportunity seekers in the first instance and would-be skinny people in the second.

Next give some details that will stimulate interest ("I did it myself, and now you can do it too by following my simple method").

Mix in a strong element of desire. Help the reader visualize what life will be like with a bulging bank account or the most beautiful body on the beach.

Finally, tell the reader how to take action to make this dream a reality. ("Call us now at 1-800, etc.") Don't forget to seal the deal with a free trial period and a money-back guarantee. ("Try it for 15 days. A full refund is yours if you are not completely satisfied.")

A personal, narrative style is a strong seller when line or per word rates are not too high. But concise, telegraphic ads can also be effective.

TEST AS YOU GO

One of the keys to success in selling merchandise by mail is to collect and carefully analyze response data so that you will know which ads pulled best. If you write two versions of an ad and you believe both are good, then try a split run. Available in some publications, a split run allows you to include one version of your ad in half of the printed copies and another version in the other half. You then key your response so that you will know which version generated the business. This is done through such techniques as adding a "department code" for written orders and an extension code for call-in orders. Version one of an ad will instruct readers to write you at your address, Dept. A, for example, or to call Extension 21. The second version will ask the reader the reader to write you at Dept. B, or to call Extension 22.

Sometimes a simple change in a headline can make a dramatic difference in response, as can the *title you give to your book*. But vary only one element at a time. Otherwise you will not know which change brought the desired results.

Julian Simon gives all the ins and outs of testing in *How to Start and Operate a Mail Order Business*. Consult his book for further details and other testing methods that you can employ.

DISPLAY ADVERTISING

If your classified advertising works well for you, you may wish to try your luck with some display ads — that is, ads which include some art, types of different styles, special layouts, etc.

Display ads come in various sizes. Most affordable are the classified displays. These are small, often no larger than the type-only ad you will have been running, and they are included in the classified advertising sections (the most read section, by the way, in any newspaper or magazine, including sports pages and the comics).

Study the examples of these small but powerful ads in John Caples' book and in Melvin Powers' book. You will be amazed at the amount of information you can get into a one or two inch ad.

If you find you have a real winner on your hands, you should test the response you will generate with a one-third page ad (vertical is best) or even a full page. These may be more affordable for test purposes in regional runs of national editions of magazines.

What are these full page ads like? Generally they are written in a lively style and chock full of information about your product. Ted Nicholas of Enterprise Publishing has been running full page ads for years for his book *How to Form Your Own Corporation for Under $50 Without a Lawyer*. Recently he has been running a new ad publicizing a book which promises to tell the reader how to obtain his own trademark or copyright, again very inexpensively and without the services of an attorney. The ads are costly, but they obviously generate more than enough business to turn a nice profit for Nicholas' Enterprise Press.

ONE STEP OR TWO

The ads I have been talking about are of the "one-step" variety. They present the product and ask the reader to order it directly.

When you begin to accumulate an inventory of books you may

want to market all of them simultaneously. If this is the case your ad will ask the reader to call in or write and send for a "free catalog." You then send a list of your books by return mail. In addition, whenever you fulfill an order from any source, you will slip into the envelope an inexpensive flyer listing your other publications.

The strength of the two-step approach is that you can include far more sales-pulling material in your direct mail packet than you can stuff into a small classified advertisement. As long as you are selling a single, relatively inexpensive item that can be adequately described in a small ad, I would recommend the one-step system. It is easier, quicker, less expensive and, within its limitations, works just as well.

How Flyers Work

Before I leave the subject of selling information by mail I will mention two other marketing techniques: the direct mail flyer and the catalog.

As your business grows you will gradually develop a mailing list of satisfied clients. To these you will mail simple one page flyers announcing each new title. You will also want to mail a flyer to the acquisitions librarians of schools and public libraries that may be interested in your book.

I have experimented with elaborate bound booklets listing each of my publications, and I have found that these do not generate the kind of return that could justify the cost of printing and mailing them. What does work, however, is the single printed page, just as it comes out of the laser printer or the office copier. The flyer will contain several paragraphs of copy telling what the book is about and an 800 number or an order blank to facilitate the purchase.

The fancy mailing pieces get filed away. The simple, one sheet jobs get acted on. They are cheaper and pull far better.

Piggyback Cataloging

While you may not want to print your own catalog, you can get a lot of mileage piggybacking on the catalogs of others. Remember Brantley's book on selling printing by mail. I found the advertisement for it in *Printer's Shopper*. That's why, as soon as this book is in print, I will contact the publishers of *Printers' Shopper* to see if they can find space for it. I will sell them all they want at a discount, so that they can make a profit too. This would be a very good deal for me since *Printers' Shopper* has a large and faithful clientele and a good track record for selling specialized books by mail. They also bear all the costs of advertising, collecting orders, and filling them. Though my up-front income (gross) will be lower, my net profit may well equal or surpass what I would otherwise have made selling these books myself.

There are catalogs serving every interest known to man. The people who put them out are constantly on the lookout for new products that will heighten reader interest and bring in orders. If one of your information book ideas seems to fall into one of these categories, by all means approach the catalog company with your product. If they take it you stand to do very well for yourself.

WHAT IS A TABLOID?
SOME SUCCESSFUL TABLOIDS
THE ADVANTAGES OF TABLOIDS
GETTING YOUR TABLOID PRINTED

11.

The Tabloid Alternative

The tabloid format represents a very attractive alternative to other techniques of publication design and production. Ease of production and affordability are its hallmarks. The tabloid does not work in every case. A quality of life magazine, for instance, requires a much slicker appearance. But when it does work, it is hard to beat. With some imagination you will find more and more opportunities for very profitable tabloid publishing.

The strengths of the tabloid for the local and regional publisher will become more apparent to you every day. I am using it in three upcoming projects, and I foresee this side of my business growing steadily.

The *tab* (as it is called in the trade) has great flexibility. One can be created quickly for just about any purpose. Although my company is committed mainly to the publication of traditional, slick-paper magazines, the tabs we bring out constitute a very strong and important secondary profit center. For many other companies, as we shall see, tabs alone are all that is needed to generate a very generous return on time and investment.

WHAT IS A TABLOID?

The word "tabloid" originated in the newspaper business. A newspaper of normal size is known as a "broadsheet." Folded in half and trimmed accordingly, the broadsheet becomes a tabloid. *The New York Times* and *The Washington Post* are broadsheet publications. *The Christian Science Monitor* and *The National Enquirer* are tabs.

The tab is also known as a "half-fold," since a regular newspaper page is folded in half to produce it. It is also possible to fold the tab itself in half (a "quarterfold"), producing a publication of near magazine size. Some TV guides and other inserts are quarterfolds.

Tabs are not usually stapled or glued but consist of loose pages, just as your evening newspaper does. Many of the newer news presses now have bindery capability and for a small additional charge will add glue, thus producing a tab that can look more like a magazine than a newspaper. This procedure is most often used for quarterfolds.

Tabloids are often printed on newsprint, the same stock that your newspaper is printed on. Usually some higher grades of paper will also be available — again for a modest additional charge. You will already be familiar with some of these better papers. Tabloid inserts for companies like J.C. Penney are often printed on better and somewhat heavier paper than the rest of the newspaper.

You can use full process color in a tabloid, although it is expensive and, in my opinion, not the way to go unless there is some compelling business reason to do so. Spot color, on the other hand, is very simple to do and can be used as required without incurring too much additional cost. It is true that more and more newspapers are beginning to use color photography and that the newer newspaper presses are much better at printing full (process) color than older ones were. This comes in response to the lavish use of color in papers like *USA Today*. Still, in the news pages of the *Post* and the *Times*, color is almost never seen.

SOME SUCCESSFUL TABLOIDS

There are many instances of successful tabloids in any trade area. Here are just a few from my part of North Carolina. A few years ago a young entrepreneur named Zack Taylor started mailing a tabloid publication to heads of businesses across the eastern part of the state. Progress was slow, but it was steady. Advertising sales increased from issue to issue. Because a tabloid is the least expensive publication to produce, Zack was able to stick with it until profits became substantial. Advertising rates are affordable and the circulation is perfect for anyone whose goods and services are marketed to other businesses.

A short time later Zack took note of another market gap. The North Carolina Rural Electric Cooperatives had, for many years, published a slick-paper magazine called *The Carolina Farmer*. Because of changing demographic patterns the co-op changed the name of its magazine to *Carolina Country*.

Zack, believing that a tremendous market existed for agri-business advertising sales in this rich, agricultural part of North Carolina, immediately created a tabloid called *The Carolina Farmer*. *The Carolina Farmer* filled an important market niche, and ad revenues began to pour in. A South Carolina edition was added, as were many special events editions.

Just a few years after start-up a group of investors approached Zack and bought *The Carolina Farmer* from him for a very substantial sum of money. As of this writing it is still going strong.

An Upscale Tab

The Raleigh-Durham-Chapel Hill area of North Carolina is the home of the famous "Research Triangle," headquarters of many of the most important high-tech companies in the U.S. It is also the home of Duke University, the University of North Carolina at Chapel Hill, and North Carolina State University — as well as a half dozen or so less well-known colleges.

It was clear that the area included far more than an average share of highly educated individuals for whom the cultural environment — arts, entertainment, intellectual commentary and discussion — were of great interest. Against this background an entrepreneurial publisher launched a weekly tabloid called *The Spectator*.

The Spectator is well written, well designed, and widely distributed. It pulls advertising dollars. It has become the foundation for many spin-off publishing activities.

The success of *The Spectator* has encouraged others to get into the market. The most successful, so far, is *The Leader*, a tabloid which does many of the same things as *Spectator* but does considerably more analysis of political and governmental issues.

The high-tech Research Triangle itself is now spawning imitators. One of these is an area to the east of Raleigh (the state capital of North Carolina) which calls itself "Triangle East" and is working to capitalize on spill-over development from the original Triangle. Along with the development of Triangle East came a tabloid of the same name. It, like *Carolina Business*, is a free circulation business-to-business publication. You can look at the rate card, count the number of ad inches and easily determine that *Triangle East* — the tabloid — is a successful business venture.

Such opportunities abound. A tabloid is easy to organize and quick to get into the market. Opportunities reveal themselves on almost a daily basis, and at every level. There is a local tab in Greenville, NC, a city of 40,000, called *The Greenville Times*. Its editorial content is oriented toward culture and local history. It is a low energy, free circulation publication which, as of this writing, appears twice monthly in a modest printing. It is nicely designed and well written, but essentially very easy to do. It could become much more profitable (by coming out weekly, for example) but the owner-publishers are content to rock along as things are. *The Times* furnishes them a decent living and leaves plenty of time for other ventures . . . or just for themselves. This is an alternative many of us might choose.

THE ADVANTAGES OF TABLOIDS

Tabloid publications, then, have a great deal to offer the publisher-entrepreneur. There are powerful advantages to taking this route whenever it is possible to do so. Here are some of the most important of them.

Quick Turnaround

Tabloids offer the quickest, most efficient turnaround time in the whole of publishing. You can take your pasted-up pages to the printer at two in the afternoon and drive away before closing time with thousands of printed, folded, and bundled tabloids ready for distribution.

Low Cost and Ease of Pre-press Work

No publication is as easy to prepare for the printer as a tabloid. After all, it is a newspaper derivative, and newspapers have to come out day after day, with no delay. When you think about it, it is truly amazing to realize that each edition of *The New York Times* is written, designed, pasted up, and printed in no more than a twenty-four hour period. All of this means that design and preparation techniques are far, far easier to implement in newspapers and tabs than in the simplest slick-paper magazine.

Black and white photos, especially, are very easy to manage. You simply lay down a black or red "window" (I use a material called "parapaque") where the photograph is to appear, and hand the printer a copy of the photo that goes in that spot, with crop marks and the enlargement/reduction percentage indicated. The photo is in place in minutes.

Frequency of Publication

Another advantage of tabloids is that you can come out as frequently as you wish. I currently publish a slick-paper magazine called *NCEast*. This magazine began as an annual publication. It now appears quarterly with plans in the works to increase the schedule to every other month publication. The increased frequency of the publication will stretch my small staff to the limit. Monthly publication would result in a very considerable increase in overhead due to the editors, writers, and art department people we would have to add.

With a tabloid, there's never a problem with frequency of publication. Every other month? A snap. Monthly? No problem. Weekly? Still quite manageable by a relatively small staff.

You Can Achieve Saturation Coverage

If, like most periodical publishers, you depend on advertising revenues to run your business, then you must get results for those who buy space in your publications. You do this by getting their message into the hands of as many readers as possible. Tabloids are so economical to print that you can afford to expand the print run far beyond what would be possible with a more expensive magazine. There is an absolute correlation between the results you get for your advertisers and the number of copies you can print. And more results yield more ad sales.

Cheaper Cost for Advertisers

The high-dollar magazines must get premium prices for a page of advertising. This effectively eliminates many small enterprises that would otherwise choose to buy space. In a tabloid these costs are much lower because your expenses are lower. The pages of a tabloid are open to virtually every business that has its doors open. A shop that can't afford the space really can't afford to be in business. There is a vast reservoir of advertising prospects for tabloids, and a gold mine for your ad sales staff.

Special Editions

You can seize any opportunity that presents itself to do a special edition. If you are geared up to do tabloids you will find ideas for additional publications popping into your head by the dozens. Are state Olympic trials being held in the capital city? They were in North Carolina not long ago and *The Spectator* brought out a highly profitable "NC Olympics" edition, including programs, venues, things to do and places to go, accommodations, news, etc. It became an indispensable reference tool for the thousands of athletes and visitors who came to the show. Advertising was easy to sell.

In the city of Greenville, where my offices are, I noted a market gap when we heard that the Chamber of Commerce would no longer publish its *Students' Guide to Greenville*. (East Carolina University is located there, and the thousands of students who attend bring many sought-after dollars into the local economy.) We cranked up a tabloid edition, sent a salesperson out, and netted (after all expenses) an additional $10,000 for our small company. It was easily done. We seized the opportunity on a moment's notice. And it generated a nice profit for us.

Look around your own community. Opportunities are there for any publication-conscious person to see. Brainstorm it with your friends and associates. You will surely come up with some ideas that will make you money.

GETTING YOUR TABLOID PRINTED

Tabloids are printed on the same presses that print newspapers. Any daily newspaper, and a few of the large weeklies and biweeklies, will have the web presses and other production services that you will need.

This kind of printing is a secondary profit center for the established newspaper. They have to have the equipment — and very expensive equipment it is — to print their own paper. They have the press crew, darkroom people, and pre-press people on the payroll. Normally they have a few hours a day that they can devote to other publications.

Simply visit the general manager of your town's newspaper. If he can't help you, he can probably refer you to someone who can. *The Daily Reflector*, the Greenville afternoon newspaper, has a large printing plant, but since they also print a number of weeklies that the company owns, they have little time for taking in outside work. But in the nearby town of Tarboro a small daily, also with excellent printing facilities, has time available and delights in taking in the tabloids that I bring to be printed.

In order to get a price from the printer you will need to furnish the following information:

☐ number to be printed
☐ number of pages
☐ number of photographs (note his quoted price per photo)
☐ the amount of color, if any, and the pages where it occurs

The printer will give you a price and set a day and time for you to bring your project in. You, in turn, will take care to arrive when you promise to do so. Otherwise some very expensive presses and very costly workmen will be standing around with nothing to do.

The newspaper that is to do the printing will furnish you with ruled layout sheets for you to paste up your tabloid on. Broadsheet sizes vary from newspaper to newspaper. Twenty years ago newspapers were considerably wider than they are now, and some older presses still turn out this size product. Since your tabloid is simply a broadsheet folded in half, the size of your tab will vary according to the size of the broadsheet you started with. Obviously, you need to check all this out before you begin your design work. You should also ask to see the grades of paper the printer has available so that you can choose the one most appropriate to your project.

12.   Small Press Book Publishing

Although there is some money to be made publishing books of literary merit simply because they *are* good, it would be hard for most of us to derive a steady income from that activity. It just can't be counted on to stock the larder, make the mortgage payment, and put braces on the children's teeth.

It is always within the realm of possibility that shortly after you set up in business the postman will arrive with an absolutely wonderful first novel from an unknown writer, for which you are able to sell movie rights, book club rights, paperback reprint rights, foreign rights, and 500,000 copies of the first hardbound edition. It is also theoretically possible that the next time you pull up an onion from your backyard vegetable patch you will uncover a pot of gold.

Possible, yes. But I do not recommend that you buy your new Ferrari just yet. But if lightning did strike — if there was a doubloon or two in the garden — it might make even bigger problems for the small, undercapitalized press. You might wind up with a bestseller on your hands that can't "best sell" because you lack the cash or the credit to assume the enormous printing and production costs that will be required of you. Algonquin Books of Chapel Hill, early in its business life, had the good fortune to publish the novel *Rainey*, by Clyde Edgerton. The novel came out accompanied by a very big play in the press, since Edgerton, a teacher at a small church-related college, was denied tenure because the school's trustees disapproved of his treatment of religious themes in the book. And, into the bargain, Edgerton was a very good writer and *Rainey* was a very good book.

Big sales and book club deals followed. The problem for Algonquin lay in raising the capital required to fulfill the steady stream of orders generated by this windfall of quality and notoriety. Printers must be paid *now*, up-front, and the payback from bookstores is very slow indeed. In addition, there were returns to consider. Part and parcel of the book trade is a traditional policy of returns which allows booksellers to send back in — for full credit — unsold copies which they have on their shelves, after a suitable selling season. So the publisher, deluged with orders, must print and pay for copies of his potential best-seller without any assurance that a great number of them may not come home to roost as much as twelve months later.

BOOK PUBLISHING IS CAPITAL INTENSIVE

This is not a game for the light-hearted and undercapitalized. Indeed, as the game is usually played, there are few business enterprises more capital intensive than serious book publishing. To create a cash flow adequate to pay management salaries (you), staff salaries (your office manager), free-lance fees (your editors), rent, postage, distribution, and other overhead — would require thirty to forty sound, saleable titles in print and on bookstore shelves.

To achieve this level of activity would mean an investment of three to four hundred thousand dollars — perhaps even more — to feel in any way secure in your enterprise.

The people at Algonquin Books managed to do what was necessary to attract the large amounts of capital needed to maintain its level of success. In so doing, it became a different company with different investors and capital sources. So far, this seems to be working for them. Their list is growing, and it is distinguished. I would be surprised, however, if the investors or any employee of the corporation, from the editor-in-chief on down, are yet taking out salaries and dividends commensurate with the risk and the cash put in.

ALTERNATIVE ROUTES

Fortunately, there are workable alternatives. The key to these is the publisher's willingness to do literary publishing *in addition to* whatever other work he or she is doing, rather than taking it on as a primary source of income.

An example. A few weeks from now I will publish a collection of poetry by a very gifted young writer from my state. Since he is personable and will do effective public readings, I expect to sell out the first printing of 1000 copies by the end of the year. If I do, the book will be considered "profitable." The author will have his royalties and I will have paid my suppliers and have a small sum left over to help publish someone else's collection of verse next year.

The sums of money involved, however, are quite small, so that even if I double my investment I will still earn a return of, at best, $2000. Now there is nothing wrong with making an extra thousand or so here and there, but you can't count on it and you can't run a household on it. This kind of publishing is a sideline and not a career. I can afford to publish this collection of verse because my company is already well established and produces a reasonable living for me from the tourism guides, quality of life magazines, and apartment directories that we publish.

Your books may be very much admired and, in fact, be distinguished both for their literary merit and for the quality of their design and production. They may be very important in your scheme of values and bring you much personal satisfaction. That is why most of us get involved in literary publishing to begin with.

This is certainly the case with a friend of mine who runs a typography studio in a nearby town. He and his wife pay their bills with their type business. But on the side, Moreland Hogan at Briarpatch Press brings out some of the most beautifully designed and elegantly printed books of any regional publisher I know of. He is able to do this because his other business activities make him self sufficient. Other literary publishers may be teachers, booksellers, mechanics — I know one who owns a pig farm. But they all have in common the fact that they have enough to live on to support themselves without counting on help from their book publishing income.

How a Non-profit Corporation Can Help

For whatever reason, those who are most attracted to the business of literary and short run publishing seldom seem to have the funds on hand to carry through the publication of even one book, not to mention the dozens of titles we were talking about earlier in this chapter. They must attract money from some other source.

State and regional arts councils are a major source of such funds. So are private foundations. You have a project on hand that you consider worthwhile. You survey the arts council and foundation field, apply for a grant of funds to carry your project through and, when these funds are forthcoming, you deposit them into your corporate bank account and go to work.

I say "corporate bank account" advisedly, because to attract such funds it is almost always necessary to be chartered as a non-profit corporation. Does this mean that you cannot earn money from your publishing enterprise? No, it does not. You will be a paid employee of the corporation and as such receive whatever compensation you and your board of directors deem affordable and reasonable.

So far as the distribution of money is concerned, the non-profit corporation differs from a regular corporation chiefly in the fact that, at year's end, any profits on hand are not distributed to share holders as dividends (the non-profit corporation does not have shareholders). These excess funds are normally plowed back into the work of the corporation so that it can do even more of the good work that it was set up to do.

Gifts and contributions to non-profit corporations are tax deductible. This means that you could solicit support for your publishing activities from *any organization at all* so long as such funds are handled in accordance with the laws of your state and with your corporate charter and by-laws.

Many small presses — and all university presses — exist today as non-profit corporations. It would be virtually impossible for them to survive in any other way. Arts councils and foundations have funds available that they *must* distribute to those projects that they find worthy. In the arts this most often involves grants for the publication of books of poetry and prose of high artistic merit but with small chance of commercial success. Ninety-five percent of all collections of poetry currently published in the United States are made possible in this way.

The downside of the non-profit corporation lies in the detailed record keeping required and the care that you must take in seeing to it that a board of directors is appointed that is congenial to your vision of what you want your publishing company to be.

OTHER SOURCES OF FUNDING

You can also find the money you need for literary publishing projects through subsidies that are available from various sources. It is important to understand here that the word "subsidy" need have absolutely no pejorative overtones. It is not a dirty word, although it can be, and has been, misused. Most university presses, for instance, require that their more erudite titles with limited sales potential be subsidized. A book may indeed be a classic of scholarship, and contain work of the highest order. But there may be only a few hundred specialists worldwide in the particular field of study that it represents. Sales, therefore, are likely to be so low that to break even on the project is virtually impossible.

Yet the book clearly deserves publishing. The university press wants the prestige of bringing it out; the author wants and needs the professional recognition that will result from publication; and the school where he teaches desires to have well-published and renowned professors on its faculty.

So how is publication arranged? Very simple. A subsidy is found. Following its very rigorous procedures, the editorial committee of the university press accepts the book for publication, but notifies the author that it requires additional funds in support of the project. The author takes this letter to the dean of the college at which he teaches and requests a grant of funds. Most often, such funds can be found and dispatched to the publishing press. These funds constitute the subsidy that makes publication possible.

This scenario will play well for your publishing company too, as long as you take care to create and maintain for it a high reputation for quality books that are regularly reviewed in the media and are well received by the public for whom they are intended.

DIRECT AUTHOR SUBSIDIES

Subsidies can also come directly from the author, but these must be handled very carefully so that you distinguish yourself clearly from the so-called "vanity" presses. These firms will make a book of any manuscript that is submitted to them, as long as the author pays them enough cash to cover all expenses and generate a profit too. Such companies do not have to sell a single book in order to thrive financially.

What most people in the trade object to is that the vanity presses are often misleading in their approach to clients. They masquerade as standard commercial publishers, but in reality they are nothing of the kind.

The reputation of a literary small press is its stock in trade and is built on the sheer artistic merit of the books it chooses to publish. Foundation grants and institutional subsidies, as we have seen, depend on this reputation. Most colleges, for instance, have strict guidelines which forbid any subsidy to a company that gives even the impression of being a vanity press. Newspapers will not review their books. Most bookstores will not stock their titles.

Why would an author want to subsidize the publication of his own book? There are many reasons. If he is a teacher, he will reap substantial rewards in raises and promotions that will come his way as a published member of the faculty. Or perhaps the subject matter is so important to the author that he wants to ensure that it will be made available to the public at large. On a more mundane level, perhaps the book in question is a text that a professor, for instance, will use in his own classes.

PUBLISH BOOKS THAT YOU CAN MARKET

In order to succeed at any level of publishing — large press or small, literary or not — *the key is to reach the buyer with a book that he or she desires to purchase and will purchase.* This presents two immediate problems. How do you reach the public when you have little or no advertising budget and only yourself, perhaps your spouse, and the U.S. mail to do your marketing for you? The second question, of course, is what kinds of books do people want to buy?

Once again, you apply our overall guidelines for success. You choose titles that will have intensive sales, in a limited geographical area, to a clearly identified clientele. These criteria would eliminate, for example, most novels of general interest, no matter how good, and most collections of short stories. The problems with such books is that you have to sell a few copies in each of many bookstores nationwide to achieve success, and you do not have the sales organization that makes this possible.

Does this eliminate all fiction? Not necessarily. You may occasionally abandon your own best business sense and give in to the temptation to plow some profits back into the publication of a novel that you love even though you *know* that you can't market it effectively. The risk here is the great possibility, even probability, of eventual hard feelings between you and your author.

If you choose to publish such a book, be very, very sure that the author understands fully the limitations of your marketing capabilities and accepts them. I have found that this is a very difficult thing to make clear. No matter how clearly I explain my limitations as publisher and the fact that I cannot mount a nationwide marketing campaign, the author is so sure in his heart that he has written a real blockbuster of a book that he will be very unhappy when sales barely limp along and when, while traveling in another town, he cannot find a copy of his book on the bookseller's shelves.

NOVELS THAT YOU CAN MARKET AND SELL

A novel that *can* be successfully sold is one that has strong local themes and ties to an area where there is constant renewal of the book-buying public — a major tourist or resort area, for instance. Eugenia Price's novel *Savannah* comes to mind as a book that clearly fits this category. For such a title there are constant local sales to the many thousands of tourists who visit the town weekly. On the basis of these sales alone the publisher could make a profit and approach a mass market paperback house to sell reprint rights. And from there on the sky's the limit.

On a more modest scale I have recently published a novel by Jean Kell called *Love, Goodwill and Affection*. It is a historical romance set in old Beaufort, North Carolina. This town is a major destination for tourism — although not nearly as large as Savannah — and a favorite stop for yachts traveling the intracoastal waterway. A steady sale of this very readable book is virtually assured.

John F. Blair, a regional publishing house located in Winston-Salem, North Carolina, has for years done well with a series of books by folklorist and story teller Charles Whedbee. Typical is one of the early books in the series called *The Flaming Ship of Ocracoke and Other Tales of the Outer Banks*. Blair is one of the stronger regional houses and does have sales reps out calling on bookstores. But Whedbee's books would have done well in the hands of any aggressive small publisher because of their strong, unmistakable ties to a limited geographical area. It would take only a sales trip or two a year to get the book on the shelves of every major outlet on the Outer Banks and thus available to every one of the hundreds of thousands of vacationers visiting the area annually and spending millions of dollars on mementoes and keepsakes.

THE PROBLEM WITH POETRY

Books of poetry can sell, but these sales are almost totally dependent on the reputation, personality, and contacts of the poet. Most books of poetry are not bought in bookstores but at readings given by the poet. If your poet is not outgoing enough to do well at a public reading and not aggressive enough to arrange a regular schedule of these, the book will not sell. The more colorful and endowed with showmanship your poet is, the more books you will sell.

It was the quality of Dylan Thomas' work that earned him a place as one of the major British poets of the mid-century. It was his colorful, quotable, feisty — even self-destructive — personality that made his books sell in relatively large numbers in paperback and cloth.

I stress that these readings will be arranged by the poet himself, because you will not have time to do so nor will you have access to the same opportunities that he has. He is where he is. You are where you are. You can't be both places at once.

My small press is currently bringing out the first book in what we expect to be a series of collections by younger poets. The work itself is superb, and that is why we liked it in the first place. It was also intelligible to the general reader. Our decision to publish it, however, was also based on its marketability. Joseph Bathanti, the author, had been active in many state writers' organizations. He taught creative writing in a number of community colleges and did workshops and seminars in others. During the summer months he served on the faculties of writers' conferences and workshops. He kept a very active schedule of readings and appearances. He was personable and came across well on a one-to-one basis. I judged that he would be quite successful in his readings and could sell books. I therefore felt confident in planning a modest printing with the reasonable expectation of eventually selling them all.

Within these narrow guidelines, yes, you can indulge your love of fine writing and publish some books of literary merit. You may find them too restrictive and wish to try a more adventurous approach. If so, I wish you luck, and I remind you that you should develop strategies for dealing with, in advance, the substantial difficulties that you will surely confront.

HOW TO MAKE MONEY PUBLISHING BOOKS

Once you get your small press up and running you will find that profitable and commercially viable book ideas abound. Here are some book ideas that have been successful for me or for other publishers that I know about. Books in each of the following categories represent prime opportunities, especially for the small, desktop publisher. Such titles are successfully published as money-making ventures without a subsidy or grant of any kind. They can be easily adapted to the personality, needs, interests, and strengths of your individual market area. Here is my list of prime nonfiction candidates for your small press list:

An Illustrated History of Your Town or County

This idea can be done at many different levels, but it is potentially so strong and can be so profitable that it is treated in a chapter of its own.

An Institutional History

Has anyone ever done a real history of the high school in your town? Put together from newspaper files, recorded reminiscences, photographs culled from yearbooks, and other sources, such a book could be a real winner. Handsomely packaged it could be quite successful. Obviously it would work better in the smaller towns and cities where the high school has fulfilled the role, along with the churches, of providing a center around which community activities revolve.

In a college or university town the same kind of book could be done for that institution. Although alumni will have scattered to the four corners of the earth, they can still be reached by direct mail. Perhaps a joint venture between your press and the institutional development office might be profitable.

I am sure that in your area other similar ideas will occur to you. It is important in such projects to put the emphasis on the photographic and illustrative side of the book. This is what sells copies. You do not need to do years of research to bring it off. You, or your writer, need only do a narrative thread to tie the book together, provide very full cutlines for each illustration, and use names, names, names.

The institutional history also has the important by-product of transferability. Once you do one and have the routine down pat, you can do the same job, more easily this time, for a nearby town, school, or other institution. You might even begin to sell your services on a contract basis, publishing a history not only about but *for* the institution involved, for a flat fee — in the five figure range. This would take the speculation out of it entirely.

Historical Narratives and Documents

Journals of explorers and letters and diaries of early settlers can make interesting and popular books. If the material is good and the book is well-designed, an ongoing, steady, but modest flow of sales should make your venture a successful one.

In my home state of North Carolina, there is a rich literature dealing with the exploration and settlement of our state, much of it quite dramatic. Everyone who made the trip, and could write, composed memoirs, journals, and letters in which they recorded their experiences for the folks back home. The same is true of settlers who left the eastern towns and cities for the uncertainties of life on the western frontier.

Many of these narratives are now out of print and unavailable to any but specialists who use large library manuscript collections. It is exciting to realize that some have never been published at all. They exist undiscovered, in attics, trunks, and badly catalogued manuscript collections all over the country.

Check the collections, for starters — and consult the appropriate librarian — of your town and state university libraries for leads. Are there any historical narratives that are unpublished or unavailable to the general reader? If you come up with some positive answers, then you may have a book.

The Reprint Market

Related to the historical narrative is the market for new editions of older, out-of-print books. You can't choose just any book, of course. You must find one that is in the "public domain," that was never copyrighted in the first place or whose copyright protection has expired.

Here are the rules of the game. Before January 1, 1978 (when the new copyright law went into effect), the maximum copyright protection for a book published in the United States was fifty-six years.

But the copyright protection on many books may have expired after twenty-eight years rather than fifty-six. The old copyright law — the one you're concerned with — granted an author copyright protection for an initial period of twenty-eight years. This was extended to fifty-six years only if an extension was applied for during the last year of the initial period. The larger publishing houses routinely do this, but the smaller companies sometimes simply go out of business during the first period and so never get an extension. Others — and especially individuals who register copyrights — simply neglect to do so.

In sum: If you find a book you are interested in reprinting and it was published more than fifty-seven years ago, you can be sure that it may be in the public domain. Books copyrighted more than twenty-eight years ago may or may not be in the public domain. You will have to do some research to find out for sure.

What kind of book makes a successful reprint publication? Look for a title that is in demand, that has no serious competition from more recent books, and that is out of print. It must also be within your marketing capabilities.

When I first began to do research for my picture history of Greenville, I had to consult a a book called *Sketches of Pitt County,* by one Henry T. King. This book had been out of print since 1911, and it was in the public domain. It was the only county history available.

Libraries where I worked treated *Sketches* as a rare and valuable book. I often had to get special permission to use it.

In addition I became aware that any copies that happened to find their way onto the marketplace (which was rare, since most families considered their copy an heirloom) always sold for as much as $100 each. *Sketches of Pitt County* was a natural for the reprint market. I wrote a new introduction and provided an index — a very useful feature that the earlier edition had lacked.

The nice thing about reprints is that they are economical to produce. The cost of typesetting is entirely eliminated, except for the few pages of introduction to the new edition that you provide and perhaps an index. The printer will simply photograph the original pages and make his plates from these.

So you have a fortunate combination — an inexpensive product whose market value will be well above that of most books that you will publish. I printed 500 copies of King's *Sketches*. They cost about $4.50 each. I sold them for $29.95. Many of these I sold directly, but even allowing for bookstore discounts the return on investment was more than satisfactory.

An Oral History

This kind of book will not be a dramatic success, but in areas that are history conscious it can bring you some community recognition and at least what the French call a *succes d'estime*. That is, your book will be well-received and admired even though it is unlikely to do much more than break even in the sales department.

The fact that I include such a book here is due to my personal interest in *lived history*. The old-timers in our communities know more about the human reality of our past than we can ever deduce by studying records, statistics, and other paraphernalia of library-type research. They know — and can tell us — what it *felt* like to live back then, the color, smell, and taste of it.

You will need only a few simple tools, chief among them a small tape recorder with a built-in mike. This less obtrusive microphone is not as inhibiting as the external ones that you stick in someone's face. Then you will introduce yourself to your first informant and get things under way.

There are some interviewing techniques that you will want to use. You can find out about these from books like Selden and Pappworth's *By Word of Mouth* (Methuen, 1983), which also may suggest specialized topics for treatment as oral history. While an oral history of your hometown may be only mildly interesting, one written for your state capital or, better, of the state legislature, or of a particularly important era in your state's history will generate much wider interest and much more active sales.

How to Buy it Cheap, and Where

We live in a consumer society, and most of us want more things than we have money to buy. A book that can tell us how to get hold of them is a natural seller. Such a book will provide detailed instructions on where and how to buy expensive things cheaply and cheap things even cheaper.

Here's just one success story. A few years ago a saddle-stitched (stapled) paperback book of a few dozen pages appeared on the counter of my favorite bookstore. It was rather ordinary looking — unambitious in format and content. It simply listed the factory outlet stores in my area where clothing and other items could be bought at prices considerably below wholesale. It told the name of each outlet, gave precise instructions on how to get there, and described in detail what you would find when you arrived.

This little book was an immediate and great success. It quickly went into an expanded and revised edition, covering a wider and wider area. Pages of paid advertising, in addition to the original editorial content, soon began to boost revenues well beyond any level the publishers had thought possible.

If such a book is not available in your area — or if any that are available are inadequate — you have a publishing opportunity before you. It will be successful if you do it well and market it actively. It will be inexpensive to print and bind, and the profit will be substantial.

The Strange, the Uncanny, and the Supernatural

Are there strange beings in outer space? There may be, but our own world is as mysterious and inexplicable as any world could possibly be. Readers are convinced of that and love to read about it. Books that plug into that thirst for the supernatural in a marketable way sell thousands of copies across the United States every day.

When I was living in France a few years ago, I traveled around the country a good deal and read a lot of guidebooks. (The French are masters of the art of writing guidebooks.) Alongside the standard models I discovered a parallel series that focused on the darker, stranger side of life. Called *Mysterious Paris, Mysterious Normandy*, or mysterious whatever part of the country I happened to be visiting, these little books were fascinating, and I always bought one. Would this idea work in Savannah, Charleston, or New York? You bet it would, and in many a smaller city, too. If a writer came to me with such a book tomorrow, I would publish it.

This is just one idea. Many others will occur to you. The important thing, as with any book project, is the unusual slant that makes your book unlike others that may be on the market.

Informational Books

The sale of specialized information is big business today. See Chapter 10 on "How to Sell Information by Mail."

WORKING WITH AUTHORS AND COLLABORATORS

If you are not a writer you will have to depend on others to write and/or edit some of your book projects. Tips on finding and dealing with writers are given in other chapters of this book. Several observations are appropriate here.

Writers come in all shapes and sizes, and as a small press publisher you are likely, at one time or another, to deal with all of them. At one end of the scale is the professional writer, the person who makes a living by the written word. At the other end may be the hobbyist or researcher who has accumulated a fund of knowledge or expertise that warrants publication but whose writing skills are slender. Though these specialists may produce a first draft of a book, the actual writing of the final text will be in large measure the work of the editor (perhaps you) who puts the project together.

There are fairly standard and well-accepted ways to compensate your authors for their work. With respect to books, the publisher and author normally negotiate a contract which pays a royalty (a fixed percentage of the retail cost of the book, normally 10% or less for hardbacks and as little as 10 to 12% of the wholesale price for paperbacks) to the author at regular intervals. Should subsidiary rights be sold — foreign rights, movies and television, mass market paperback rights — the fees received from the sale of such rights are generally split 50/50 between author and publisher. If the writer has an agent, all monies due the writer are paid to the agent, who passes the money along to the author after deducting his own commission.

The many details of book publishing contracts are discussed in two recent books, both of which are recommended for further reading: *An Author's Guide to Book Publishing*, by Richard Balkin and *How to be Happily Published*, by Judith Applebaum. These books generally approach the topic from the writer's point of view, but all the information is there. And you, as publisher, need to understand the process as seen by the writer.

It is also possible, especially when assigning a book topic to a free-lancer, to negotiate a flat-fee payment for all the work. Such a book becomes what the copyright law terms a "work made for hire," and you, as the person who assigned and paid for the work, own the copyright. In the case of a flat-fee project, no royalties are paid. This kind of arrangement is advantageous to the publisher only when it is as certain as can be that adequate sales can be expected.

The larger publishers often pay an "advance against royalties" to the author. As royalties accrue they are credited against the advance. If the book, for some reason, does not sell as well as expected and royalties do not accumulate in sufficient amounts to defray the advance, the publisher sustains the loss. Smaller presses, in general, do not pay advances because they simply cannot afford to do so.

The fee basis is also used when you assign chapters of a book to a number of different individuals. A few years ago I was asked by Westminster Press to write a chapter on the southern French city of Montpelier for a book to be entitled *Shoestring Sabbatical*. I agreed to write this chapter for a fixed fee, did so, and the book was subsequently published. Since I had already been paid I received no royalty or sales reports from the publisher.

It is also possible to devise a shared royalty contract for a book made up of the work of several authors. In your contract you would specify the overall commission and also the portion of that commission to be paid to each contributor.

BOOK DESIGN

The appearance of your book is important if you expect to sell it in bookstores. It is less so if you intend to sell it exclusively by direct mail. This presents a challenge. Most small press books are published in fairly short print runs, ranging from 500 to two or three thousand on the first printing. Because of this fact, your per unit cost will be considerably higher than that borne by larger publishers who regularly print their titles in quantities of 10,000 to several hundred thousand copies.

In spite of your higher costs, your books must possess all the quality of design and appearance of any other title on the bookstore shelves. Indeed, since your retail price is likely to be just a bit higher,

"Restraint is probably the most difficult design principle to apply in a consistent manner. That's because desktop publishing presents you with tremendous design power — power which just a few years ago was limited to those who had years of training and tens of thousands of dollars worth of equipment.

"With so much power at your fingertips it's easy to forget that straightforward simplicity is a virtue and that graphic design should be invisible to the reader."

Roger C. Parker
Looking Good in Print
Ventana Press

your book must, whenever possible, look even better than the others. It should be beautiful to look at, to hold, and to read.

If you are inexperienced in book design I recommend that you spend some time with the many excellent books on that subject. See the suggestions for further reading in the back of the book for details.

Not the least of your problems will be communication in matters of design — even if you know precisely what you want. The problem lies in the technical vocabulary. You will pick this up soon enough, but you are not likely to be familiar with all its terms in the beginning. Words like *pica* (a measure of line length), *leading* (a measure of the space between lines), *trim size, type page area, signature, front matter,* and many others may puzzle you.

You will soon be able to talk in these terms as easily as anyone else. Meanwhile, however, you can use the tried and true method that I used when I was getting my own first book into production: I browsed through the library, found a book that I liked, took it to the printer and said, "Make my book look like this one."

Never hesitate to ask questions. "What do you mean by that?" and "Why do you want to do it that way?" will elicit much useful information that you can store up for future reference.

Since design elements are often linked to the costs of production, which you want to keep under control, there is another question that can save you a great deal of money over the long run: "Can you think of a better and less expensive way to do this?" Your printer will be glad to begin your technical education for you if you will only ask.

The way you bind your book will have a significant influence on the cost of production and on the retail price you can charge. As surprising as it may seem it is not necessarily advantageous to publish a book in paperback.

A short book of forty-eight pages will be paperbound of necessity. It is just not thick enough to look good when casebound in hardcover. But longer books tend to be both more attractive and more profitable when casebound. Libraries, for instance prefer casebound books and will purchase them more readily than paperbacks, which do not stand up well under circulation pressures.

The main consideration, though, is retail price. A casebound book may cost anywhere from $2 to $3 more to produce than an paperback book. However, you can sell it for more than *double the price of the paperback version.*

Many of your books will be of the kind that people want to buy and keep permanently on their shelves. This kind of buyer prefers a casebound book.

When I published Henry T. King's *Sketches of Pitt County* I could have brought it out in a paperback version and sold it for ten or twelve dollars, tops. I had it casebound in a numbered edition of 500 copies and sold out the edition at $29.95. The same book, packaged differently, sold at nearly three times the paperback price.

HOW MANY DO YOU PRINT?

Deciding how many books to print on your first run will be one of the earliest and thorniest problems that you will have to face. My own rule has always been to print only those I was pretty sure I could sell, then go back to press for additional copies if and when demand warranted. Many publishers who market books by mail order don't print *any at all* until the orders begin coming in. Thus the little notes one sometimes sees: Please allow four to six weeks for delivery. The inventory is created only *after* the demand is established.

Obviously you want to have enough books on hand to fill the orders that come in from bookstores, libraries, and individuals. Just as obviously you don't want to pay out good money for more books than you are likely to sell. A good deal of the decision you make will rest on intuition, with healthy amounts of rule-of-thumb and informal readership survey thrown in.

I have noticed that most inexperienced publishers — or self-publishers — overestimate the size of the market for their product. There are fewer book buyers — and even readers — out there than most of us who love books would like to admit.

How do you estimate a print order? How many copies do you print, say, of a picture history of a town or county? Surely you can sell a great many of them. Everybody, you think, will want one.

Well, let's see. In a city of 40,000 inhabitants there are roughly 10,000 households. Of these at least half either can't read or don't read. That leaves 5000. Of this 5000, half read only the daily paper and *TV Guide*. That leaves 2500. Of this 2500, half would not mind having a copy of your book, but either can't afford one or won't get around to buying one. That leaves 1200. Of this core of 1200 qualified prospects, at least half just won't get around to buying the book. The other half, if you do a good marketing job, will.

So, in a town of 40,000 population there is a core market of 750 households where you have a good chance of placing a copy of your book. I recommend printing this 750 in a relatively expensive, limited edition, signed and numbered — thus creating a collector's item. This will, believe me, handle your initial orders and provide enough additional copies to keep the book alive on bookstore shelves through the Christmas season.

Adjust downward for books of purely literary interest and upward for those of more general interest or of appeal to a larger (in numbers) market.

STAGES OF PRODUCTION

You can set up in business as a small press publisher with little or no experience in the field, relying totally on the jolt of high quality know-how that comes with on-the-job training. It helps, though, to be forewarned so that you can prepare for the work to be done.

Once you have your manuscript in hand, the job is just beginning. There is a definite number of steps, in a definite order, that you must take before you hold a finished book in your hands and place it for sale on the bookstore shelf.

Step One

Edit the manuscript for style, correctness, organization, etc. Return it to the author for whatever rewriting and revisions are needed and for retyping. Careful work at this stage will save many a problem — and many an unnecessary expense for alterations — later on.

Step Two:

Once you have the edited, clean copy in hand, **analyze** the book. Count the number of characters. How long a book are you dealing with? Will there be photographs, drawings, diagrams, graphs? How many pages will be devoted to these elements?

Step Three:

Develop a tentative design. You may well have to adjust some details as the book takes shape, but you can determine fairly well how long your book will be, what kind of paper you want it printed on, the number of photographs you will include. Contact one reliable short-run book printer. For details on obtaining quotes see Chapter 13, "Better Printing for Less Money."

Step Four:

Once you have developed a design format that you can live with, **set the type** on your desktop system. All corrections and alterations are made at this level, as well as the final page layout. When page proofs are approved, run out clean pages and use these to paste up your book. If you decide to use high resolution type, take the floppy disk on which the book is stored to a nearby printer who owns high resolution phototypesetting equipment, and have the pages run out on resin coated paper.

As of this writing there are two basic typesetting systems that desktop shops use: the Apple and the IBM and its clones. When you look for a shop to convert your desktop copy into high resolution type keep in mind that Apple-generated type is compatible with Allied-Linotype (formerly Merganthaler) equipment and the IBM with Compugraphic.

Step Five:

Prepare galley proofs. Return one copy of these to the author for corrections. Extensive rewriting should be strongly discouraged at this time. Editing will have taken place in the first step, above. You will retain two copies. On one of these you will enter the corrections that you or your proofreader discover. When you and the author have completed the proofing process, all corrections indicated will be evaluated and those that you determine should be made will be entered on the third copy of the galleys, which you will return to the typographer for corrections.

Step Six:

You will **run out a second set of galley proofs**, which you will study to be sure that all corrections have been made.

Step Seven:

When galleys are clean, the **front matter and chapter**

heads are designed and page proofs are prepared. At this point you should, ideally, discover no further errors. Some few, however, may be found and these are then corrected.

Step Eight:

You now know *precisely* how long your book is. **Contact your initial printer** with these specs if they differ from the original ones. Also contact at least two additional printers for quotes.

Step Nine:

Send your book off to the printer and begin to schedule press releases, prepare a list of review copies to be sent, design promotional pieces, plan autograph parties, and set up radio and television appearances.

13.

Better Printing for Less Money

Newcomers to publishing typically pay far more for the printing of their books and magazines than they should. In fact, unreasonably — and unnecessarily — high printing costs have jeopardized the profitability of many an otherwise strong project.

The time that you put into writing a book and the care with which you design it are valuable, of course, but at least these are not paid for with money directly out of your pocket. These are sweat equity elements. They cost you weeks of work but very little hard cash. Printing, on the other hand, *is* a cash transaction. It drains the bank account as well as the sweat glands, and it can do so very rapidly. For new accounts, especially for new accounts that are also new businesses, the printer will usually ask for at least 50% up front and the balance before shipping — or even on approval of blueline proofs.

So what do you do? How do you make sure that you are getting the best possible price? Simple, when you follow the rules and guidelines outlined in this chapter. By using these methods you can save thousands of dollars on printing costs, increase your profit margin dramatically, protect your all important cash flow, and often get a better product into the bargain.

A very valuable reference for understanding the trade terms and jargon you will have to learn as you get into periodical and book publishing is the Pocket Pal: A Graphic Arts Production Handbook. *The book is richly illustrated. You can obtain a copy from many paper and supply wholesalers, or you can order one directly from the publisher: International Paper Co., International Paper Plaza, 77 W. 45th St., New York, NY 10036.*

A SAD TALE

My first publishing project was a picture history of the city of Greenville. I was a quick study on research, wrote easily and clearly, and even had a pretty clear idea what I wanted my book to look like.

But when it came time to get it printed, I was in the dark. I was naive and uninformed about the whole production process. I figured that a printer was a printer, that they were all pretty much alike. I was ignorant and did not know it. As a result, hard experience taught me a very costly lesson.

It happened like this. I had a friend who owned a small print shop. I *knew* he was a good printer. How did I know it? Well, he printed the football programs for the university where I was teaching, didn't he?

We'll call my friend Jimmy. Jimmy's small company was staffed

217

by his wife as business manager, a receptionist-typographer, and Jimmy himself as master of the press room.

He had two small presses, a Multilith 1250 and an A.B. Dick 360. This machinery was perfectly adequate for the bulk of Jimmy's work, which consisted mainly of letterheads and envelopes, simple three-panel brochures, and a ton of football programs.

I took my book to Jimmy. Could he print it for me? I asked. He smiled and said, yes, he was just right for the job. And he gave me a price: $10,000. I had nothing whatsoever to compare Jimmy's price with, and I agreed to it. I figured that the generation of printing quotes was a science and that, no matter where I went, others would apply the same formula and come up with the same price.

Today, I know that I could have done the same job, far better, for under $5000. The extra five I paid came right out of my back pocket. By making a deal with Jimmy before I knew the rules of the game, I had cut my profit margin in half.

My friend was not ripping me off. He just did not have the equipment to do the job in the most economical way. Printing a 120 page, large format book on his small presses was a little like chopping down an oak forest with a penknife. It took him a long, long time to turn the job out and, as is the case in any business, Jimmy had to charge me for his time.

THE MORAL: ALL PRINTERS ARE NOT CREATED EQUAL

Printing, I would soon learn, is a highly specialized business when you get beyond the routine jobs that are the bread and butter of most small print shops. The local guy is a generalist. He has a few small pieces of equipment that can do a little of this and that, but such limited equipment is hard put to meet the needs of even the smallest publisher.

Books and magazines require million-dollar presses and sophisticated bindery equipment that work twenty-four hours a day, six and seven days a week. Because this equipment is built to do a certain kind of printing job — and to do it quickly, well, and efficiently — you will pay considerably less for the finished product. So much less, in fact, that when you start getting these quotes in you may at first find them hard to believe.

Where do you find such printers? I'll give you a list of some I know about later on in this chapter. Book printing specialists are national concerns and draw business from all over the country. There is a concentration of very good ones, for instance, in the Ann Arbor, Michigan area. One of the best known book printers, R.R. Donnelly, has plants across several states. And there are many others.

Short run magazine printers (say 100,000 copies and under) are more often regional. There are three in North Carolina and Virginia that I regularly request quotes from.

I would not know the best sources in Texas or California. You will have to trust in your own information network to ferret out their names. Word of mouth will be your best guide in this case. Ask other publishers where they get *their* magazines done, then call and ask for a quote on your own publication.

ALWAYS GET SEVERAL QUOTES

I would not want to take my book or magazine to a given printer before I had gotten and compared several quotes from shops whose work I respected. Prices will vary widely, frequently by as much as 20 or 30%, and sometimes by as much a 50 to 100%.

Why? Price differences are usually a function of work load and equipment. Sometimes a shop will need work, and the price quoted will be a little lower than usual. Sometimes the shop will be flooded with work and quote high. One company may have the equipment to do the entire job, including binding. Another may have to send it out to another shop for binding or other work. When this is the case, an unacceptable increase in cost almost always results.

Please note that I use the word "quote." I do not say "estimate." An estimate is useless for your purposes. A quote, on the other hand, is a firm price, a commitment to produce the work as described for a definite and agreed upon sum of money. If the specifications of the job do not change, the price quoted will not change.

An *estimate*, however, is another matter. An estimate represents nothing more than your printer's best guess as to what the completed job will cost. The final price may well — and probably will — be different from the estimated price. I have never, by the way, known a final charge to be less than an estimate. Somehow it is always higher.

Examples of widely varying quotes? Here is one. I recently asked for quotes on a newcomer's guide my company was publishing. It was a digest-sized publication, saddle-stitched on 60 lb. stock. I was ordering 50,000 books, each containing 112 pages in full color. The pre-press work was done by us, in house. All the printer had to do was make the plates and turn on the press. Yet one price from a large printer in Tennessee came in at $42,000. Another printer, in North Carolina, quoted $25,500 on *the very same job*. You be the judge. Was it worth my time to secure and compare multiple quotes? You bet your life it was.

A quote is furnished to you in written form, usually with an identifying number. It will be signed by a representative of the printing company and, typically, they will ask you to sign as well and return one copy to them. This document then becomes a binding agreement between you.

USE A PURCHASE ORDER

As a beginner in publishing I used to skip over some of the routine paperwork. This was another costly mistake. I assumed, in particular, that a one-man firm had no need to issue purchase orders to buy what it needed. And for small, routine purchases of supplies I may have been right. But for any major purchase I was very, very wrong.

A purchase order protects you against assorted extra or additional charges that a printer or other supplier might one day be tempted to add to your bill. It clearly and completely describes the product you are ordering (when buying printing you can reference the printer's quote number) and the price you will pay for it. You will not be obligated for any additional charges that you have not authorized in advance and in writing.

HOW TO GET A QUOTE

Your printer will need certain information to provide you with a firm quote. If you are new to the business it may be a bit tricky coming up with the specifications in the jargon of the printer, but there is no substitute for it. If you run into problems go by any local print shop and ask the owner for the information you need. Most will be glad to help, especially those from whom you have bought business cards or other routine materials. Other small publishers will usually be happy to give you a hand as well. Or give me a call at my office here in Washington, NC at (919) 975-2066. I'll be glad to help too.

QUOTATION

Client Name: _____

Title or Job Name:_____ Date:_____

Brief Description: _____

Quantity:_____

Pages: _____

Trim Size: _____

Text Paper:_____

Cover Stock: _____

Binding: ☐ Saddle Stitched ☐Perfect ☐Casebound ☐Sewn

Color: _____

Separations Provided ☐By Customer ☐

Typography, Art & Design _____

_____

Blue Lines: ☐ Yes ☐ No

Additional Specifications and Instructions:_____

_____

_____

_____

Total Price:_____ (plus freight and sales taxes, if any.)

_____

FREIGHT & POSTAGE — Billed at actual cost plus 5% handling charge or $5.00, whichever is greater unless shipped freight collect.

OVERRUNS OR UNDERRUNS — Overruns or underruns not to exceed 10% of the amount ordered shall constitute acceptable delivery and the excess of deficiency shall be charged or credited to the publisher at the overrun rate, not the unit rate.

Please sign and return the original copy of this quotation authorizing _____ to proceed with the manufacturing of this title. Note any changes in specifications and an amended quotation will be forwarded. See the reverse side for additional terms and conditions of this quotation.

Accepted by: _____ Date: _____

SETTING THE SPECIFICATIONS

Here is a rundown of the things that you will need to know about to "spec" your work for the printer.

Quantity

Do you know how many books you want to print? Probably. But each press may have slightly different price breaks. A book which costs $2 each on a run of 500 will cost only $1.50 on a run of 1000, and even less on a run of 2000 or more. At some point you will reach a level where the cost will even out so that there will be no further reductions in per unit cost based on larger quantities.

When asking for your quote you may specify several different quantities to determine which is most advantageous to you. When asked the question, "How many?" you might answer: "I'd like a quote on quantities of 1000, 2000, and 5000" or whatever numbers are appropriate to your project. You might also ask for a quote on quantities of, say, 3000, 5000, and additional thousands.

Trim Size

Trim size refers to the size of the pages themselves. When telling your printer which trim size you want, always let the first number represent the width of the page and the second number represent the height. "Nine by six" means nine inches wide and six inches high. "Six by nine," on the other hand, means six inches wide by nine inches high. (It can, by the way, be much more expensive to bind a book that is wider than it is high — a fact that I learned too late to save a sizeable chunk of my hard-earned cash.)

Certain trim sizes have become standard: 5½" x 8½"; 6" x 9"' and 8½" x 11". In general, you will save money by sticking to standard sizes. And you should be aware that on certain presses it may be considerably more economical to print a slight variation of these sizes. Ask your printer for his recommendation.

Number of Pages

The printer will want to know how many pages are in your book or magazine. There are methods of counting characters and determining the number of pages. Reference books and manuals are available to help you do this. A better way is to typeset it *before* you ask for your quote and determine the number of pages precisely.

Keep in mind that all publications are printed in *signatures*. The word "signature" refers to the pages printed on both sides of a single

PURCHASE ORDER

Purchase Number _____ Date _____ / _____ / _____

Purchase order to:

Job Title:

Description of job:

Special Instructions:

Quantity: _____

Schedule: _____

_____

Price Quote: _____

Authorized Signature: _____ / _____ / _____

For more information or questions please contact: _____
at

Please sign and return to

sheet as it goes through the press. This sheet is then folded, collated with other signatures, trimmed, and bound into your publication.

Some small presses may run signatures of eight pages or even four. Most of the larger presses, however, will run signatures of 8, 16, or even 32 pages, depending on the trim size.

Your page count needs to be in even multiples of eight or, in the best case, in even multiples of the basic signature size that your printer uses. When this is not done you may quickly incur needless additional expense. A 64 page magazine is fine. A 58 page or 66 page magazine would get you into real trouble.

With a little experience, such basic planning considerations will become second nature to you. In the beginning, though, you will have to plan carefully and carry on a continuing dialogue with your printer to come up with the best and most affordable size.

Text Stock

The text stock is simply the paper on which the book is printed. Text stock has four main characteristics. The first is weight. The weight of the paper is measured in pounds. The most common text weight is 60 lb. stock. If you desire pages that are heavier you will order a 70 lb. or 80 lb. paper. Very bulky publications — the Sears catalog, for instance — may be printed on a 35 or 40 lb. stock or lighter.

As a publisher you will need samples of available paper stocks so that you can judge the best weight (as well as other characteristics) for your book. You can obtain such samples by contacting a wholesale paper vendor. Such companies will be listed in the Yellow Pages under "Paper Distributors." Contact one of these companies and identify yourself as a publisher. Ask them for a sample kit. They will usually be happy to furnish such samples to you in the hope that you will specify their paper when you ask for a quote. I have on hand now two complete sets of such samples, one from Unijax, Inc., and one from the Henly Paper Company.

The color of the stock is the next characteristic to be considered. Some text stocks are highly bleached and very white. I find these papers hard on the eyes. Unbleached or "natural" stocks have an off-white and sometimes even an eggshell appearance. I find these easier to read and more restful to the eyes. You can, of course, get papers in all colors, but these are seldom used in publications.

Surface qualities are important. Some papers are shiny; some are dull. Shiny stocks are said to be "coated," or "enameled." Slick paper magazines are printed on such stock.

BETTERWAY PUBLICATIONS, INC.

P.O. BOX 219, CROZET, VA 22932 ■ (804) 823-5661

REQUEST FOR QUOTATION

DATE:	July 9, 1990
JOB:	160: How to Make $100,000 a Year in DTP
TRIM SIZE:	8½x11" (binds on 11" side)
PAGES:	280 (includes front and back matter)
COPY:	Text: camera ready without bleeds; 12 halftones Cover: camera ready with bleeds
PAPER STOCK*:	Text: 60# Lakewood White, 456 ppi Cover: 12 pt C1S
PRESS:	Text: offset press; black ink throughout Cover: covers 1 and 4 print 1 PMS color + black + liquid lamination
BINDING:	Adhesive paper cover
PROOFS:	Text: Complete bluelines Cover: Blueline or color key
QUOTE:	4,000 plus extra 1,000s 300 extra covers, trimmed, shipped flat. Working days from receipt of copy to delivery Terms

* Please supply sample of recommended stock if other than specified.

Over/underrun not to exceed 10%.

Please use book code number in all quotations, correspondence, and billing.

All boards and artwork to be returned within 30 days of printing. Please save plates/negatives for reprint.

KINDLY NOTE SHIPPING ADDRESSES:

For Ups, Fed Ex, Or Purolator: Rt. 2, Box 180 (Rt. 811, off 680)
                                 Charlottesville, VA 22901

For truck shipments over 150 lbs.: The Very Idea Building (lower level)
                                   Route 250 West
                                   Crozet, VA 22932

Thank you,

Most book stocks are not coated. As I write this I have two publications at press. One, a magazine, I had quoted on "60 lb. coated stock." The other, a book of poetry, I had quoted on "60 lb. natural."

The bulk of the paper is the final consideration. Book paper, especially, is rated as to its bulk in pages per inch (ppi). You may be concerned about the thickness of your book. If you want it thicker you will choose a stock that bulks out at fewer pages per inch. If you want it thinner you will choose a paper that bulks out at a greater number.

I recently had a problem with a book of poetry. To bind it in the way I wanted (perfect bound) I needed to have a book of a certain thickness. The paper I had chosen did not have sufficient bulk. My printer suggested another stock of the same weight but with a bulk rating that gave me more thickness per page. The problem was solved when I switched to the higher bulk paper.

Cover Stock

If your book is to be paperbound you will have to choose a cover stock. Cover stocks are measured in "points," with 8 pt. and 10 pt. being the most common. There will be a wide variety of cover stocks available for inspection in your paper sample kit. If your publication is going to be sold in a bookstore, you will have to be sure that your book looks and feels like all the others — and better, if possible. For this reason I recommend a coated cover stock which will then be "laminated" (or some equivalent process — these things change all the time) to get that extra-shiny appearance that is so popular today.

If you are printing a magazine you may also choose a cover stock that is heavier than the text stock. Most magazines, however, are "self-covered." The covers are simply a part of the text itself and of the same stock. When you ask for your quote you will specify, for instance: "64 pages plus cover," or "64 pages self-covered." The self-covered magazines are always much less expensive.

Binding

A book can be bound in several ways.

Saddle-stitched. Most magazines are saddle-stitched (stapled along the spine). Most books of forty-eight or fewer pages are saddle-stitched as well, because their bulk is too slight to support other binding methods.

Perfect bound. Perfect bound books and magazines are squared off at the spine and glued. *Playboy* magazine, once saddle-stitched, is now perfect bound. Almost every paperback you will find on the shelves of a bookstore is perfect bound.

Perfect bound books are generally considered better looking and more prestigious than saddle-stitched books, although there may not be an enormous difference in the cost of the two methods. Much depends on the equipment owned by the printer. I recently had a job quoted for 50,000 copies of a 128 page magazine. The price for perfect binding was actually $2000 less than the price for saddle-stitching.

Casebound. This is the standard term for a hardcover book. A "case" is manufactured, covered with the cloth which you will have chosen, and embossed with the name of the book, the author, the publisher, etc. The printed text is inserted into the case and attached to it with glue.

The pages of casebound books may be *sewn* or *glued*. For library use and reference use, sewn books are generally preferred, but the glues in use today are so much improved that many publishers are choosing this method for books that would almost surely have been sewn just a few years ago. The glueing process is less expensive.

Casebinding can add $2.00 or more per book to your production costs, depending on 1) the number of books you are ordering; 2) the price of the cloth you choose; and 3) the area on the cover that you will emboss with the title, publisher, etc. You will also incur the added expense of a dust jacket.

The other side of this coin is that hardback books, which may cost only two or three dollars more to produce than paperbacks, can be sold for twice as much money at retail and sometimes more.

Whether to publish a hardcover edition is really a marketing decision. Perhaps you might consider a *split run*, taking 1500 in paper and 500 (for the library market) in hardcover — or whatever variation of these percentages you consider appropriate.

There is growing acceptance of the so-called *quality paperback* as a substitute for the hardcover, especially for a book that is essentially a handbook or manual. An illustrated city history, on the other hand, would probably do better in a signed and numbered hardcover "collector's" edition. You could sell these for $30 or $40 in hardcover. It would be difficult to break the $20 barrier in paperback. And remember that your actual cost difference will be just a few dollars per book.

Endsheets

Endsheets are glued into casebound books, and in at least one instance, I have seen them used very effectively in a perfect bound book. The endsheet is a heavier stock. One side is glued to the inside of the cover and the other is glued along the fold to the text pages. The remainder of the endsheet constitutes the first turnable leaf in the book, though it is not counted as a page. You can specify that endpapers match the cover cloth in color, which gives a very nice effect. Or you can specify that the endpapers match the text.

Endpapers can also be printed before being bound in — with a map, for instance, or other art that is closely related to the text.

The Blueline

The blueline is a cheaply produced proof copy of your publication. It is made from the very film that will be used in the printing process, so the blueline is identical to the finished product with respect to page order and the text on each page. The printer will ask whether or not you want "blues" (short for bluelines). You should tell him that you do.

The blueline represents a small additional expense and it extends production time a bit, but it is an essential check. In theory every typographical error will have been caught and corrected long before you reach the blueline stage. And perhaps for a single typo you will not want to make a change this far along in the production process. But if you have misspelled the business name of your largest advertiser or if the printer has inexplicably gotten your pages out of sequence this is your last chance to do something about it. I have discovered many, many a potentially ruinous error in bluelines and I have remedied them. Whenever I have let a pressing deadline tempt me into skipping the blueline stage I have lived to regret it. You will too.

Color

Your printer will want to know whether you are using color in your publication, and if so, how much and where. If you are doing a magazine and have some pages of full-color ads and many more of black and white, your printer will be happy to furnish you with a *page imposition format* and tell you where you can place the color most economically. If possible you will want to place color on the pages printed on the same side of a signature sheet.

Halftones

The word "halftone" refers to the process by which black and white photographs are made ready for printing. The printer will want to know how many of these you will have. If you are uncertain of the number, you ask him for a *price per halftone*.

Bleeds

When ink is applied up to the very edge of the printed page it is said to *bleed*. There is a small extra charge for bleeds, and your printer will want to know how many you have designed into your book. Bleeds are far more common in full-color magazines but do appear from time to time in books — on the cover, for instance, of a paperbound book.

THE MAGIC QUESTION

When you have gotten your quotes and reviewed them, you will choose one. At this point ask your printer the magic question: "I like your quote," you say, "and we'd like to send this job to you, but we're still a little over budget. Is there any way that you can see that we could whittle this price down a bit?" And if he asks you by how much, do not hesitate to give him a number to aim for.

At this point several things may happen. The worst of these is that you will be told that no reduction is possible. You may be pleasantly surprised, however, at how deft printer's account reps can be in showing you how to save a little money when they think it is to their advantage for you to do so. Sometimes it is simply a rationalized price reduction that you have given them a face-saving way of offering to you. At other times a production department can suggest very real ways to format your publication and achieve significant cost savings. It may be merely a question of where you place your color photographs. Or it may be a slight adjustment in the number of pages.

On Ordering Printing
You may not get the exact number of books you order from your printer. There is spoilage in every operation from press setup to folding to binding. The trade customs of the printing trade generally allow the printer to deliver up to 10% more or fewer books than the specified quantity. Of course, you will be charged for the "overs" or credited for the "unders."

Sometimes, believe it or not, the addition of *extra* pages can actually result in a price drop because the larger number will better fit the presses and trimming and bindery equipment that a printer has. I recently increased a publication from 56 to 64 pages because the latter number saved a substantial amount of money in production charges.

Occasionally you will discover that your printer will have a new piece of equipment that is more efficient and that works more quickly and better. Since you did not know about this equipment, you did not specify your publication for it. The sales or service rep may be able to tell you how to prepare your work for this press and benefit from the lower cost that higher efficiency brings.

This PROPOSAL prepared   3/9/90   is for the exclusive use

of

      2409 S. Charles St.
      Greenville, NC 27858

      Attn: Tom Williams

It is subject to your acceptance in 30 days, to credit approval by Courier Printing Co., Inc. and to the PRINTING TRADE CUSTOMS on the back of this form.

Prices are based on current paper costs. Since paper manufacturers' current policy is to "bill at price prevailing at time of shipment," we must pass on price increases when they occur. We will always attempt to guarantee prices at the time your order is placed.

ITEM:	20,000 NORTH CAROLINA EAST
SIZE:	56 pages self cover, page size 8 3/8 X 10 7/8
PAPER:	60# white Surfa enamel
INK:	4 color process throughout
BINDING:	Saddle stitch with 2 stitches, skid pack.
PREPRESS:	You will furnish single page negatives to us.
PRICE:	20,000 @ $732.20/M

Jerry Cooper
Jerry Cooper

This proposal is F.O.B.   Smyrna, TN   Our terms are net with payment due the 10th of the following month. Accounts 20 days past due are subject to 1½% service charge.

I accept your Proposal on behalf of _____ on _____

                                        by _____

REQUEST FOR QUOTE

Small publishers often fill out a "Request for Quote" form, which they then send to the printers from whom they are seeking prices. This form is especially useful today when facsimile communication is becoming so widespread. You simply fax your quote form to the printer and he is able to begin work on it almost immediately. There is no two to three day delay in the mails and there are no misunderstandings. It's all there, in black and white: paper, quantities, binding . . . everything.

Nevertheless, I must say that I have had very good luck getting my quotes by phone. I telephone my contact at the print shop, read my specs, and ask him to get back to me as quickly as possible, with both a price and a turnaround time. (Often the price will be right, but it may take longer to produce your publication than you can afford to wait.)

I ask that the quote be telephoned back to me as soon as it is ready. This call will then be followed by the quote in written form. I never do business without a written quote, on my form or theirs.

STAY ON SCHEDULE

At any print shop, but especially at the larger ones, schedules are important. Press time is scheduled well in advance. If you promise that your camera ready copy will arrive on a certain day, do everything in your power to see that it does so. If you are going to be delayed, and you know this in advance, call the printer at once and reschedule.

If your work does not arrive at the printer's facility on time, it creates major problems. At the very least you risk being bumped from your spot on the printing schedule. Another job will be moved up and it may be days or even weeks before your turn comes around again.

Printers have long memories. They have their own business to protect. If you develop a reputation for not getting your materials in as scheduled, the printer will not be as likely to do rush production for you when you truly need it. He is also likely to ease his prices up a bit to cover the loss of time that occurs due to last minute press changes.

TRADE CUSTOMS

You should be aware of the "Customs of the Printing Trade." These trade customs define the relationship between the printer and the printer's clients in many important areas, and they are usually explicitly or implicitly made a part of any agreement between printer and client. Typography studios, by the way, also have their trade customs.

SOME PRINTERS I RECOMMEND

Listed below are the names, addresses, and telephone numbers of printers with whom I have done business in the past, and whose services I have used and highly recommend. There are doubtless many other good shops out there, and I encourage you to investigate those in your part of the country. At the very least the quotes you elicit from those on this list will give you a standard by which to judge the prices and services that others will offer you.

Book Printers

Crane Duplicating Service, Inc.
PO Box 487, Barnstable, ME
(508) 362-2441

This is an unusual source for a highly specialized product. Crane provides bound review copies for galleys for most major publishers, but their work is also suitable for short runs of paperback books, as long as you can be satisfied with the very basic cover and text stocks available and a very basic level of printing. I will use them for a short-run poetry series that I am currently planning. I am also test marketing a 64 page specialized paperback that is being sold by mail order. Crane is printing 100 of these for me for less than $150. If the book pulls orders as expected I will take it to another press for a much longer press run.

McNaughton and Gunn
PO Box 2030
Ann Arbor, MI 48106
(313) 429-5411

An excellent source for both paperbacks and casebound books. Careful, with great attention to detail.

Bookcrafters
140 Buchanan Street
Chelsea, MI 48118
(313) 475-9145
Paperback and casebound books. Rock bottom prices. There are sometimes communication problems between Bookmasters, which sells Bookcrafters' services, and Bookcrafters offices.

R.R. Donnelly & Sons
2223 Martin Luther King Drive
Chicago, IL 60616
(312) 326-8000
(main office)
An old, established printer with very wide capabilities. Has plants in many locations across the country. Can handle any print run. Sometimes (in my experience) a bit higher than some others on super short runs, but the quality is superb. Offers very valuable *Book Planning Guide* to publishers. Ask for a copy.

Magazine Printers

Hickory Printing Group, Inc.
PO Box 69
Hickory, NC 28603
(800) 222-4171
I have been doing business with Hickory for a number of years. For jobs that fit their presses (half webs) Hickory is, in my experience, unsurpassed in quality. Their quotes are consistently the most favorable that I get. Does not do perfect binding. Strong customer service.

William Byrd Press, Inc.
2901 Byrdhill Road
PO Box 27481
Richmond, VA 23261
A major shop for magazine printing. Can handle the longest runs and is capable of printing 32 page signatures on its full web presses. Very competitive in pricing, especially on perfect bound magazines. Quality is second to none.

14.

Making Money from Secondary Profit Centers

My wife Christina owns a ballet school. Her principal source of income comes from the monthly tuition fees that her students pay for their instruction. This tuition income is sufficient to pay all her expenses and generate a comfortable income in addition.

But from time to time she develops other sources of income. At recital time, for instance, she photographs each student in costume and sells these photos to the parents. The sale of these photos is a nice *secondary profit center*. It is not her main job. Teaching ballet is. But it is available to her because she is in the ballet business. The opportunity to sell the photographs simply comes her way, and she takes advantage of it.

THE PLEASURES OF "CHUNK MONEY"

Secondary profit centers will come your way, too, once you become known as a publisher. These can be very important to you as you work to build income from your publications. Later on you will want to leave by the wayside some of the more marginally profitable of your sidelines. But you will surely want to keep others. In addition to the magazines I currently publish I have been asked to develop a sixteen page image-enhancing publication for a five county consortium in my part of the state. This consortium came to me because they had seen and liked my regional magazine, *NCEast*.

The contract will bring in about $5000 in profit. I can do the project with the same facilities and free-lancers I use in my other work. There are no ads to sell, no risks to take. The client is simply paying me for my expertise. The money, needless to say, is a very welcome addition to my bank account, the kind of usable lump sum cash that James R. Cook, in his book *Start-up Entrepreneur*, calls "chunk money."

There is not enough of this kind of work available for me to do it full time. For me the custom design of publications for others is a very profitable *secondary profit center* that I will continue to take advantage of as long as I am in business.

You will be aware of secondary profit centers available to you because of your particular combination of talents and publishing activities. Here are some that have been important to me.

PRINT BROKERING

In the chapter on buying printing, you learned that small local print shops do not have the equipment to handle most publication work economically. From time to time you will get a call from someone who wants you to print a publication for them. Often this is a paperbound or hardcover book. Because you know where to get the best prices you can often get such a favorable price from your printer that you can mark the job up 30 to 40%, quote this to the customer, and still come in under the price that the local printer has quoted. Sometimes the customer will not even have gone to the trouble of getting another quote. You can also handle any design or typography work that needs to be done to get the book ready for the printer.

Get It in Writing

You should take care to undertake such projects only when you have a signed agreement in hand and when you have taken the trouble to determine that your client is credit-worthy. One reason this person may be coming to you is that no other print shop will give him credit. I never take on such an assignment without a credit check and a substantial advance payment of no less than a third. Half is better. I also insist that the final payment — I make exceptions for large companies of impeccable credentials — be made prior to shipping the completed print job.

I have never lost money on such a job but I certainly could, if I did not take the necessary precautions. Often there is a fairly large sum of money involved, so that a single sour deal would be a damaging blow for you. Handled carefully, though, print brokering can be a nifty secondary profit center.

Utilize "Printers to the Trade"

A customer goes into the neighborhood print shop and orders 1000 business cards. A week later he returns, picks up his cards, and pays his bill. He assumes that his cards were printed locally. He would be surprised to learn that they were actually printed 2000 miles away in Mankato, Minnesota, headquarters of the Carlson Craft company.

The same company can provide local printers with letterheads, envelopes, business forms, and many other products — all at wholesale prices. It also specializes in the printing of wedding invitations.

The truth is that many routine printing jobs are done by

"printers to the trade," highly specialized print shops that do work sent in by small printers who pay for them at discounts of 40% and more.

You can use the services of these wholesale houses, too. While you may or may not want to bother with single business card orders, where the typical profit ranges from $10 to $30, orders that include business cards, letterheads and envelopes, statements and invoices, and perhaps a logo design can certainly be worthwhile.

Since you will have a great deal of contact with many businesses, large and small, while selling advertising and doing feature articles, you will be in a position to pick up such orders. You can get other leads by reading the newspaper carefully for stories about business start-ups and looking over the new business license applications at the local register of deeds office.

You can check the back pages of trade magazines like *Printing Impressions* and *American Printer* where the printers to the trade advertise. You will find everything available there from the paper products mentioned above to embossed foil labels and four color presentation folders.

CAPABILITIES BROCHURES

With the capabilities brochure we get into the higher levels of income potential from secondary profit centers. Such a project gives you the opportunity to make money in several ways. You can profit from writing, from design, and from brokering the printing of the job.

A capabilities brochure is a company's chief sales piece, and it must be very well done. Elsewhere in this book I emphasized the necessity of an impressive capabilities brochure for your own company.

The customer is usually willing to pay whatever it takes to get the job done right. He is not, however, interested in wasting money. The advertising agencies that will compete for such jobs are likely to be much more expensive than you will have to be. You can do a 100% mark-up and still be competitive. Agencies typically have a much higher overhead than you will have, and they will be staffed with highly paid graphic artists. You will be using free-lancers for the most part, and you do not have to maintain the expensive image in your offices that the ad agency does. For the agency, remember, such brochures represent primary rather than secondary profit centers.

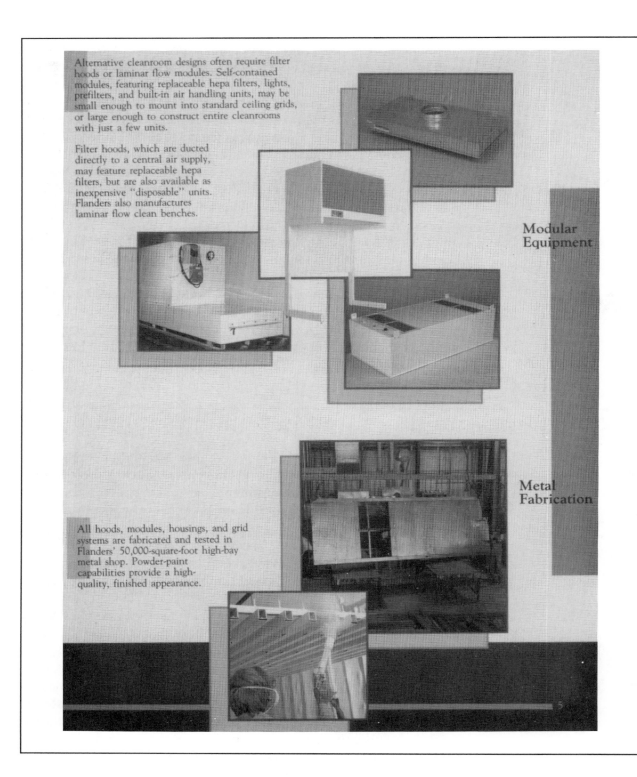

Alternative cleanroom designs often require filter hoods or laminar flow modules. Self-contained modules, featuring replaceable hepa filters, lights, prefilters, and built-in air handling units, may be small enough to mount into standard ceiling grids, or large enough to construct entire cleanrooms with just a few units.

Filter hoods, which are ducted directly to a central air supply, may feature replaceable hepa filters, but are also available as inexpensive "disposable" units. Flanders also manufactures laminar flow clean benches.

Modular
Equipment

Metal
Fabrication

All hoods, modules, housings, and grid systems are fabricated and tested in Flanders' 50,000-square-foot high-bay metal shop. Powder-paint capabilities provide a high-quality, finished appearance.

They have much less room to play around with pricing since they have to factor a major portion of their overhead into their quotes on such work. Your own overhead is covered by your publishing business.

I am talking about full-fledged, multi-page capabilities brochures. The small, three-panel jobs will not be profitable for you, and your prices will not be competitive. Any print shop can, and will, throw one of these together at rock-bottom prices, often including the (admittedly unimaginative) design work into the bargain at no charge. Stay away from these. They bring too much grief for too little money.

PRODUCT CATALOGS

Once you have assembled the necessary talent — whether free-lance or in-house — you can begin to keep an eye out for work designing and producing product catalogs for your clients.

Product catalogs are photography and design intensive, and the printing is likely to be expensive. You will be dealing with a considerable sum of money, so no matter what your percentage of mark-up you are likely to make a good profit on the job.

Another nice thing about such jobs is that they tend to be repeated. If you do a good job at a competitive price this year, the client will come to you again next year for an update. Sometimes you will get requests to reprint the very same catalog.

ANNUAL REPORTS

Corporations that are publicly traded must prepare annual reports for their shareholders. These reports are typically showpieces of design and printing. If the shareholders knew how much the report actually cost them, they might decide to instruct management to send out photocopied sheets with the same information on them.

But, happily for you, they do not do this, and the fancy, expensive annual report has become a fixture in American business. Your clients will be those corporations that are large enough to require such an annual report but small enough that they do not have an ad agency or a public relations firm on retainer.

Utility Trailers

LU 4X8 with sides extra

LU 6X10

LU 4X8

LU 6X12 T

MODEL	BED SIZE	CAP	TIRE SIZE	HUBS	SPINDLE	BETWEEN FENDERS	DECK	WOOD SIDES	FENDERS	BRAKES	TONGUE JACK	AUTO LUBES
LU 700	4x6	600	480x8 OR Equal	4 H	1 1/16	48"	N/A	N/A	Square	N/A	OPT	OPT
LU 4x8	4x8	1000	480x8 OR Equal	4 H	1 1/16	48"	OPT	OPT	Square	N/A	OPT	OPT
LU 5x8	5x8	1200	480x8 OR Equal	4 H	1 1/16	72"	STD	OPT	Square	N/A	OPT	OPT
LU 5x10	5x10	1800	20.5x10 L/C OR Equal	5 H	1 3/8	60"	STD	N/A	Square	N/A	OPT	OPT
LU 6x10	6x10	1800	20.5x10 L/C OR Equal	5 H	1 3/8	72"	STD	N/A	Square	N/A	OPT	OPT
LU 6x12	6x12	2000	F78x14 OR Equal	5 H	1 3/8	72"	STD	N/A	Round	OPT	OPT	OPT
LU 5x10 T	5x10	2500	20.5x10 L/B OR Equal	4 H	1 1/16	60"	STD	N/A	Square	N/A	OPT	OPT
LU 6x10 T	6x10	2500	20.5x10 L/B OR Equal	4 H	1 1/16	72"	STD	N/A	Square	N/A	OPT	OPT
LU 6x12 T	6x12	5000	F78x14 OR Equal	5 H	1 3/8	72"	STD	N/A	Round	OPT	OPT	OPT
LU 6x14 T	6x14	5000	F78x14 OR Equal	5 H	1 3/8	72"	STD	N/A	Round	OPT	OPT	OPT
LU 6x16 T	6x16	5000	F78x14 OR Equal	5 H	1 3/8	72"	STD	N/A	Round	OPT	OPT	OPT

Pontoon Boat Trailer

PT 2700-G

LONG TRAILER CO., INC.
PRICES ARE F.O.B. TARBORO, N.C.   RFD #2 BOX 1
PHONE 823-8104   TARBORO, N.C. 27886
AREA CODE 919

LONG TRAILER CO., INC. reserves the right to change construction, specifications, prices and terms without notice and without obligation as to trailers already shipped and sold.

There are many such firms. Local and regional banks and savings and loan institutions are excellent prospects. Your proposal will have to be made to the corporate headquarters. If you live on the east coast and discover that the corporate headquarters of the business in question is in Los Angeles, then you cannot service that prospect.

In my area the giant, multi-national drug manufacturing firm Burroughs-Wellcome has its American headquarters nearby. But it is obviously too large a company for my small firm to approach successfully. On the other hand, a new regional system of banks has just begun to do business. This is a prime candidate for my company. So is the small plastics manufacturing firm that has set up shop in the industrial park nearby, and there are many others.

How much time do you spend prospecting such potential customers? I find that a phone call or two, each day, to purchasing agents or others in charge of getting the reports, catalogs, and capabilities brochures done, will land an opportunity to make a proposal and generate as much of this kind of work as I can handle.

If you find that you are really good at getting this kind of business and producing documents that please your clients, you can profitably spend more and more time doing it. It could in time move up from secondary to primary profit center or become the nucleus of a separate business.

BUSINESS DOCUMENTS

There are many business documents that owners and managers require but which they cannot themselves generate. Usually a limited number of copies is needed, so printing is not an important factor in the cost. It is the writing and desktop design services that you will provide.

A short time ago a young entrepreneur came to my office. He had developed an idea for a chain of fast food restaurants that he would place in shopping malls throughout the region. In order to franchise his idea he had to develop a complete operations manual. He asked if we could help, and we immediately said that we could.

The entrepreneur, whom I will call Stan, was not a writer. It is doubtful if he had ever even written a long letter. But he was a man of action and knew the fast food business from top to bottom. Since Stan could not generate even a rough draft of his ideas for me to revise, I took another approach. I interviewed him and got everything down on tape. Some sections he dictated into my recorder while driving from one of his business locations to another. I transcribed all of this material and edited it.

This constituted the first rough draft. I then gave it to Stan for revision. He dictated new passages, filled in the blanks, and we followed the same process through again. After we had a second draft, I asked him to have his operations manager, his attorney, and his accountant read through the manual and add their own notes. Their observations were noted and their additions duly incorporated into the text.

I then generated a final proof copy. After correcting the typos and making a few minor textual changes, this became the final version. Stan signed the authorization to print form that I always use, and I printed the operations manual and had it bound in looseleaf form so that later additions and changes could be made easily. There were just fifty copies.

Since I am a writer and had time to take it on, I did the manual myself. Had I not been a writer, I could easily have assigned it to a free-lancer. My profit on this job, after all expenses, was several thousand dollars. In a major metropolitan area I would have made much more than that, but of course my overhead would have been much greater and my chances of getting the job reduced because of the more competitive environment.

There are many other such business documents that you can generate. Two that I have found profitable are business plans and employee manuals.

Business Plans

The business plan is a key document for any business, especially any new business. The care and professionalism with which it is written and designed will favorably influence the decisions of bankers and others important to the financial success of the enterprise.

The business plan is also important to the entrepreneur himself, since it is his own map of the commercial terrain he intends to conquer and his guidebook to the way his business should operate and grow.

I have developed many business plans over the years for my own businesses, so I have learned what the elements of a good one are. When developing a business plan for a client I often use the same interview method that I used with Stan and his fast food franchise. I

"Spin-off is an important concept. Re-packaging the same information for various markets will bring in more money . . . Magazine articles may be extracted from a book, book chapters may be used as a basis for a conference workshop, a series of magazine articles may be combined into a book, or the book may be re-written and directed toward a new audience. With a computer, it is easy to pull out part of the book and add an introduction and a conclusion."

Dan Poynter
The Self-Publishing Manual

simply ask the appropriate questions and help the client work through his ideas to develop good answers. I am not a lawyer, so I steer clear of giving hard legal advice. But I do get the facts down in such a way that they become clear to any interested reader.

From time to time I insert house ads in one of my own magazines offering a business plan service. Each time I place the ad it draws a couple of responses from entrepreneurs who become paying clients. Many of these people are under-financed, so you cannot always get top dollar for your work. Nevertheless, it is a profitable sideline, a financial gap-filler par excellence.

Another approach is to work with accountants. You call on them, make them aware of your capabilities, and ask for the opportunity to do their business plans (and annual reports of their clients) for them. Often they will be very happy to farm their work out, and they will pay well for the service.

The accountant deals with the customer, you deal only with the accountant. As a result you know from the very beginning precisely what is to be included in the plan, and you are furnished with raw copy that is usually in pretty fair form. You simply take and edit this, design the financial tables, graphs, spreadsheets, etc., and provide the accountant with the necessary number of copies.

Employee Manuals

There comes a time when every growing business needs an employee and operations manual. For larger enterprises these are separate documents, but for smaller businesses they are easily combined. My own company uses the combined version.

In the first months we simply communicated our company policies, procedures, and benefits to each new person individually. There came a time, however, when this was no longer sufficient. We are still a very small firm by many standards. But I do delegate some authority to those who work for me. I do not always see everyone every day. I needed a written statement of what I offered my employees and what I expected from them.

An employee manual is very simple to do. You can prepare a questionnaire for your client and put together the manual by collating and rewriting his answers to your questions. There are many good books on this subject that will provide an outline for you of what should be included. The Small Business Administration has a free booklet on this subject.

DEVELOP A SEMINAR

If you have a flair for speaking and think well on your feet, you can put together a menu of two to three hour seminars that you can do under the sponsorship of your Chamber of Commerce, the Small Business Center of your local community college, or some other agency.

The seminars you give will grow out of your background and abilities. They are generally directed toward small business people. Sample topics might be: "How to Advertise for Success"; "How to Market Your Services"; "How to Prepare a Business Plan"; "How to Write an Employee Manual"; "How to Position Your Product or Service in the Marketplace"; "How to Design and Publish a Company Newsletter or Magazine"; and many others in the same vein.

You can profit from these seminars in two ways. First of all, you get paid the usual fee as seminar presenter. In addition to this you make contact with business people who are impressed by your knowledge of the subject, unsure of their own, and who will contract with you to prepare the materials that they need.

Since I spent some years in the classroom before becoming a publisher, seminars are right down my line. I enjoy doing them and find the fees I earn to be quite pleasant additions to my bank account. I have prepared a separate brochure for my seminars under a company name.

GHOST WRITING AND EDITING

This kind of work just appears on your doorstep from time to time. There is usually not much you can do to attract it. If you live in a town where a good deal of scientific research is going on, you can let the researchers know that you are available to rewrite their scientific papers.

I have done this kind of work profitably, although it was often more time consuming than I anticipated. You have to be careful to deal only with those who can afford your services. I ghosted an "autobiography" for which I had a wonderful collection of memoirs, diaries, and letters to draw upon. My subject was a good natural writer, and this helped. I set the fee at $10,000. Based on the time it took, I should have asked $20,000 or more. Next time I will know better.

On shorter jobs I generally will work for $50 an hour. The client usually wants a firm price, so I estimate how long it will take and multiply that figure by my hourly rate. Ghost writing requires concentrated effort and attention. To try to do it at a fire-sale rate is neither possible nor profitable.

BE A CONSULTANT

I occasionally send a mailing piece to CEOs and purchasing agents in my area advertising my services as a publications consultant. I also find it worthwhile to advertise these services in the pages of my more prestigious magazines.

As a consultant I help business, government, and industrial clients develop publications that accomplish the goals that they set for them. I develop editorial formats and physical formats. I show them how to write, edit, lay out, and print their publications. I help them set up schedules and procedures that assure a timely, quality product. All of these services are very valuable, and I find that whenever a client who does need my services comes my way he is generally willing to pay a reasonable price for them.

For those who want to read up on the consulting business I recommend the books of Herman Holtz, starting with *How to Succeed as an Independent Consultant* (John Wiley & Sons, 1983).

GIVING A QUOTE

When you are selling an ad for a publication, the terms of the purchase are clearly set forth in your rate card. Your insertion order, or contract, gives all the details. Almost anything that can happen is covered in it: price, payment terms, ad size, etc.

Financial understandings with your secondary profit center activities should be just as clear, otherwise you risk trouble. Verbal agreements are too easily misinterpreted. We all remember the terms of an agreement differently — and generally in our own favor. Ambiguity has no place in a financial transaction. You need a written agreement signed by you and by your client specifying *precisely* what goods and services you agree to deliver and what sum of money your client agrees to pay for them, and how and when payment is due.

The following is a simple agreement that has worked for me. It is very adaptable. As many items as necessary may be added to the list.

INSERTION ORDER

Advertiser's Name _____

Address _____
_____

Ad Size
- ☐ sixth page
- ☐ third page
- ☐ half page
- ☐ two thirds page
- ☐ full page
- ☐ business card size
- ☐ amplified listing

- ☐ process color
- ☐ spot color
- ☐ special position
- ☐ creative services

DATE _____

SALESPERSON _____

Explanations and Instructions _____
_____
_____
_____

————————————— **AD COPY** —————————————

Authorized By (Print) _____

Title _____

Signature _____

Accounts are due and payable on publication. Advertiser must provide copy by closing date, otherwise an advertisement will be inserted on behalf of the advertiser. Publisher not responsible for typographical errors when ad copy has been approved by advertiser. Publisher's liability is limited to the cost of the space involved.

PREPARATION BEGINS EARLY
WHAT IS YOUR PUBLICATION WORTH?
WHAT YOU ARE SELLING
THE SELLING PACKAGE
STRUCTURING THE DEAL
CAN BUSINESS BROKERS HELP?

15.

Selling Out for Pleasure and Profit

One of the benefits of being a periodical publisher is that when your magazine or weekly newspaper is successful it becomes a valuable property in the publishing marketplace. You can expect that from time to time, especially after you have come out for two or three years and established a track record of profitability, you will have an occasional nibble from some individual or company who wants to buy you out.

I was in my third year as publisher of my weekly newspaper when one of the large chains began to buy up newspapers in my part of the state. Eventually their interest turned to my newspaper, and I had a brief telephone call from the president of the chain. Would I be interested in selling? he wanted to know. Since I had already considered putting the newspaper on the market, I replied that I was. He asked me what my circulation base was. I told him. He asked if all those readers were actually paid subscribers. I said yes, they were. He asked me how much I wanted. I replied that my previous year's gross was a certain amount of dollars and that I would take that amount for my paper. He replied that that sounded okay to him and, in fact, six weeks later I was sitting in the conference room of my bank filling out and signing an impressive stack of papers and getting, in return, a check for a very substantial sum of money.

PREPARATION BEGINS EARLY

Selling out is something you can just let happen, as I did in this case, or make happen. Either way somebody, someday is going to offer to buy one of your publications. When that happens you want to be ready. Some of the most important things you can do with an eye to profiting from the sale of your publication are done in the very beginning, as you organize your business.

Here is a prime example. Under U.S. tax laws, the money that is made from the sale of a corporate asset is taxed as a capital gain of the corporation, not as ordinary income to you. You will still have to get the money out of the corporate account and into yours before you can spend any of it.

There have been times when tax rates on capital gains were very much lower than any other rate. When I sold my newspaper, treatment of capital gains income was very favorable. After the Tax Reform Act of 1986, those benefits largely disappeared.

Your accountant needs to be aware that you want to be set up to take maximum advantage of any possible sale. He will study your financial situation and make recommendations. One thing that he will probably recommend is that you organize as an "S" corporation rather than as a regular "C" corporation. That way you can avoid double taxation.

What is double taxation? Well, if you are set up as a regular corporation and sell off an asset such as a magazine, it is the corporation that makes the money from the sale, not you. This is true even if you own every single one of the outstanding shares. So the corporation pays whatever taxes are due on the profits from the sale. When the money passes from the corporation to you it does so as ordinary income, and you pay income taxes on it all over again. So if you are organized as a regular "C" corporation and sell an asset for, say, $500,000, the corporation would first pay approximately 30% in capital gains taxes, and you would pay an additional 30% or so as your personal taxes on whatever was left and came through to you. On top of that there are the state income taxes to pay. All in all, you could pay out as much as $300,000 of your $500,000 profit in taxes. Quite a bite.

On the other hand, if you organize as an "S" corporation you avoid the double tax burden. Since you cannot change from "C" status to "S" status at the last minute, you should select the status that is best for you from the beginning. This is all amateur accounting on my part, although it grows out of considerable personal experience. You should consult your own accountant and do what is best for you.

I should add here that most accountants are not experienced in the sale of publications, which are valued differently from most other businesses. You might give him or her this chapter to read and evaluate.

WHAT IS YOUR PUBLICATION WORTH?

How do you set a price on your publication? What is it worth? Essentially, it is worth what anyone will pay for it, but such an observation is obviously not very helpful.

Publications are not valued like businesses whose asking price is related to net income. In the world of periodical publishing, price is more likely to be related to gross income. If you have a solidly established weekly newspaper or magazine, but one which has not been published over a long period of time, a fair asking price might be one equivalent to the previous year's gross income. That's the price I got for my weekly in spite of the fact that just three years before, when I bought it, it was on the brink of bankruptcy. It was still not showing much of a profit on the corporate level when I sold it, although it was generating a decent income for me in my role as editor and publisher. And it was beset on all sides by competitors, ranging from big city dailies to free-circulation shoppers.

If you are showing a good profit, if you are in a growth market, if you are the only such publication in town (a monopoly), if you have a long track record of successful publication, then the percentage goes up from one times gross to one and a half, to two, three, or even more in exceptional cases.

WHAT YOU ARE SELLING

Never forget that you are selling, in essence, the goose that lays the golden egg. Say you are taking a modest $30,000 a year from this particular publication. What is $30,000 a year worth to you? What will you trade a $30,000 a year income for? How much money would you have to have in the bank to generate that in interest?

Put in that perspective you can see how important it is for you to get top dollar for something that you have worked so hard to build.

To begin with, understand clearly what you are selling. It is more than first meets the eye.

- You are selling not only all the profit that you are currently making but all that you will make in the future.
- You are selling the entire future potential of the publication.
- You are selling hard-won market position.
- You are selling name recognition and good will.
- If you have paid subscribers you are selling access to a faithful, signed-up group of readers. Your subscriber list is an extremely valuable item. You built this list of subscribers slowly, over time. It would cost someone else tens of

thousands of dollars to come in and even *attempt* to duplicate your list. They would still have no guarantee of success.

So if a buyer wants to get into your market in a hurry, and has the money to pay, it makes sense for him to pay you a substantial price for the successful publication you have already built. It would cost even more to try to duplicate the work you have already done. Big buy-out corporations do not operate on the kind of sweat-equity you invested to get your magazine up and going. They have to pay for everything with real dollars — lots of them.

THE SELLING PACKAGE

When you set your company up and were trying to impress the bankers and others with your prospects, you prepared a business plan with great care. Now you should prepare another report with the same care, this time with a view toward furnishing a prospective buyer with the information he believes he needs and the information that you want him to have.

This report will share many of the same features as the business plan. Your own credentials may be important if, as part of the deal, you are to stay on to run your publication. You will want to characterize your publication, explain its editorial policy, and show how it has developed over the years in response to market needs and challenges.

- It should summarize the financial history of your publication and project its growth curve four or five years into the future. A graph showing an income line rising continually can be quite effective.

- Describe your circulation methods, and if you have paid subscribers tell how you got them and how you keep them.

- Tell why your publication worked and became a strong presence in the market. If you have a success story to tell, tell it well.

- Discuss competing publications and tell how you have positioned your magazine to overcome the challenge offered by the competition.

- Be certain to include a discussion of growth patterns in

your trade area that will increase the profitability of your publication.

- Put as much of this information in graphic form as possible. Everyone will study the diagrams. Fewer will read the entire report.

Be absolutely certain that all the information you put into your report is accurate. In the financial summary, particularly, you must be scrupulously correct. The facts are what they are. You can state them in such a way as to make their strong points apparent and easy to grasp, but state them you must. Any deviation from this path will surely come back to haunt you.

STRUCTURING THE DEAL

When you agree on a purchase price, the real negotiations begin. The way the deal is structured is all-important.

An example: The buyer will want to pay you part of your compensation in the form of a non-compete agreement. He does this for at least two reasons. First, he really does need a formal agreement that you will not simply move across the street, start another paper or magazine, and take all your customers with you. Second, the money paid by way of a non-compete agreement is wholly tax deductible to the buyer as an expense of doing business.

For you this money becomes ordinary income, and it is taxed as such. As I write this (early 1990), this fact makes little difference. It could even be a boon to you as well if you are organized as a "C" corporation and thus subject to the perils of double taxation. But when, and if, favorable treatment for capital gains income is reenacted it may not be favorable at all. In fact, it could cost you considerable money.

The buyer will want to assign other values to parts of his purchase: so much for the subscription, so much for good will, so much for your fixed assets and equipment, etc. All of these things can have tax consequences. You will want to have a very sharp accountant on your side throughout this process. The way the deal is structured can have a major impact on how much of the money you make actually sticks in your back pocket.

The buyer may also want to stretch payment out over three, four, or even five years. As tax laws now stand there is no benefit to you in this; only risk. Work to get your money in as short a period of time as possible. If you do go for a long period, be sure that the purchaser is entirely credit worthy before you enter into an agreement. Be sure that he pays the highest going rate of interest on any unpaid balance deferred to future years. Also try to be sure that *he pays a higher overall price* for your business if he wishes to make payments year by year.

If you do accept a note as partial payment be sure that the note obligates the parent corporation and not merely some new subsidiary set up only to run your magazine and with few assets to back up its promise to pay. Otherwise, through mismanagement or other errors, the publication and its new corporation might fail, and your balance due would go down the tubes with it.

A good rule: Do not sign anything at all that is not carefully reviewed by your attorney and, especially, by your accountant.

Can Business Brokers Help?

In every profession some practitioners do better work than others. Unfortunately, when most of them get into water that is too deep for them or unfamiliar to them they prefer not to let you know about it. They just go home, do what reading up they can do, and handle the matter as best they can.

Because the sale of a publication is not an everyday event, you may find that your accountant and attorney are not adequate when it comes to negotiating the particular structure the deal takes. They may simply not be aware of all the alternatives.

There are business brokers who specialize in publication sales. They can be most helpful to you in seeking out potential buyers, since they will know the players in the publications game. They will know who is looking for what, who will pay top dollar. And they will know all the ins and outs of structuring a deal. (Conversely, business brokers who are not experienced in publication sales, no matter how impressive their credentials in other areas, are not likely to be of any help to you and can actually get in the way.)

The typical broker wants 5 to 7% of the gross sales price, though this can be negotiated. The 7% covers the tab when they actually do a national search for prospects. If you already have an interested buyer and wish to retain a broker to handle the deal, you may negotiate 5% or less.

Not every broker of reputation will be interested in handling the smaller deals. For some, any transaction under $10,000,000 is small potatoes. For others, such a deal is right up their alley. Find out about a broker before you retain him. Ask for references. What successful transactions has he concluded in the last one to three years? How does he think he can find a buyer for you?

Whether the sale of your company or one of its publications is an immediate goal or not, it is comforting to know that when retirement time comes, or when you wish to change career directions for some reason or other, the publication that you have put so much of yourself into — heart, soul, sweat, and pocketbook — has a real value that you can turn in for cash.

Appendix

The following is an explanation of the forms that follow. Photocopy any of the forms or redesign them yourself. The following is a description of each and its possible use.

Job Jacket for Ad Design: Have this printed on a 9x12 envelope so art marterials are in one package. This will provide you an easy way to store the many pieces of art work that accompany ads. I suggest that you designate a drawer just for the purpose of holding the materials that come in these folders.

Advertisement Proof Form: This gives the advertiser the chance to make any changes to the overall look of the ad. At this point, no major changes should be made.

Purchase Order: As a I talked about in Chapter 13, use the Purchase Order for any big purchase. All dealings with the purchase of large equipment or printing services should be done in this manner. The space for "Job Title" usually holds the name of the publication you are printing.

Weekly Sales Report: Keep this file on each of your sales people so to keep track of sales commissions. The important column is the "Dossier Complete" column. Check and date this when all materials are in and filed.

Freelance Contract: Though this may seem like one more piece of paperwork, it is extremely important to not only have a binding contract that the artist/editor/writer signs, but also to provide a written down description of their assignment. This could save a lot of phone calls.

Quote Recap Form: This is a handy form for comparing different printers' quotes. Note that price is not always the issue. Sometimes a printer's quote will be lower because they are using a lower grade paper than you requested because they do not have the one you ordered in stock.

Color Separations Transmittal List: This is a helpful checklist for sending your mechanicals to the color seperator. This gives the separator one sheet of instructions and helps him to be clear on your requests.

JOB JACKET FOR AD DESIGN

┌─────────────────────────────────┐
│ **Insert all artwork,** │
│ **logos, photos and** │
│ **materials inside** │
└─────────────────────────────────┘

Date: _____ Publication _____

Ad Design Information

Company and or name _____

Contact _____

Address _____

City _____

State _____ Zip _____

Phone _____

INFORMATION TO BE INCLUDED IN AD DESIGN

Line drawings _____ Color/B&W photos _____

Photo: Supplied by customer ___ Supplied by W&S ____

Date to be taken _____ Rain date _____

Subject of photos _____

_____

_____

PMS colors _____

Ad design information _____

_____

_____

_____

_____

Image to be portrayed in ad design _____

_____

Target Audience _____

_____

_____

Special features which may be included _____

_____

_____

Notes from ad representative _____

_____

_____

_____

INFORMATION CHECKLIST

Layout _____

Headlines _____

Copy _____

Logo _____

Photo/Line art _____

Map _____

Brochures _____

Old ad _____

Ad size _____

Color _____ B&W _____

CUSTOMER WILL FURNISH

Film: Date _____

Camera Ready: Date _____

Photos: Date _____

Rough Layout: Date _____

Other: _____ Date _____

ADVERTISEMENT PROOF FORM

Important!...
ORDINARY QUALITY
PROOF COPY FOR YOUR AD IN

Beaufort County Magazine

Williams & Simpson, Inc.
223 W. 10th Street, Suite 120
Greenville, North Carolina 27834

- Please check carefully.
- If this ad as it appears meets your specifications please give your signed approval below. Failure to return this ad in (10) days constitutes approval to advertise as is.
- If there are any alterations make desired changes on proof and return to us. Williams & Simpson, Inc. will send you a second proof for your approval.
- If you have any questions please call us at (919) 758-4093 (Local) or 1-800-682-0080.

Advertisers Approval _____

PURCHASE ORDER

Purchase Order

Purchase Number: _____ Date _____

Purchase order to:

Job Title:

Description of job:

Special Instructions:

Quantity: _____

Schedule: _____
_____

Price Quote: _____

Authorized Signature: _____ Date_____

For more information or questions please contact:_____
at:

Please Sign and Return to:

WEEKLY SALES REPORT

Weekly Sales Report

Name _____ Week of _____

Name of Advertiser/Client	Name of Publication	Amt. of Sale	Contract Attached	Dossier Complete	Comm.	Comm. Paid	Date Comm. Paid

FREELANCE CONTRACT

Freelance **Contract**

deadline _____

amount to be paid _____

total due upon completion _____

printed sample requested by artist? _____

description of sample:

description of work:

I understand that should I fail to complete the assignment according to specifications set by Wiliams & Simpson, Inc. by the necessary deadline, I will not be paid for my work, unless arrangement for a specific aspect of the job is separate from the completion, such as a design fee, above and beyond the finishing of work.

I also understand that all reproduction rights become property of Williams & Simpson, Inc. unless prior arrangement is made.

artist's signature _____

date _____

authorized signature _____

date _____

QUOTE RECAP FORM

QUOTE RECAP FOR _____

Title					
ISBN Code					
Author					
# of pages					
Size					
Qty requested					
Paper stock					
PRINTER:					
Contact:					
Base price					
+ 1,000s price					
Paper stock					
Work days					
Notes					

PRINTER:					
Contact:					
Base price					
+ 1,000s price					
Paper stock					
Work days					
Notes					

PRINTER:					
Contact:					
Base price					
+ 1,000s price					
Paper stock					
Work days					
Notes					

COLOR SEPARATIONS TRANSMITTAL LIST

COLOR SEPARATIONS TRANSMITTAL LIST

To: _____

Code: _____ **Title:** _____

Date: _____ **Shipped via:**_____

☐ Job Order or Quote Acknowledgement

☐ Cover mechanical

☐ Cover photographs or art

_____ transparencies _____ slides ____ reflective art

☐ Insert mechanical

_____ transparencies _____ slides ____ reflective art

☐ Assembly sheet or dummy layout

☐ Shipping instructions

FOR QUESTIONS, CONTACT: _____

SPECIFICATIONS:

_____ Random _____ Position

_____ Press proofs _____ Progressives _____ Chromalin

_____ Other:

150 line screen − right reading emulsion down − negative film − sheet fed press − coated stock

OTHER:

_____
_____
_____
_____
_____

SUGGESTIONS FOR FURTHER READING

The books listed below are few in number but very solid in content. Each of them has been a valuable source of information and inspiration for me in setting up and managing my publishing businesses. Each contains concrete, usable information and techniques that can make you money. I highly recommend them to you. Since many of these books exist in a variety of editions, some expensive and some much less expensive, I suggest that you consult *Books in Print* and *Paperback Books in Print* at your library or bookstore to find the one that best fits your needs and pocketbook.

Bodian, Nat. *The Publisher's Direct Mail Handbook.*

Book, Albert C. and Schick, Dennis. *Fundamentals of Copy and Layout.*

Brabec, Barbara. *Homemade Money, 3rd Edition.*

Caples, John. *Tested Advertising Methods.*

Carnegie, Dale. *How to Win Friends and Influence People.*

Cohen, William A. *Building a Mail Order Business.*

Cook, James R. *The Start-up Entrepreneur.*

Felice, James and Nace, Ted. *Desk-top Publishing Skills: A Primer.*

Ferguson, R. *Editing the Small Magazine.*

Glenn, Peggy. *Publicity for Books and Authors.*

Graham, Walter. *Complete Guide to Paste-up.*

Haldeman-Julius, Emmanuel. *The First Hundred Million.*

Hill, Napoleon. *Think and Grow Rich.*

Hopkins, Claude. *My Life in Advertising.*

——. *Scientific Advertising.*

Hurlburt, Alan. *The Grid.*

Kamaroff, Bernard. *Small-time Operator.*

Kennedy, Bruce M. *Community Journalism: A Way of Life.*

Kleper, Michael. *Desktop Publishing and Typesetting.*

Kremer, John. *Directory of Book, Catalogue and Magazine Printers.*

Kuswa, Webster. *Big Profits from Small Budget Advertising.*

Levinson, Jay Conrad. *Guerilla Marketing.*

Louis, Gordon H. *How to Handle Your Own Public Relations.*

McKinney, John. *How to Start Your Own Community Newapaper.*

Mancuso, Joseph. *How to Start, Finance and Manage Your Own Small Business.*

Middleton, Tony. *A Desktop Publisher's Guide to Paste-up.*

Mogel, Leonard. *The Magazine.*

Nelson, Roy. *The Design of Advertising.*

— —. *Publication Design.*

Ogilvy, David. *Confessions of an Advertising Man.*

Parker, Roger C. *Looking Good in Print.*

Powers, Melvin. *How to Get Rich in Mail Order.*

Poynter, Dan. *The Self-Publishing Manual.*

— —. *Publishing Short-Run Books: How to Paste-up and Reproduce Books Instantly Using Your Own Copy Shop.*

Romano, Frank. *How to Build a Profitable Newspaper.*

Simon, Julian. *How to Start and Operate a Mail Order Business.*

INDEX

This manuscript was typeset and designed using Microsoft Word 5.0 with Bitstream Fontware on an AST 286 (IBM-compatible) machine and printed out on Hewlett-Packard LaserJet Series II at 300 dpi. The body text is Zapf-Calligraphic 11/14.